environmental
MISSIONS

environmental
MISSIONS

planting churches AND trees

LOWELL BLISS

WILLIAM CAREY
LIBRARY

Published by William Carey Library
1605 E. Elizabeth St.
Pasadena, CA 91104 | www.missionbooks.org

Aidan Lewis, editor
Brad Koenig, copyeditor
Alyssa E. Force, graphic design
Josie Leung, graphic design

William Carey Library is a ministry of the
U.S. Center for World Mission
Pasadena, CA | www.uscwm.org

Printed in the United States of America
17 16 15 14 13   5 4 3 2 1 BP500

Library of Congress Cataloging-in-Publication Data
Bliss, Lowell.
  Environmental missions : planting churches and trees / Lowell Bliss.
     pages cm
  Includes bibliographical references.
  ISBN 978-0-87808-538-5
  1. Human ecology--Religious aspects--Christianity. 2. Missions. I. Title.
  BT695.5.B56 2013
  266--dc23

                                                    2013029403

Dedicated to my dear wife,
Robynn, who loves me more
than she does
the Indian subcontinent,
who loves Christ more
than she does herself.

*If you want to build a ship,
don't drum up people to collect wood
and don't assign them tasks and work,
but rather teach them to long
for the endless immensity of the sea.*

Antoine de Saint-Exupery

CONTENTS

FOREWORD

I n this passionate and personal account of his embrace of creation care as an integral part of biblical mission, Lowell Bliss invites us on a journey. It is a journey that begins on familiar ground—an American missionary to Asia, full of love and compassion for those he is called to serve, who is wrestling with all the complexity and glory and pain of serving Jesus in a very broken world. But as he literally embraces the body of a "throwaway" man and literally gives his blood in a futile attempt to save the life of his six-year-old neighbor, so he is impelled to ask what significance God's very material creation has for his personal calling, and how the evident distress of creation that he sees on every side shapes the way the church understands its mission in the world.

It is a privilege to accompany Lowell through the twists and turns of his reflection. He engages with those who disagree with him with courtesy and with the understanding of a true disciple who has come a long and difficult path towards his present biblical convictions. He shares those scriptural explorations with us too, frequently offering insights that he has both developed and gleaned, many of them unusual within the growing library of biblical environmental writing. Furthermore he generously takes his place within a global community of other Jesus followers from whom he is eager to learn, and with whom he wishes to grow in understanding and in a commitment to showing the love of God for all he has made.

It is clear that this book is rooted deeply in the particular North American missions world from which Lowell has come. This too is important, because the American global footprint remains the deepest and the most influential, even as we witness the very rapid rise in influence of other voices and other mission movements from all over the world. It is well known that the American experience is quite distinct, as is the American response to the multiple environmental crises we all face. This book goes a long way towards both exegeting those particular responses and helping to draw them into a wider, more global discussion.

We can all pray that the profound and heartfelt experiences and longings that Lowell shares with us in these pages touch our hearts too. The creation is groaning, but the kingdom of God is coming—it is vital that our proclamation of Jesus should bring hope to all creation, and authentic missional callings should, whatever their nature, extend to the healing of our fractured relationship with the world around us that is God's handiwork, created for his glory and to witness to his character. The inspiration of those like Lowell and Robynn, his wife, who have poured themselves out in pursuit of such callings is a gift indeed.

Peter Harris
Wiltshire, UK
June 2013

This is a book about definitions, but not strictly about the definition of a word or phrase. If that were the case, our task could be completed in a paragraph:

en·vi·ron·men·tal mis·sion·ar·y
/enˌvīrənˈmen(t)l ˈmiSHəˌnerē/ noun. 1. one sent cross-culturally to labor with Christ—the Creator, Sustainer, and Redeemer of all creation—in caring for the environment and making disciples among all peoples; 2. arguably, a new category within missions; 3. analogous to medical missions; 4. terminology attributable to Peter Harris (A Rocha), Ed Brown (Care of Creation), and the Environmental Missions Consultation (July 2010).

Indeed, we'll explore this definition in detail, but environmental missions is also the definition of a *calling*, which invariably means self-definition, the tale of a stirring of the Spirit of God in the hearts of his disciples. For example, there is the story of William Carey, the father of modern missions, who early in his career in India feared that his extensive botanical studies, if the church in England found out about them, would "mock the expectations of our numerous friends, who are waiting to hear of the conversion of the heathen and overthrow of Satan's kingdom."[1] William Carey went on to help found the Agricultural and Horticultural Society of India, an organization which still blesses that nation today.

Admittedly the transitional stages of self-definition are an uneasy time. My wife and I were church planting missionaries of the most traditional variety in India and Pakistan for fourteen years. We served with Christar, the mission agency in which my wife, Robynn, grew up. Now, as the director of Eden Vigil, I call myself an "environmental missionary." I can trace my transformation to, among other things, a single mosquito bite, and you will hear that story.

The Lausanne Movement's creation care "Call to Action" claims, "We are faced with [an ecological] crisis that is pressing, urgent, and that must be resolved in our generation."[2] This statement suggests that our book about definitions appears during a *defining moment* for the church. Environmental issues can be controversial, and currently none more so than the topic of global climate change. And yet, will our generation choose to be defined by the love of Christ which compels us (2 Cor 5:14), a love that compels us to navigate through the controversy? On the other side of that controversy, Bangladeshi villagers are already dying of arsenic poisoning, Chinese urban populations of respiratory illnesses, and Indian children of giardia. I am of the opinion that the church is at her worst when she *engages* a controversy, and at her best when she sees *through* it with the elemental eyes of love.

For four decades now, the Lausanne Movement has been a force to cut through controversy, including that moment in 1974 at the first Congress on World Evangelization when Ralph Winter's seminal paper on unreached people groups suggested that the church should reprioritize her mobilization. In October 2010, over 4,200 evangelical leaders from 198 countries converged on Cape Town, South Africa, for the Third Lausanne Congress on World Evangelization. The Congress' stated goal was to present "a fresh challenge to the global church to bear witness to Jesus Christ and all his teaching—in every nation, in every sphere of society, and in the realm of ideas,"[3] and they embodied that challenge in a remarkable document entitled *The Cape Town Commitment*. Among the many issues touched upon by the *Commitment* is what the church is calling "creation care," or a Christian stewardship of the environment. What the *Commitment*

says about creation care is unprecedented in the history of the modern evangelical church. For example: "The earth is created, sustained and redeemed by Christ. We cannot claim to love God while abusing what belongs to Christ by right of creation, redemption and inheritance."[4] Following the Congress in Cape Town, the Lausanne Movement embarked on a series of topical and regional "consultations," each charged with taking up the challenges specified in the *Commitment*. I was one of the fifty-seven theologians, scientists, church leaders, and creation care practitioners from twenty-six countries who met in St. Ann, Jamaica, in October 2012 for the Lausanne Global Consultation on Creation Care and the Gospel. We also produced a document, the "Call to Action," which you can read in full in appendix 1 of this book. I will refer repeatedly to both the *Cape Town Commitment* and the "Call to Action," because I'm convinced that they represent environmental missions' founding documents. Here is item #5 from the "Call to Action":

> **Environmental missions among unreached people groups.**
> We participate in Lausanne's historic call to world evangelization, and believe that environmental issues represent one of the greatest opportunities to demonstrate the love of Christ and plant churches among unreached and unengaged people groups in our generation (*CTC* II.D.1). We encourage the church to promote "environmental missions" as a new category within mission work (akin in function to medical missions).[5]

This is not the first call to environmental missions, but it is one of the most powerful and widespread. It establishes environmental missions as a new category within the labors of the church. From the human side, new categories in the period of their infancy require two things above all else: legitimation and rigor. These are two things that definitions confer, and they are the two primary purposes of this book. Legitimation, precisely because it is so central to this book, could benefit from a quick definition itself. It is simply the act of providing legitimacy. One source writes: "Legitimation in the social sciences refers to the process whereby an act, process, or ideology becomes legitimate by its attachment to norms and values within a given society. It is the process of making something acceptable and normative to a group or audience."[6] Roman Catholic canon law uses the term "legitimation" to refer to the process by which a child born out of wedlock can nonetheless be welcomed into the regular practice of the church. This is a helpful analogy, because there are some who believe that the traditional gospel-preaching, disciple-making, church planting missions that, for example, Robynn and I practiced in India with Christar, could never marry a hippie like environmentalism, even if some well-meaning Christians dress her up with terms like "creation care."

The legitimation of environmental missions means making this new category "acceptable and normative" to the evangelical church, and this is accomplished by making "attachment to norms and values" within the society of the church. In this book, we'll make theological, historical, and missiological attachments. Theologically, we'll discover a biblical basis for environmental missions by looking at creation care from a Christological perspective. In other words, what does it mean for the second person of the Trinity, whose gospel we preach, to be additionally "the Creator, Sustainer, and Redeemer of all creation"? Just how full is the redemption we have in Christ Jesus? Historically we'll discover that environmental missions is simply new terminology for a labor of love that missionaries like William Carey, Robert Moffat, and generations of others have worked in so faithfully. Whether in sustainable agriculture, pure water supply, or reforestation, previous generations of missionaries intuitively cared for the environment—that which surrounds the people we love, those for whom Jesus died. Finally, missiological legitimation means that we will demonstrate how creation care fits and feeds into the structures and the strategies of the missionary work of the church, not only as we seek to obey the Great Commission but as we reach out to those people groups that remain unreached or unengaged.

A good definition also provides rigor or discipline, by which I mean it demands we do good, authentic, effective work. Environmental missions, by definition, lives at that point of integration between church planting

and creation care. We must ruthlessly keep ourselves at that point. It is too easy to "greenwash" our efforts, whereby our missions projects have a green veneer about them—perhaps to obtain a convenient visa in our passport, perhaps to appeal to a new generation of recruits—without actually benefiting God's creation at all. Rigor, in our case, also means scientific rigor. In the time-honored practice of the church (though occasionally lost in our current controversies), environmental missionaries proclaim that "all truth is God's truth," and so we apply the best possible science to our labors. Thirdly, rigor in environmental missions means that we avoid "mumbling" the gospel in our creation care efforts, so consumed with our environmental activities that we fail to open our mouths to proclaim that Christ is our only hope for this world and the next. Finally, environmental missionaries are invariably activists. We want to dig a hole and plant a tree. We want to grab a wrench and install a solar panel. I'll devote a whole chapter to the rigor of prayer. I believe there is a type of prayer ideally suited for a new category like environmental missions.

Who is the audience for this book? It's likely that this book will start out with two audiences, which hopefully by the end of the book will converge into one. One initial audience are those traditionally understood as "the missions minded." Maybe you are like Robynn or I were: cross-cultural church planters already on the field, cultivating a love for your people group, a growing witness to how those people are daily affected by "that which surrounds them." Maybe you are a missions student at a Bible college or seminary, in that intense period of self-definition: "What is my calling? What kind of missionary will I be?" Maybe you are a missions leader or a missiologist intrigued by the "Call to Action" claim that "environmental issues represent one of the greatest opportunities to demonstrate the love of Christ and plant churches among unreached and unengaged people groups in our generation."[7] Maybe you are a church leader who diligently seeks to stay attuned to what might advance the kingdom of God.

Another initial audience is the creation care minded. If you are in this group, you might be like the environmental studies majors (or engineers, or biologists, or resource managers, etc.—I'm using this term in the broadest

possible way) who have come up to the Eden Vigil booth at the last two Urbana mission conferences and said, "Do you really mean I can use my environmental skills in missions?!" Our answer is that you can plant both trees *and* churches; you can help save both soils *and* souls. Even the most secular of environmental studies majors have an altruistic bent. They aren't in it for the money. They actually want to "save the planet," or at least some species or ecosystem of it. When that altruism is biblically informed in a student who is also a follower of Christ, environmental missions is a natural expression of "God's love . . . poured out into our hearts through the Holy Spirit, who has been given to us" (Rom 5:5). Those who are already development professionals might also be among the creation care minded audience of this book. If you are in this group, then your counterpart is the professional church planter, and the message is the same: a humble suggestion as to how to do better, more authentic, more effective work. After all, the most polluted river in the world—that which pollutes all other waterways—is the river that flows out of the human heart, and our only hope for the human heart is transformation in the Spirit of Christ. How strong are the evangelistic and discipleship components of your creation care ministry?

I can demonstrate these two audiences by describing where my family lived while in India. (For security reasons, I'll not mention this city by actual name.) Our house on the western banks of the Ganges River was surrounded, even overwhelmed, by Hinduism. In fact, a loudspeaker situated outside our bedroom window would often fire up at 4:30 in the morning during festival times and blare out its chants. Our landlord maintained a family temple on the property and every year at Diwali performed a blood sacrifice of a goat. If the wind was blowing from the north, you could smell the smoke of the cremation fires where the Dom caste attended to the dead. However, if you climbed up to our roof at night—particularly when a power outage eliminated the light pollution—you could stare up at the galaxies and feel the worship of the Creator God well up within you. Or you could stare out across the river, or down at the water's edge, at the stone steps known as *ghats*. You would see the kids playing in the water and shudder to think that the thin edge of eternity is often defined for them by a sip of that

 Preface

polluted river. In other words, however much you might be surrounded by the "spiritual" on the western banks of the river, just one mindful glance to the east would indicate how much God's creation, both its glories and its abuse, impinges upon your most heartfelt desires in ministry.

If you stood on the eastern bank of the Ganges looking west, you would be surrounded by environmental issues. Maybe you've just caught a glimpse of a river dolphin—*Platanista gangetica*—a remarkable creature that hunts by sonar and swims on its side. There are only between 1,200 and 1,800 of them left in the world. They are an endangered species, red-listed by the International Union for Conservation of Nature and Natural Resources (IUCN). But maybe your work on the eastern shore is with the Kewat people, the traditional fishermen on the river. In 1975 the Indian government built the Farraka Barrage downstream in the state of West Bengal. The hilsa fish, which used to swim 850 kilometers upstream to spawn, were hindered from traveling as far as our city. The fishery collapsed for the Kewat, and so now, in search of a way to supplement their livelihood, the Kewat plant watermelons and cucumbers in the sand bar on the eastern bank, hoping to harvest them before the monsoon rains again flood the river bed. So maybe you are helping your Kewat friend lay an irrigation pipe, but then you look up toward the west and you see the city rising on the man-made bluff on the other side. The temples are easily recognizable with their distinctive *shikara* shapes and fluttering flags. You hear the clangs of bells and can imagine the *puja*, the worship. Even though the river dolphin is an endangered species, you know it is still being occasionally slaughtered, particularly downstream, by fishermen who chop it up to use as bait. We might say it is being sacrificed on the altar of commerce. And your Kewat friends will lie on their own pyres when they die, the cremation grounds just visible off to your right. Plagued by casteism, hounded by alcoholism, they will go to their cremations having trusted in gods that, like the hilsa fish, were never able to save them. In other words, however much you might be surrounded by the "environmental" on the eastern banks of the river, just one mindful glance to the west would indicate how God's spiritual world, both its glories and its abuse, impinges on your most heartfelt desires in ministry.

❧ ENVIRONMENTAL MISSIONS ❧

Every year, after the monsoon flood has receded, city officials build a small, narrow pontoon bridge that traverses the river, west to east, east to west. It looks like a rickety structure, but it is solid enough that pedestrians, rickshaws, bicycles, and oxcarts all cross with confidence. Books can also be rickety structures, but I'm hoping that legitimation and rigor will fortify the definition of our calling during a defining moment of the church. From that bridge, just a couple feet above the water, you find yourself not living in one world or the other, but in both at the same time, that point of integration known as environmental missions.

NOTES

1. William Carey, quoted in George Smith, *The Life of William Carey: Shoemaker and Missionary* (Middlesex, UK: Echo, 2006), 204.

2. Lausanne Global Consultation on Creation Care and the Gospel, "Call to Action" (St. Ann, Jamaica: Lausanne Movement, 2012), http://www.lausanne.org/en/documents/all/2012-creation-care/1881-call-to-action.html.

3. Third Lausanne Congress on World Evangelization, *The Cape Town Commitment*, ed. Julia Cameron (Peabody, MA: Hendrickson, 2011), foreword: 4.

4. Ibid., I.7.A.19.

5. Lausanne, "Call to Action."

6. "Legitimation," *Wikipedia*, http://en.wikipedia.org/wiki/Legitimation.

7. Lausanne, "Call to Action."

ACKNOWLEDGMENTS

Thank you, triune God, for creating such a wondrous place for us to live. If this planet and the starry host above it are so beautiful, how much more beautiful must you be.

Thank you, Robynn, to whom this book is dedicated. The difficult transition from India into Eden Vigil is just further proof of how adept you are at love. Thank you as well to my beloved kids—Connor, Adelaide, and Bronwynn—not only for the stuffed Lorax you gave me one Father's Day, but for how valiantly you've tried to answer the question, "What is it that your Dad does?"

Thank you, Mom and Dad, for taking me out in the woods of Michigan, Kansas, and Colorado as a kid.

Thank you, Steve Coffey and our other colleagues at Christar. Eden Vigil would not exist if you, Steve, hadn't encouraged and defended it along the way.

Thank you to my newfound friends in the creation care community who welcomed me and a missionary approach. Ed Brown (whose mentorship you will amply see in the text of this book) as well as Susan Emmerich and Tom Rowley have been my closest colleagues, a true honor to work alongside.

Thank you to Gary Allyn and John Miller, Eden Vigil's first teammates and helpful in formulating the concepts in this book.

Thank you to the participants of the Environmental Missions Consultation, held in Manhattan, Kansas (July 2010). The first manuscript of this book was subtitled *Notes from a Consultation*. Certainly the definition of environmental missions is the product of the experience that you brought to those four days. So thank you to Katie, Bob, David, Yvonne, Tim, Vern, James, Neil, Gary, Steve, Walter, Eric, Celeste, Joan, Robynn, and Kraig.

Thank you to the libraries of Kansas State University and Manhattan Christian College, which accommodated much of my research.

Thank you to the staff of William Carey Library. Jeff Minard, Greg Parsons, and Suzanne Harlan took a risk on a controversial subject, and I appreciate their persevering trust in me through three versions of this manuscript. Greatest thanks go to Aidan Lewis, my developmental editor. Thank you, Aidan. Your skill at shaping a manuscript is surpassed by the godly and gentle spirit you bring to your work. As you embark on your career and ministry, I pray that the Lord will use you greatly for his glory and for the sake of the least reached among his elect.

Finally, thank you to a person, now deceased, who in this book I call Golu. Thank you for being my friend in India. Jesus in his generosity knows that in many ways all of Eden Vigil is also dedicated to you.

1

THREE WAYS MISSIONARIES
CLEAR THE POLLUTED AIR

I 've always assumed that the "sons of Issachar," as described in 1 Chronicles 12:32, represent a model for missionaries. They were "men who understood the times and knew what Israel should do." In the context of this passage, this meant gathering around David at Hebron "to turn Saul's kingdom over to him, as the Lord had said" (1 Chr 12:23). Of all the military contingents, Issachar's was likely among the smallest, but their value to the new kingdom was unique: they discerned the *kairos* moment, the time of divine opportunity.

Robynn and I returned from India in 2007. Any cross-cultural experience has the potential of becoming a universe unto itself, especially one as chaotic as our North Indian city. We had allowed ourselves to get isolated and weren't greatly aware of the global news. So returning to North America, it was natural as per the missionary model of Issachar to ask, "What's happening in the broader world? What is the nature of these times?" Apparently, we were told, the planet was getting warmer. While in India, I had heard only the briefest mention of the greenhouse effect or global warming. I had heard that former vice president Al Gore had won an Academy Award for a documentary built around a PowerPoint presentation. And so we rented his DVD documentary *An Inconvenient Truth* in order to learn more.

In this introductory chapter, I want to recognize upfront that an environmental approach is a controversial topic in the North American evangelical church of the twenty-first century. You'll notice how thoroughly

❧ ENVIRONMENTAL MISSIONS ❧

I've delimited my audience. An environmental approach is generally well accepted outside of the US and Canada, and even in North America had remarkably few evangelical detractors until around 2008. Nonetheless the audience for this book is largely North American, and the record temperatures of the year 2012 were surpassed only by its political heat. So I am aware that I have lost many potential readers who have judged my book by its cover. They saw the title and left the book on the bookstore shelves. You can imagine some of the consternation of my editors when they learned that I wanted to recognize the controversy, as if to confront it head on, by leading not only with the prickly issue of climate change but also with the one environmentalist most vilified by evangelicals: Al Gore.

But look back. I didn't lead with climate change and Mr. Gore. I led with the sons of Issachar. I led with a missionary mandate that we understand the times and that we humbly apply influence as to what the Great Commission church should do. The spirit of Issachar is just one of the three ways in which a missionary approach can clear the smog-ridden air around the environmental controversy. We'll never be able to sustain an honest consideration of environmental missions as a new category within the labors of the church unless there is enough initial oxygen in the room for us to breathe. Let's see if we can clear some of the air.

One Lone Villager from Issachar Investigates

For however much we might want to dissect Gore's argument in *An Inconvenient Truth*, here's an indisputable fact from my first viewing of it as a recently furloughed missionary: the Indian subcontinent was mentioned throughout the movie. At one point, a satellite map of India flashes to the screen and the imagery is of such high resolution that you can identify the Ganges River and where it bends from south to north past our old home. The statistic accompanying the map claims that in June 2003, temperatures in Andhra Pradesh reached 122° F, killing more than 1,400 people. In another segment, Gore reports how on July 26, 2005 in Mumbai, thirty-seven inches of rain fell in twenty-four hours, the most an Indian city has ever received in one day. Water levels reached seven feet, and the death toll in Western India reached a thousand. I actually have my own memories of that event. Mumbai is the financial capital of India. On the day of the flood, banks across the country, including in our city, were forced to close. The documentary went on to discuss how climatic changes are increasing the range of disease vectors, and I heard names with which I was familiar: malaria, dengue fever, avian flu. Both Robynn and I had contracted dengue in the past year. Al Gore quoted Tony Blair's science advisor, who has claimed that "because of what is happening in Greenland [i.e., addition of land-based ice melt to the world's oceans] the maps of the world will have to be redrawn." He then showed what would happen if the West Antarctic ice shelf or the Greenland ice shelf collapsed, or half of both. We saw animated satellite photos of Florida, the Netherlands, and Beijing, of sea levels encroaching on these populated areas. And then there was a photo of Calcutta and Bangladesh, and the threat to 60 million people there. The movie spent a year in production, so the producers felt obliged to invite Gore back for a Special Features update. Gore referred back to the heat wave in Andhra Pradesh in 2003, but then he said, "This past summer, not too far to the north in Pakistan, on the Indian subcontinent, it reached 125.6 degrees Fahrenheit."[1] The slide showed the city of Multan on the map. Multan is in the lower Punjab of Pakistan, near where Robynn grew up.

I am well aware of the accusations of political demagoguery and scientific sensationalism that surround *An Inconvenient Truth*, but here's the question I wrestled with: what kind of missionary would I be if my ears didn't perk up at every mention of my people group; if I didn't at least wonder, "What if even half of this is true?"; if I didn't feel compelled to investigate further? Hadn't our church sent Robynn and I to India specifically to love those people portrayed in those photos of suffering? We just happened to be back in the US for meetings in the weeks following the Bush vs. Gore election of 2000, so we got to experience firsthand the acrimony of the evangelical Christian population toward Gore, some of it from our own family, our own mission colleagues, our own missions supporters, and

our own church. We heard the evidence that made many people think that when it came to the truth, Al Gore was, at the least, a serial exaggerator.

It's not surprising, considering recent political history, that evangelical Christians have treated Al Gore and his global warming documentary like the character in Aesop's fable, ascribing to the Boy Who Cried Wolf the approbation, "No one listens to a liar, even when he is telling the truth." But actually there's one last scene in Aesop's fable that none of us ever stop to extrapolate. On the day after the exasperated villagers chase the boy out from among themselves, they go up to the hillside only to discover that, this time, there actually was a wolf, but now their flocks are all dead. Yes, the boy is foolish, but in the end, so are the villagers. You should always send at least one person up the hill to investigate. There is too much at stake if you don't. And so maybe I felt like that one villager, compelled by a missionary love for the parched of Multan and the displaced of Bangladesh, for the drowned of Mumbai and the dengue-fevered of our city. I went off to investigate. It seemed like the responsible thing to do.[2] In January 2008 I submitted to my leadership at Christar a fifty-page report entitled "A Church-Planting Missionary Looks at Global Climate Change."

Environment's Most Basic Definition

I believe that missionaries possess a second unique investigative capacity, one which I describe as the ability to "lop off the -*ism*." My best Indian friend was a Hindu Brahmin, whom I will call here by a different house name, Golu. One of the first things that Golu taught me was that Hindus rarely refer to Hindu*ism*; that is, to an organized religion. At the most, the term is *sanatan dharma*, a rule of life. My initial interactions with Golu proved that, for whatever my training had taught me about Hindu*ism*, it was more important to know the individual Hindu—in other words, "lop off the -*ism*" as soon as possible. For that matter, my friendship and growing love for Golu drew me away from religious labels altogether. I tried to understand him as a human being, to know and to be known. In a similar fashion, I have no desire to write this book as a defense of environmental*ism*. I believe we are well advised to be wary of anything that has an -*ism* attached to it. This can also apply to movements within the church, such as Evangelical*ism*, for which we can multiply examples: Methodism, dispensationalism, creationism. It's not that these movements, as *-isms*, are unbiblical, but because they are not *de facto* biblical. We must hold every *-ism* up to the light of Scripture and "test the spirits."

If environmentalism in recent times has not been offered an opportunity to be addressed by Scripture, has not had a fair trial in the testing of the spirits, it may be because of *-isms* other than its own. Some evangelicals fear that environmentalism is a modern paganism: half-naked druids worshiping the earth, hugging trees, preferring the life of a California condor over the life of a human fetus. Even taking a step back from these stereotypes isn't reassuring. Environmentalists seem too quick to invoke Henry David Thoreau, transcendentalism, even Buddhism. Scientism as well leaves many of us wary of environmentalists. Since *creation care* is still a relatively new term within the church, you are more likely to hear the word "creation" brought up in a discussion of *creationism*, and thus in the context of an antagonism: creationist versus evolutionist, faith versus science. In other words, even the word "creation" seems to unconsciously put many of us on the defensive. We can't quite bring ourselves to trust the scientist whose lament over the loss of biodiversity doesn't extend to the extinction of Jesus in our universities. And finally, we can be upfront about the current politics of environmentalism, what we might call factionalism, or partyism, a term for political partisanship. It is a documented fact that most voters in the US who identify themselves with Evangelicalism also associate with the Republican party. Some of these evangelical voters are surprised to learn that the modern conservation movement began under the Republican administration of Teddy Roosevelt. Environmentalism's greatest policy successes—the Endangered Species Act, the Clean Water Act, the Clean Air Act, the formation of the Environmental Protection Agency—were all signed into law by Richard Nixon. As recently as 2008, the most faithful introducer of climate change legislation was Senator John McCain. Newt Gingrich wrote the book *A Contract with Earth* in 2007. But American politics have rarely been so polarized as today. While

❧ ENVIRONMENTAL MISSIONS ❦

many environmentalists are profoundly disappointed in President Barack Obama's first term, nonetheless environmentalism seems more associated with the Democratic Party, and thus becomes part of the antagonism of Republican voters, including the evangelical ones.

With all these conflations—paganism, transcendentalism, scientism, Democratic partyism—it's no wonder that evangelicals are wary of all things environmental. But what if that three letter suffix *-ism* acts like a closed nodule on a sauce pan? If we could somehow lop it off, we might find that much of the pressure of the pot has dissipated. We are certainly left with the question: What is this thing now that it is devoid of the emotional and ideological construct that a fallen humanity has built around it? What is environmentalism without its *-ism*? Grammatically, the root is simply "environment."

I trace the definition I use—and I believe it is a missionary definition—of the word "environment" to the lifting off of a blanket. I know that the phrase "a blanket lifted" is often used metaphorically to refer to the uncovering of a truth, an epiphany; but in my case, I literally lifted the edge of a thick cotton *razai* and found myself staring in the eyes of a young Pakistani girl, a victim of an earthquake. The 2005 Kashmir earthquake resulted in a Pakistani death toll upwards of eighty-six thousand people. The story of my participation in this relief effort is the story of a church planter's epiphany; namely, that "environment" can be understood as "that which surrounds those we love, those for whom Jesus died"—environment as context, and thus environmentalism as simply contextualization, if you will. When you love someone, you are keenly interested in what crumbles down on their head. I loved that little girl.

An armed police officer stood at the front flap of the field hospital where our team was stationed and maintained a queue, but this was mostly for those patients who were using our facility as a clinic, as a replacement for the civil hospital that had collapsed down the road. But when the military helicoptered in a patient, or if the police officer saw a particularly desperate case, he would send them in through the side entrance. One evening after dark, a group of big, burly Pathan men came in through the side entrance carrying a rope bed between them, piled high with blankets. They had hiked in from their village. I lifted the covers to reveal a girl, perhaps age fourteen, sallow-skinned, bony-wristed. She lay on one side, her legs curled up. Her mouth gaped. She breathed as if the blankets were water and she was a fish. She had cerebral palsy.

Her father told us a stone had fallen from the wall of their house and had struck her during the quake. Since then she had regressed; she no longer ate solid food but was back to drinking from a bottle. She whimpered continuously. Our doctors examined her and discovered only minor bruises. They asked me to translate: "Tell them that the earthquake is not responsible for her cerebral palsy."

I didn't need to tell them; they knew that.

"Tell them that there is nothing wrong with their daughter."

I couldn't tell them that either. It wasn't true. What could be more fundamentally wrong than to be trapped in innocent incomprehension, unable to make sense of a formerly safe home that is suddenly shaking, crumbling, and falling upon you?

Therein lay the flash of understanding, the epiphany that can change a ministry, the heartbreak that is furrowed soil for the seed of a new calling. Environment surrounds those we love, those for whom Jesus died. And those we love have bodies—sallow-skinned, bony-wristed, gaping like a fish. Their environment is crashing around them. Our team was fundamentally helpless to do anything about this girl's hurt, except to turn to Jesus—the Creator, Sustainer, and Redeemer of all creation. The doctors prescribed aspirin in liquid form in case her bruises were hurting her. I explained to the family that they should take her home, keep her warm, continue with the same tender affection they were showing, and not worry about her reversion to the bottle. I asked them if we could pray together. And so we stood around this girl's bed, doctors who didn't know Urdu, Pathans who didn't know Jesus. We lifted our hands up to pray, Muslim-style, and then we asked *Hazarat Isa Masih*, the Lord Jesus Christ, to speak words of comprehensible comfort into this girl's soul, a depth to which none of us were capable of reaching.

ENVIRONMENTAL MISSIONS

Environmental Missions as Strategic Opportunity

There is, however, an -*ism* which constitutes another missionary strength. Pragmatism is a determination to let no good opportunity rest only in theory. We are like mother birds that push fledgling ideas to the edge of the nest. It's not a bird if it can't fly, if it can't do the work of wing and wind. Our goal is the evangelization of the world, including its least-reached peoples. It's not surprising that when I finally wrote up my conclusions—after having watched *An Inconvenient Truth*, after having been an investigating villager, after having reflected on my own experience in India and Pakistan—I did so in the form of a SWOT analysis: strengths, weaknesses, opportunities, and threats. How does the current ecological crisis affect the fulfillment of the Great Commission? After Christar's leadership read my report, they turned to me and asked, "Okay, so what do we do about it?" Pragmatists, every last one of them! There is no prayer more central to the missionary enterprise than the one Jesus taught us in Matthew 9. Jesus sees the people. He knows they are distressed and downcast, like sheep without a shepherd. He is moved to compassion. But Jesus retains his eyes of faith by which he can see that the harvest is plentiful. "Ask the Lord of the harvest, therefore," he tells us, "to send out workers into his harvest field" (9:38). Implicit in this prayer is a yearning: we want to get the job done.

The Lausanne creation care "Call to Action" declares the belief that "environmental issues represent one of the greatest opportunities to demonstrate the love of Christ and plant churches among unreached and unengaged people groups in our generation."[3] I had a hint of that in Pakistan. At one point while our earthquake relief team was still in the town of Battagram, the Pakistani military approached our team and offered us a three-year project to rebuild the entire medical infrastructure in Battagram District. Our team leader came back from a meeting to report this offer. Everyone on the team was gratified—"Cool!"—but I was a church planter; my jaw dropped! Three hundred and sixty-one thousand Muslims living in 1,300 square kilometers in one of the 10/40 Window's most politically inaccessible regions—and we were being offered protected and sanctioned access to every single home! Surely this was one of those once-in-a-lifetime moments for a church planter. But in that November of 2005, we weren't church planters; we were relief workers. Most of us—including myself—were short-termers. We needed to head home to our families and to our stewardships. The work of SIM, the agency that sponsored our team, wasn't normally up in the mountains but down in the plains. The same was true of Christar workers. All agencies in Pakistan were working with diminished staffs, doing the best they could with what they had for the ministry opportunities that they knew God had already given them. It would actually have felt cruel to try to sell this new opportunity to my colleagues in SIM or Christar. A three-year project to rebuild the entire medical infrastructure in Battagram District—in the end, we just let the opportunity pass. The harvest is plentiful, but the workers are few.

But what if the church had a vision for a reconceptualized type of worker, one which didn't separate relief work from church planting? On the day my two friends from India and I took our leave, teammate Dr. Steve Duncan called me aside and told me of his firsthand experience of the heartening stories about tsunami relief efforts in Islam's most populous country. This integration of relief and church planting was precisely what was happening there. Church planters have long been burdened for that region, as effectively kept at bay as the missionaries who longed to minister in Pakistan's Northwest Frontier Province. But the tsunami opened a door, and a group of workers saw it not only as an opportunity to provide relief but as a chance to preach the gospel, make disciples, and establish local indigenous churches. Disasters open doors. They open previously closed borders, but also previously closed hearts. One day, one of our hospital guards told my friend, "Allah will surely grant you paradise because you have come here to help our Pakistani people." My friend, a fervent evangelist, didn't let that opportunity go to waste. (In chapter 4, I will profile a different Muslim country—the sixth most religiously repressive country in the world, according to the World Watch List—for which its many environmental issues also represent an open door.)

Pragmatism, however, has a weakness. It has a temptation. You can hear it if I speak of disasters with more opportunistic excitement than with

the lament and grief they deserve. Pragmatism's great temptation is to lapse into utilitarianism, to treat everything as just a means toward a greater exclusive end. Environmental missionaries want to evangelize the world, but as we'll see when we turn to the biblical basis of environmental missions, the creation care they engage in must be *bona fide*. It must be recognized as a good calling in its own right, an act of worship to the Creator, an act of love for our neighbor. While I am thrilled that an environmental approach will supply more visas for church planters to enter closed countries, creation care must mean more than a creative access strategy. While I believe that environmental missions represents a way to pass the baton of church planting on to the next generation, a generation that seems to have intuitively embraced environmental stewardship, creation care must mean more than just a relevant recruitment strategy. (The younger generation will quickly see through such inauthenticity anyway.) So we must diligently keep working at the point of integration between creation care and church planting. The true pragmatist will be willing to embrace such diligence, spurred on by a belief that "environmental issues represent one of the greatest opportunities to demonstrate the love of Christ and plant churches among unreached and unengaged people groups in our generation."

"If You Ask Me as a Person"

Admittedly, earthquakes and the tsunamis they may spark—in other words, the main examples of this chapter—are not caused by global climate change, the other major example of ecological crisis. Whether earthquakes can even rightly be called an environmental disaster, or whether it even matters what they are called, the earthquake of 2005 in Pakistan taught me about opportunity, and about church planting opportunity at that. It taught me about the most basic definition of environment when you strip away all the -*isms* like blankets from a smothered bed. I have thought often about this region of Pakistan in the years following 2005. I thought of it, of course, when Osama bin Laden was discovered in Abbottabad, our staging ground (though reportedly he hadn't moved there until 2006). I thought of the region when news arrived that the Northwest Frontier Province had once again been largely overrun by the Taliban. Christian witness, I imagine, has once again been expunged, an opportunity lost. But I thought often about this cerebral-palsied girl when record floods devastated Pakistan in the summer of 2010, deluging 20 million people. Was she one of them? I tracked down regional statistics. Thirty-five people in her area, Battagram District, were reported dead. Was she one of them? I watched the news obsessively, letting statistics and aerial shots float by. I looked for footage of people. I looked for her.

I've worked hard in the intervening years to study the science and policy of environmental issues, including that of global climate change, but I've never developed a taste for the politics. Let others debate it; it's our obligation to always search out and find the human face. In truth, I believe it's one of the responsibilities of the church. One difference between the 2005 earthquake and 2010 floods is the link to human-caused global climate change. Regarding the floods, the director of the World Meteorological Organization claimed, "There's no doubt that clearly climate change is contributing, a major contributing factor."[4] Pakistan's foreign minister said his country's flooding "reconfirms our extreme vulnerability to the adverse impacts of climate change."[5] Nonetheless it wasn't long before climate change skeptics threw the blanket of "natural variability" over the disaster, thereby absolving us all from blame and responsibility. While it is true that a single weather event—however extreme—can never be traced definitively to climate change, I was struck by the dilemma faced by Dr. Gavin Schmidt, a NASA climate researcher. Commenting on another summer 2010 disaster, Schmidt told the *New York Times*, "If you ask me *as a person*, do I think the Russian heat wave has to do with climate change, the answer is yes. If you ask me *as a scientist* whether I have proved it, the answer is no—at least not yet."[6]

So my question is: what's wrong with answering *as a person*? Answering as a person will sustain us in ministry long after the son of Issachar, like Dr. Schmidt, investigates and still finds himself confused. It will sustain us long after our pragmatism has succumbed to utilitarianism and been found wanting.

A year after we had left India, we received news that my best friend there, Golu, had died. He died of cerebral malaria. He died of a single mosquito bite. My love for Golu extends to that air space that surrounded him, a space in which that lethal insect flew. My love for him extends to the stagnant waters of the Gangetic Plain in which that insect was bred. There are many reasons why I now call myself an environmental missionary, and I'll refer to them throughout this book in our task of supplying legitimation and rigor, but I can trace my conversion to one red raised spot on the brown skin of someone I loved in Jesus' name.

NOTES

1. Al Gore, *An Inconvenient Truth*, dir. Davis Guggenheim (Hollywood: Paramount, 2006), DVD.

2. For those who would like to like to retrace a few of my steps, particularly on the science of climate change, let me recommend two respected climatologists who are also evangelical believers: Sir John Houghton and Dr. Katherine Hayhoe. Sir John Houghton is the former director of the UK Met office and was the chairman of the Scientific Assessment Working Group, which collected and summarized the research of global climate change, publishing it in the Summary Reports of the Intergovernmental Panel on Climate Change (IPCC). Dr. Katherine Hayhoe is a climatologist at Texas Tech University and also an IPCC scientist. Katherine is the author of *A Climate for Change: Global Warming Facts for Faith-based Decisions* (FaithWords, 2009), a book she coauthored with her husband, Andrew Farley, the lead pastor of Ecclesia in Lubbock, Texas. A good place to start with Houghton is with his addresses at Wheaton College. I recommend John Houghton, "Sir John's Word to Pastors" (speech at Center for Applied Christian Ethics, Wheaton College, January 24, 2007), http://www.wheaton.edu/CACE/CACE-Audio-and-Video (accessed February 14, 2012).

3. Lausanne, "Call to Action."

4. Nathanial Gronewold and Climatewire, "Is the Flooding in Pakistan a Climate Change Disaster?," *Scientific American*, August 18, 2010, http://www.scientificamerican.com/article.cfm?id=is-the-flooding-in-pakist (accessed May 16, 2013).

5. Anwar Iqbal, "Climate Change Responsible for Floods: Experts," *Dawn*, August 23, 2010, http://archives.dawn.com/archives/41768 (accessed May 15, 2013).

6. Justin Gillis, "In Weather Chaos, a Case for Global Warming," *New York Times*, August 15, 2010, A1.

2

WHAT IS ENVIRONMENTAL MISSIONS?

The seeds for the current emergence of environmental missions were sown in the late 1980s. The Second Lausanne Congress on World Evangelization met in Manila in 1989, and the resulting *Manila Manifesto* proves that creation care is not just some twenty-first-century innovation of the Third Congress and the *Cape Town Commitment*. The *Manifesto* makes only one brief reference to creation care, but it places it at the heart of the Lausanne Movement's great premise that the modern world still desperately needs a Savior:

> *A. The Whole Gospel: 1. Our Human Predicament:*
>
> Human beings have become self-centered, self-serving rebels, who do not love God or their neighbour as they should. In consequence, they are alienated both from their Creator and from the rest of his creation, which is the basic cause of the pain, disorientation and loneliness which so many people suffer today. Sin also frequently erupts in anti-social behavior, in violent exploitation of others, and in a depletion of the earth's resources of which God has made men and women his stewards. Humanity is guilty, without excuse, and on the broad road which leads to destruction.[1]

Around the same time, Ghillean Prance, soon to be appointed director of the Royal Botanical Gardens in Kew, UK, presented a paper at the Au Sable Institute of Environmental Studies near Traverse City, MI. The title of the paper was "Missionary Earthkeeping," and thus Prance coined the term in which our definition of environmental missions has its origins. (Here in my book, appendix 2 is entitled "Origin of the Terms" and gives a brief survey of how evangelical leaders, in their language, have tried to reframe environmentalism from a Christian perspective. In that appendix, you can also read the reasons why I prefer the term "environmental missions" over "missionary earthkeeping.")

The first time I ever encountered the words "environment" and "mission" together in print was in a short article about Ed Brown of Care of Creation. Ed is the author of *Our Father's World: Mobilizing the Church to Care for Creation*, offers a seminar by the same name, and most recently has been appointed as the Lausanne Senior Associate for Creation Care. Ed has become a personal friend and is Eden Vigil's closest colleague. In 2007 I read these words of his:

> The basic idea [behind forming Care of Creation] was to combine the environment and missions in a way we don't think anyone else is doing. On an organizational level, no mission organization in North America is openly both environmental and missional. It's very similar to medical missions in its approach to the mission field. When you take out the word "medical" and put in the word "environmental," that's what we are. We want to do practical things where we help people by sharing the Gospel, but we want to serve people and serve the church by helping to heal the land through various means. In Kenya, this means reforestation.[2]

Now actually Ed's statement stops short of offering a formal definition of environmental missions. Instead it offers an analogy—"very similar to medical missions." This analogy has made its way into the Lausanne creation care "Call to Action": "We encourage the church to promote 'environmental missions' as a new category within mission work (akin in function to medical missions)."[3] The analogy is a helpful explanatory device. Evangelicals have had long exposure to medical missions and intuitively know how missions-minded doctors can treat both body and soul, and how mission agencies can deploy a care-giving infrastructure.

Over the next couple years, Ed helped organize the Environmental Missions Consultation that met in Manhattan, Kansas, in July 2010. This is the gathering that wrote the specific definition we use in this book. The background behind the Consultation is also described in appendix 2, as are quick references to the earliest usage of the term "environmental missions" (Peter Harris in 2000) and some of the earliest calls to it as a new category within missions. All that background information is meant to convey that our definition has the weight of progression, reflection, comparison, and collaboration. That definition is:

> *Environmental missionaries are those sent cross-culturally to labor with Christ—the Creator, Sustainer, and Redeemer of all creation—in caring for the environment and making disciples among all peoples.*

The remainder of this chapter unpacks this definition phrase by phrase. Subsequent chapters will test whether sound biblical, historical, and missiological study corroborates it.

"Environmental missionaries"

In the end we don't really have a definition of a category of missions at all; it's the definition of a type of people: "environmental missionaries are . . ." It's inevitable that the personal approach to missionaries would have emerged at the Consultation. We were friends helping to bless and define each other, and offering that definition to others who would join us. That probably explains the plural usage as well: "Environmental missionaries *are* . . ." as compared to "An environmental missionary *is* . . ." We intend to be many, and a team, and a movement.

"those sent"

The quality of "being sent" is inescapable in the etymology of the word "missionary" ("apostle," "sent one"). Romans 10 establishes sending as the baseline activity for all preaching, hearing, believing, calling on, and being saved: "And how can anyone preach unless they are sent?" (v. 15). The opening scene of Acts 13 indicates that the sending of missionaries has its locus in two sources: the Holy Spirit, who said, "Set apart for me Barnabas and Saul for the work to which I have called them" (v. 2), and the church at Antioch who obeyed the Spirit. This is more than just a matter of missionary technicality. What hope does an environmental missionary have in addressing the current ecological crisis, let alone raising the spiritually dead to newness of life in Christ? Only if we speak in the authority of the Holy Spirit who sent us can we hope for success. Bob Blincoe, US director of Frontiers, teaches that the word "apostle" has its roots for Barnabas and Saul in a common Hebrew word, *shaliakh*: "The messenger arrives as though the one who sends had himself arrived."[4] Whether we stand before an unbelieving audience, beside the demon-possessed, or over an eroded riverbed, we'd best stand in the authority of Christ. The same applies for the local church's participation in our sending. Environmentalist Bill McKibben argues in his book *Deep Economy* that a renewed sense of community is the primary hope for our deep environmental problems.[5] A missionary sent from a healthy local fellowship is steeped in a sense of community and is equipped to cultivate that in others.

"cross-culturally"

Maybe in the end, the crossing of cultures is the difference that the "-s" makes between the way the two words "mission" and "missions" are used in the church, at least as a North American evangelical understands them. Both words demand that we go and bring forth the good news of Christ the King through word and deed. But *mission* can be exercised within our own culture with no necessary reference to those who live on the other side of our cultural and linguistic borders. It took a couple centuries for Zinzendorf, Carey, and Judson to transcend the insular *mission* of the Reformation, and to bring the Protestant church into obedience to the Great Commission. Making disciples of all nations (*ta ethne*) will invariably require us to transcend our Northern European roots just as much as the apostles were required to step out beyond the Hebrew-speaking world.

What Is Environmental Missions?

Strong churches have been established in countries once considered "mission fields" for the West. As they rise up and assume responsibility for evangelizing their own countrymen, they too need the challenge to send cross-culturally.

"to labor with Christ"

We know all about laying down our lives in missions. Does it look any differently in environmental missions? In chapter 8 I'll tell the story of Dorothy Strang, martyred for her work among the Anapu people of the Amazon rain forest. At the least, environmental missionaries intend to work hard and sacrificially. But laboring *with Christ* makes all the difference in the world. However discouraged we might become in our work, we are colaborers with Christ, with a full share in his glory (Rom 8:17). Dallas Willard reminds us that our colabor with Christ is of the nature of being in the yoke with him (Matt 11:29–30). His yoke is easy, his burden light, because Christ bears the weight of it and determines the direction and pace. Willard writes:

> What we most learn in his yoke, . . . beyond acting with him, is to abandon outcomes to God accepting that we do not have in ourselves—in our own "heart, soul, mind, and strength"— the wherewithal to make this come out right, whatever "this" is. We simply have to rest in his life as he gives to us.[6]

A labor that is also rest is a mystery that all Christians, missionary or otherwise, must learn.

Laboring with Christ presumes that spreading the gospel and doing "creation care" is something that Jesus is already doing. That's Henry Blackaby's famous dictum: discover what God is doing and join him there.[7] This is a privilege and a joy.

"the Creator"

Maintaining a Trinitarian perspective on life requires discipline. When someone prays, "Thank you, Father, for dying on the Cross for us," we all know what he or she means, but something is lost in not recognizing that it was the second person of the Trinity who was crucified to the sorrow and satisfaction of the first. It's natural when we talk of creation care that our reference to "the Creator" be of God the Father. *Our Father's World* is a fitting title for Ed Brown's book. But even in the Genesis passage, it is the plural name *Elohim* who calls all things into being. The persons of the Trinity are apparently conversing among themselves: "Let us make mankind in *our* image, in *our* likeness" (Gen 1:26, emphasis added). In the New Testament of course, Trinitarian language comes to light. Colossians 1:15,16: "The Son is the image of the invisible God, the firstborn over all creation. For in him all things were created: things in heaven and on earth, visible and invisible, whether thrones or powers or rulers or authorities; all things have been created through him and for him." John 1:1–4 (NLT):

> In the beginning the Word already existed. The Word was with God, and the Word was God. He existed in the beginning with God. God created everything through him, and nothing was created except through him. The Word gave life to everything that was created, and his life brought light to everyone.

It is appropriate to refer to Jesus, as well as his Father, as "the Creator."

"Sustainer"

Colossians 1:17 (NLT): "He existed before anything else, and he holds all creation together." First Corinthians 8:6: "Yet for us there is but one God, the Father, from whom all things came and for whom we live; and there is but one Lord, Jesus Christ, through whom all things came and through whom we live." This is an important consideration. Deism easily creeps into our debates about creation*ism* (i.e., the origins debate) and can also do so in creation care. Do we believe that the Jesus who set the hydrological cycle in motion still attends to precipitation and evaporation? When we labor with Christ the Sustainer, we find hope that he who created the earth is still actively caring for it and desires to empower our small efforts as we join with him. We'll take up the topic of "Christ the Sustainer" further in our biblical basis chapters.

What Is Environmental Missions?

"Redeemer"

Christ the Redeemer is more familiar language. The great paean of Colossians 1 that begins, "The Son is the image of the invisible God, the firstborn over all creation" (v. 15), ends with, "For God was pleased to have all his fullness dwell in him, and through him to reconcile to himself all things, whether things on earth or things in heaven, by making peace through his blood, shed on the cross" (vv. 19–20).

"of all creation"

The question remains, however, how much of creation participates in the redemption that Christ has bought? The title *Redeemer* itself appears only in the Old Testament, primarily in Isaiah and Ruth, as one might expect. In the New Testament, Christ *redeems*, as an action, but the recipients invariably seem to be people, whether Israel (Luke 24), "those under the law" (Gal 4:5), or the 144,000 witnesses (Rev 14:3). Does Christ's redemption extend to his nonhuman creation? Or does this further confuse the strange language of Mark 16's commission: "Go into all the world and preach the gospel to all creation" (v. 15)? We'll seek to answer these questions in the biblical basis chapters. For now, here is a quotation from theologian George Caird's references to the book of Revelation (with allusions to Isaiah):

> Nothing from the old order which has value in the sight of God is debarred from entry into the new. John's heaven is no world-denying Nirvana, into which man may escape from the incurable ills of sublunary existence, but the seal of affirmation on the goodness of God's creation. The treasure that men find laid up in heaven turns out to be the treasures and wealth of the nations, the best they have known and loved on earth redeemed of all imperfections and transfigured by the radiance of God. Nothing is excluded but what is obscene and false, that is, totally alien to the character of God. Nowhere in the New Testament do we find a more eloquent statement than this of the all-embracing scope of God's redemptive work.[8]

"in caring for the environment"

In this phrase, the practical nature of our labor with Christ—Creator, Sustainer, Redeemer—is spelled out. What do environmental missionaries do? They care for the environment. What does this look like practically? One can usually throw out a few examples, and the inquirer will easily identify the category without needing an exhaustive list of the jobs: reforestation, sustainable agriculture, watershed management, drinking water supply, waste management, renewable energies, toxic mitigation, wildlife conservation. Green industry jobs are the fastest growing worldwide, but what this really means is that almost every profession can have a green expression of it. Does the construction of the massive blades for a wind turbine represent a set of "green jobs," or are they good old-fashioned "manufacturing jobs" now redirected to a renewable energy purpose? Similarly, there can be green lawyers, green journalists, or even green schoolteachers. I was recently asked whether Eden Vigil could provide an environmental missionary to help write a nationwide environmental curriculum for the high schools of a Muslim North African nation. This is a government initiative of that nation.

Medical missions, veterinary missions, Bible translation, and missionary aviation are missions categories in which, when one explores them even a little, one discovers a wide range of practical jobs, roles, and contributions. An X-ray technician or a hospital chaplain is no less a medical missionary than the physician leaning over the hospital bed administering chloroquine to a malaria patient. Nonetheless these categories tend to be suitably self-proscribed. Seen in context, we know what activities qualify as "medical." Environmental activities seem to cut across an unwieldy number of disciplines. It actually makes it hard to organize environmental missions as a category. Christian Veterinary Mission finds many of their long-term recruits in the CVM chapters that they've organized in university vet schools and in the professional associations in which they participate. It's relatively easy to call CVM missionaries back together for a focused training that can extend their effectiveness. There are no comparable associations for Christian environmental professionals. Precisely because there are so many possibilities for environmentally described activities, defining the work as a category will depend on the full phrase "caring for the environment." Any activity that intends to extend care qualifies.

Christar found me in that traditional recruiting pool of traditional missions agencies—namely, Bible colleges and seminaries; Moody Bible Institute in particular. Whatever additional education I have is in the arts and humanities, not in the sciences. How will Bible college and seminary grads contribute to "caring for the environment"? First, I would say that the point of environmental missions is integration, so that these grads, as members of an environmental missions team, may find themselves taking the lead in the other component of environmental missions: making disciples. But secondly, they can easily find the training that will give them the skills necessary to make an important contribution to an environmental project. For example, one of the easiest skills to acquire is how to go into a new region and collect the data for an environmental assessment. That data can then be sent off, even off the team, for analysis. Any solutions proposed for a local environmental problem should be simple enough to communicate to the local believers—simple enough for the environmental missionary to understand it himself or herself in the first place.

Environmental missionaries who come with professional degrees will likely need training in Bible, theology, and cross-cultural ministry—making disciples being the other core activity. The biggest challenge for professional grads, however, since they intend to "labor with Christ," is to cultivate and apply the character and mission of Christ to their creation care. In other words, their work will need to be creative, sustaining, and redemptive in ways they may have never learned at university.

I asked the Consultation if we should change the word "environment." The emerging "Christian" terminology is "creation care." No, the group said, we've used the words "creation"/"Creator" already in the definition. Besides, we've given sanction to the word "environment" already in the name "environmental missionary." I think our chosen phrase was also a means to talk in the language of the wider world. In other words, environmental missionaries intend to enter into good-faith partnerships with secular or unbelieving environmental professionals. The other question I asked the Consultation was, "Should this phrase precede or follow 'making disciples'?" Leave it first, they said. The issue in placing these two phrases isn't priority; it is integration. If we had put "caring for the environment" after "making disciples," it would have been too easy to dismiss creation care as an add-on, a hobby, something to do only when the *real* work is done.

"and making disciples"

"Make disciples," we know, is the only command given in the Great Commission (Matt 28:18–20). All other verbs—as you go, baptizing, and teaching—are key participles which inform our disciple making, but "make disciples" is the core element of our stewardship. I'm not sure that anything new needs to be said about discipleship from an environmental missions' perspective. Care of Creation Kenya, as described in Craig Sorley's profile (appendix 3), would challenge environmental professionals to pause before they jump in with their expertise to "fix the problem." Our task is to disciple local believers to care for their local piece of creation. The problem, whatever it is, will have its roots in sin, and so we evangelize and disciple with a view to transforming the human heart for the glory of God. Church planting addresses how you make disciples when there is no healthy local body of Christ as a context for that discipleship. Church planting honors the value that Christ—the head of the church—places on local fellowships.

Church planting also keeps us honest as missionaries. It can be easy to organize and supervise a project; planting a church verges on the impossible and certainly eludes any formula that we try to bring to it. Combine the unsearchable riches and wisdom of God, the desperate deceitfulness of the human heart, and the prowling opposition of Satan—nowhere is this glory and agony played out more fully than in a fledgling church plant, whether among the least reached or not. Church planting also encourages the long view of things. Plant geneticist Wes Jackson once said, "If your life's work can be accomplished in your lifetime, you're not thinking big enough."[9]

What Is Environmental Missions?

"among all peoples"

I saw Christar's former president Pat Cate recently, and our visit brought back many fond memories. Pat used to stand up in front of students, candidate classes, even struggling veterans and say, "God did not call us to the E-A-S-Y people; he called us to the A-L-L people." Going to the least-reached Buddhists, Hindus, Muslims, and East Asians will require from environmental missionaries the same degree of courage, perseverance, sacrifice, vision, and creativity as it requires of the current missionary task force. Environmental missionaries will go to the unreached with the same conviction that motivated generations before them: Jesus is worthy of the worship of *every* tribe, tongue, people, and nation.

NOTES

1. Second Lausanne Congress on World Evangelization, "The Manila Manifesto," *The Lausanne Movement*, http://www.lausanne.org/en/documents/manila-manifesto.html (accessed July 15, 2013).
2. Ed Brown, quoted in Tri Robinson and Jason Chatraw, *Saving God's Green Earth* (Norcross, GA: Ampelon, 2006), 64.
3. Lausanne, "Call to Action."
4. Bob Blincoe, "'Unleashing the Gospel': Perspectives Lesson #5," PowerPoint slide, http://www.perspectives.org.
5. Bill McKibben, *Deep Economy* (New York: Holt, 2007).
6. Dallas Willard, *Renovation of the Heart* (Colorado Springs: New Press, 2002), 209–10.
7. Henry Blackaby, *Experiencing God* (Nashville: Broadman & Holman, 1994).
8. George Caird, *The Revelation of St. John the Divine* (New York: Harper & Row, 1966), 279-80.
9. Wes Jackson, quoted in interview by Majora Carter, *The Promised Land*, American Public Media, http://www.thepromisedland.org/wes-jackson-transcript (accessed July 15, 2013).

3

WILLIAM CAREY,
AN ENVIRONMENTAL MISSIONARY

William Carey sailed to Calcutta in 1793 and has subsequently become known as the "Father of Modern Missions." In 1993, to commemorate the bicentenary of Carey's arrival, the Indian government issued a six-rupee postage stamp. Carey is portrayed on the stamp at his desk. Serampore College—cofounded by Carey in 1818 and still educating students today—stands in the background. Carey with pen in hand has an open book in front of him. He leans into his writing.

My missionary career began in India in 1993, and I found the Indian government to be quite antagonistic to missions. I can't imagine that they were celebrating William Carey the preacher of the gospel of Jesus Christ. So the postage stamp begs the question: for which of Carey's contributions does India wish to commemorate him? Certainly he was a linguist of Indian languages, publishing dictionaries, grammars, or Bibles in Sanskrit, Bengali, Hindustani, Marathi, Telinga, Kurmata, Orissa, Punjabi, and Assamese. Carey was also one of India's first social reformers. His written appeals to the British government resulted in the abolition of *suttee*, the ceremonial casting of the widow onto her husband's funeral pyre. In the end, all we know of the reason behind the government's respect is embodied in the accompanying declaration: "The Department of Posts is privileged to issue a stamp on Dr. William Carey, who adopted India as his country and strived to serve her people."

Robynn and I often advised new missionaries arriving in India that living there would feel like living in exile. Unpack your bags and, almost as a spiritual discipline, throw out the cardboard boxes with which you had purchased your appliances and other supplies. Why keep this cardboard flattened and dusty in a storage space, where it would only grow moldy and attract earwigs? Jeremiah 29:4–7 was our inspiration:

> This is what the Lord Almighty, the God of Israel, says to all those I carried into exile from Jerusalem to Babylon: "Build houses and settle down; plant gardens and eat what they produce. Marry and have sons and daughters; find wives for your sons and give your daughters in marriage, so that they too may have sons and daughters. Increase in number there; do not decrease. Also, seek the peace and prosperity of the city to which I have carried you into exile. Pray to the Lord for it, because if it prospers, you too will prosper.

If William Carey did anything in India that demonstrated he had "adopted India as his country," he planted a garden. Those five acres of his garden grew to become the second largest botanical collection in India. In a sense, while Indian education, linguistics, and social reform have all moved on in the last two hundred years, botany has a way of always mindfully attending to its roots. Botanical pioneers have their names preserved in the scientific designations of growing, reproducing plants (e.g., *Careya arborea*). Textbooks and indexes are republished year after year. Seed varieties and hybrids (as well as invasive species) are launched and centuries later flourish even to the point of domination. William Carey was a world-class botanist. Among his luggage when he first traveled to India in 1793 were 108 botanical journals. Two trees and an herb (*Careya arborea*, *Careya spherical*, and *Careya herbacea*) bear his name. He introduced the Linnaean system of classification, edited Roxburgh's *Florica Indica*, and almost singlehandedly founded the Agricultural Society of India.

If his own personal garden was the surest sign of "adopting India as his own country," then the Agricultural Society may be the surest demonstration of "striving to serve her people." After just one year of his arrival, Carey sent a detailed list back to England, requesting farm implements

and seeds. "Apply to London seedsmen and others," he writes, and then casts his appeal in the language of adoption and service, "as it will be a lasting advantage to this country; I shall have it in my power to do this for what I now call my own country."[1] One of the earliest biographers of Carey writes:

> After lengthened experience and observation he arrived at the conclusion that much might be done for the welfare of India by improved agriculture, better fencing, better implements of husbandry, and the introduction of useful cereals and plants. The cultivation of the soil was carried on in the most wretched manner; the cultivators were miserably poor and ignorant; the landowners wrung all they possibly could out of them, and left them for the most part without the inspiration of hope. It appeared to Carey that if an Agricultural Society could be formed for India, it would show the proprietors of the soil that their interest lay not in rack-renting the peasantry, but in developing the resources of the country, and might besides be a preparation for the time when men should beat their swords into ploughshares and their spears into pruning hooks.[2]

Dana Robert, in her paper "Historical Trends in Missions and Earth Care," writes:

> Protestant missions from William Carey forward were consistent with Catholic and Orthodox practice in recognizing that controlling the human relationship to nature was essential to the success of Christian mission. The vision of subduing nature and replacing the wilderness with the fields and farms of "civilization" was a common trope among early Protestant missionaries.[3]

In the language of power encounter, Robert notes, "In the context of modern science, Protestant missionaries used their observations of nature as a way to attack the perceived superstitions of non-Christian religions and world views, and to affirm God's creative and providential power."[4]

Certainly the "modern science" of the era, probably better labeled "natural history," was obsessed with classification of genus and species. Ever since Adam named the animals, we've understood that naming an item is a form of exercising dominion over it. William Carey may even have been something of a control freak in this matter. His own son said of Carey's garden, "The arrangements made by him were on the Linnaean system; and to disturb the bed or border of the garden was to touch the apple of his eye."⁵ Nonetheless there are modern witnesses—Wendell Berry and Wes Jackson among them—who appreciate Carey's variety of "modern science" as compared to the modern science we know today. They would say that our care of creation took a hit when science moved from trying to understand "the way things *are*" to "the way things *work*." Carey seemed to exhibit a genuine wonder over the piece of tropical creation where God had placed him. The wonder is lost when a materialistic, reductionist knowledge of "the way things work" is employed to manipulate nature so as to appropriate its power—technology as power grab. And Carey's wonder over creation was genuine. He valued it often with no apparent hint of utilitarianism. His son Jonathan eulogized:

> In objects of nature my father was exceedingly curious. His collection of mineral ores, and other subjects of natural history, was extensive, and obtained his particular attention in seasons of leisure and recreation. The science of botany was his constant delight and study; and his fondness for his garden remained to the last. No one was allowed to interfere in the arrangements of this his favourite retreat; and it is here he enjoyed his most pleasant moments of secret devotion and meditation.⁶

In fact, in an oft-told story, Carey was once chided by his friend Joshua Marshman for not wearing a wide-brimmed hat while working in his garden, thus overexposing himself to the sun. Carey, we are told, retorted in mock anger, "What does Marshman know about a garden? He only appreciates it, as an ox does grass!"⁷ No hint of utilitarianism there.

Often when I do an environmental missions presentation at a new church, I'll begin with a slide of *Careya herbacea*. It has a teardrop-shaped leaf with a white bud that when in blossom reveals a red, wispy flower. Its taproot juts off to an angle and, closest to the surface of the soil, resembles a green caterpillar. I ask the audience if they can identify this plant. They can't. I then show a slide of William Carey and ask if they can identify this man. A goodly number can. Maybe it's that distinctive bald head. (Kingdom: *animalia*; Phylum: *chordata*; Genus: *Homo*; Species: *sapiens*; Name: *William Carey*.) I then explain how the Father of Modern Missions was also a world-class botanist. It's all good fun and has a surprising legitimatizing effect on my environmental missions presentation. Such is the respect we grant Carey. Is William Carey the first (modern) environmental missionary? If our definition of environmental missions demands a high degree of integration between gospel preaching and creation care, then that's the same standard we should apply to our historical inquiry. Was William Carey an environmental missionary, or was he an environmental hobbyist? Does it matter?

Six years into his time in India—still a "newbie" in many respects, still keenly under the authority of others—Carey confided to a friend in a letter:

> Mudnabati, 17th July 1799—Respecting myself I have nothing interesting to say; and if I had, it appears foreign to the design of a mission for the missionaries to be always speaking of their own experiences. I keep several journals, it is true, relating to things private and public, respecting the mission, articles of curiosity and science; but they sometimes continued and sometimes discontinued; besides, most things contained in them are of too general or trivial a nature to send to England, and I imagine could have no effect, except to mock the expectations of our numerous friends, who are waiting to hear of the conversion of the heathen and overthrow of Satan's kingdom.[8]

Even years later, when he filed a report with the Society back in London and commented on the status of his physical health, he wrote:

> I have also a great fondness for natural science, particularly botany and horticulture. These, therefore, furnish not only exercise, but amusement for me. These amusements of mine are not, however, enjoyed without expense, any more than those of my brethren, and were it not convenient for Brother Marshman's accusers to make a stepping stone of me, I have no doubt but my collection of plants, aviary, and museum, would be equally impeached as articles of luxury and lawless expenses; though, except the garden, the whole of these expenses are borne by myself.[9]

Robynn and I kept a garden in India. In our first houses, we gardened the way most urban Indians do: with potted plants out on the balcony, up on the roof, and in the courtyard. When we moved to the ashram, we even hired a *mali* (gardener). He planted bougainvillea around all our entranceways. We had a poinsettia bush that bloomed, as promised, over the Christmas season. (While the family *Euphorbiaceae* has members native to India, our poinsettia probably came from the Americas, but everyone considers it now "naturalized" to India. Carey, as we'll see, wouldn't have minded.) While providing a beautiful and pleasant "green space" is integral to the ministry of ashram, nonetheless the garden was often nothing more than the simple joy of Robynn puttering around in the dirt. Her favorite day-off activity was a trip to the nursery with her best friend. They would come home with plants piled up on the back of flatbed bicycle trolleys. Robynn has coauthored a book about missionary burnout.[a] We, like Carey, know the health benefits of "amusements" and the therapeutic value of flowers in bloom. But we also know some of the unease that Carey must have felt. (In fact, the full title of Robynn's book is *Expectations and Burn-*

---

[a] Sue Eenigenburg and Robynn Bliss, *Expectations and Burnout: Women Surviving the Great Commission* (Pasadena: William Carey Library, 210).

out.) Is gardening just an amusement, an expense and luxury, a distraction from the "conversion of the heathen and overthrow of Satan's kingdom"?

For that matter, what do we make of David Livingstone? In 1857 he published *Missionary Travels and Researches in South Africa*. Published today, if you picked a book by that title off the shelf of your Christian bookstore—the only store that carries missionary titles as a matter of course—you would know what to expect. Your first clue, however, that something was different with Livingstone's book would be the front page, which shows an etching of the tsetse fly instead of any overtly Christian symbol. "Livingstone described flora and fauna, including the habits of animals, waterways and topographical features, varieties of trees, diseases of animals and people, species of birds and animals, the state of the soil and prospects for farming and animal husbandry, and so forth."[10] Was Livingstone really a missionary on his missionary travels? Was evangelism just a hobby?

Integration is important, so we'd best not invest William Carey yet with the fatherhood of environmental missions, but I do intend to argue that Carey's garden (and Robynn's too for that matter) is where we start. Wendell Berry reports, "My daddy used to say, 'If you want people to love their country, let them own a piece of it.'"[11] We never owned the ashram, but we felt like we owned the soil in which every one of the plants grew. For that matter, I guess we did have legal ownership of the soil at one point. We purchased a few trolley loads of clay and *khad* (desiccated cow manure) to be mixed into the sandiness of the soil that was there. We nurtured that land. We loved India.

Actually my most profound experience of Indian soil involves a whole different type of planting into the ground. Robynn's best friend since childhood was Amy Jo Boone. They were dormmates at boarding school in Pakistan. Amy Jo and her husband, David, were living in New Delhi and expecting their first child when Amy Jo was diagnosed with a brain tumor. She is buried in Delhi, in a Christian cemetery in the military cantonment out toward the airport. Her coffin is a simple wooden box. I was one of the men who held the ropes that lowered her coffin down into the ground. My end of the rope—I can still feel its rough texture—was too short, and

I almost fell into the grave. My foot desperately dislodged the dirt at the edge as I tried to retain my balance. With her body placed in the ground, I then joined some of the others in picking up a small handful of Indian soil in our hands. I held it in my palm, and then let it drop with a gentle *thump* on the lid of the coffin. Was Amy Jo just another missionary buried on foreign soil? Not anymore. It was home.

"Build houses and settle down; plant gardens and eat what they produce . . . Seek the peace and prosperity of the city to which I have carried you into exile. Pray to the Lord for it, because if it prospers, you too will prosper." As we seek the environmental peace and prosperity of our new homes, Jeremiah 29:4–7 takes on the flavor of a Great Commission. Jonathan Wilson-Hartgrove's new book is about the Benedictine vow of stability. Benedict apparently considered stability so important that he includes it in the first chapter of his Rule. Wilson-Hartgrove picks up the phrase "stability with roots of love" from Anselm of Canterbury, a twelfth-century monk:

> Without roots of love, we easily become slaves to our own desires, using the place where we happen to be as a staging ground for our own ambitions and manipulating the people around us so they might serve our objectives. We do this, of course, with the best of intentions—even in God's name. But until we give ourselves to a place—until we care enough to learn the names of its flowers and its second cousins—stability's wisdom suggests we cannot know very much about the One who so loved the world that he gave his only Begotten Son . . . If I really want to learn to love my neighbor, I have to pay attention to the details of life in this place. Stability's wisdom calls me to learn the ways and means of grafting onto this place.[12]

Ed Brown has a perspective on William Carey which summarizes our discussion:

I am not sure if I would want to call William Carey's horticultural work a "hobby." (Maybe "avocation" would be a better word?) Though his scientific pursuits were a sideline to his primary vocation of evangelism and Bible translation, he produced world class results which is why we have the strange situation where half the world knows Carey as a great missionary but knows nothing of his scientific renown, and the other half lauds his science without being aware of the work he did as a missionary. Whether hobby or avocation, he offers us an example that evangelists and church planters everywhere could emulate: You don't need to give up your primary calling to be effective in understanding and working to heal God's creation.[13]

A historical inquiry into William Carey yields one more helpful thing. I am going to propose it as a test of whether such "missionary" activities as gardening represent a fruitful rootedness into a sense of place, or rather a mere hobby, a pleasant diversion. I call it "the test of invasive species." Carey had no compunction about freely swapping seeds and seedlings between India and Great Britain. In one famous episode, a botanist near Sheffield sent him a package of seeds that included daisies. Carey wrote, "I know not that I ever enjoyed, since leaving Europe, a simple pleasure so exquisite as the sight of this English Daisy afforded me; not having seen one for upwards of thirty years, and never expecting to see one again."[14]

John Montgomery was inspired to write a poem of this incident that includes this homesick stanza:

Thrice welcome, little English flower!
To this resplendent hemisphere,
Where Flora's giant offspring tower
In gorgeous liveries all the year:
Thou, only Thou, art little here,
Like worth unfriended and unknown,

Yet to my British heart more dear
Than all the torrid zone.[15]

The capitalized *Thou* pronouns in this stanza are troubling because the reader begins to wonder whether the daisy is being addressed as a metaphor of Christ, also "little" in India, unfriended, unknown. By the last stanza, the daisy is a "pledge of Hope." During times of overpowering sorrow Carey can "call to mind, how—fresh and green, / I saw thee waking from the dust, / Then turn to heaven with brow serene / And place in God my trust." If the daisy is the image of the resurrected Lord, then how unsettling to see him named "little English flower," held dear primarily to "my British heart."

Of course this is sentiment that the poet Montgomery put in Carey's mouth as narrator. I can recognize the homesickness in the narrator's voice. Truth be told, that's likely what the poinsettia in the ashram's front garden meant to me. I ignored it through most of its season of bloom except for right around Christmastime when I could imagine it in a foil-covered pot, sitting near the windowsill of my childhood home, snow visible on the Kansas soil outside. I can also recognize in the narrator's voice a nagging doubt, which I would venture to guess that every missionary of any era serving in India has felt. It's in the form of a question that comes late at night with the ceiling fan swirling over your head. You look up to heaven and ask, "Is Jesus nonnative to this place? Is he unable to grow in this soil? Am I bringing a foreign god of my own spiritual horticulture to India?"

May I use the idiom that (the real) William Carey had "a devil of a time" keeping daisies alive in India? He wrote to a friend in Yorkshire:

> With great labour I have preserved the common *Field Daisy*, which came up accidentally in some English earth, for these six or seven years; but my whole stock is now only one plant.
> I have never been able, even with sheltering them, to preserve a root through the rains, but I get a few seedlings every year.[16]

Carey's report also sounds like some of the prayer letters that we used to write about our church plants. On more than one occasion our whole

stock of disciples was "now only one." Many disciples never persevered through the rains.

Parenthetically, I can mention that invasive species can work both ways. Rhododendron is prevalent in the Himalayas; in fact, one of the most enjoyable portions of the Everest Base Camp trek is the Rhododendron Forest on the far side of Tengboche monastery. In England, however, "rhodie bashing" has become the conservationist's obsession. That's the term given to clearing out *Rhododendron ponticum*, an invasive species that, in fairness to Carey's cohorts in India, was likely introduced from Spain or Portugal. Meanwhile, immigration of Gujarati Indians to Leicester, England—a city in which Carey once pastored—has become so great that Leicester will likely become Europe's first "Asian city." You can visit a church building in Leicester—one named after Carey following his departure to India—which has subsequently been sold to a Hindu society and now houses a Vishnu temple.

The difference between a plant species labeled *nonnative* and one labeled *invasive* is significant. The very word "invasive" suggests the aggression of an invasion, the power encounters of a Boniface, the missionary to Germania who chopped down the oak grove sacred to Thor. An official definition reads: "An invasive species is an alien species whose introduction does or is likely to cause economic or environmental harm or harm to human health."[17] *Nonnative* species are likewise introductions but with neutral or beneficial impacts. (It's both Christmastime and pheasant-hunting season right now in Kansas—the one time of the year when depressed Western Kansas communities are grateful for all types of Chinese imports.) I've always thought that E. Stanley Jones, author of *Christ of the Indian Road*, would find modern contextualization agendas needlessly complicated and a tad bit invasive. Jones preferred the almost botanical-sounding term: "naturalization."

Christ is becoming a familiar Figure upon the Indian Road. He is becoming naturalized there. Upon the road of India's thinking you meet with him again and again, on the highways of India's affection you feel his gracious Presence, on the ways of her decisions and actions he is becoming regal and authoritative.[18]

You can almost picture Jesus blossoming along the roadside, heartening the foot-weary traveler. And he's no English daisy. In fact, a nonnative species—introduced but noninvasive—is also an inadequate metaphor. Jones writes, "He [Jesus] and the facts not only command us to go, but he, standing in the East, beckons us to come. He is there—deeply there, before us. We not only take him, we go to him."[19] Let's call it the glorious biodiversity of the kingdom of God. "Every nation has its peculiar contribution to make to the interpretation of Christianity. The Son of Man is too great to be expressed by any one part of humanity."[20] And so my proposed test of a missionary's gardening hobby is this: are you planting more nonnative species of plant than native? If so, you may also be sowing a self-defeating vision of Christ, planted in doubt, cultivated without rest, and harvested for few others' enjoyment than your own.

NOTES

1. William Carey, quoted in Smith, *Life of William Carey*, 301.
2. James Culross, *William Carey* (London: Hodder & Stoughton, 1881), 191.
3. Dana L. Robert, "Historical Trends in Missions and Earth Care," (paper presented at the Overseas Ministries Study Center, New Haven, CT, December 2009). An edited version of this address is available: Dana L. Robert, "Historical Trends in Missions and Earth Care," *International Bulletin of Missionary Research* 35, no. 3 (July 2011): 123–28.
4. Robert, "Historical Trends," 125.
5. Jonathan Carey, quoted in Eustace Carey, *Memoir of William Carey, D.D.* (Hartford: Canfield & Robins, 1837), 431.
6. Ibid., 431.
7. S. Pearce Carey, *William Carey: The Father of Modern Missions* (London: Wakeman Trust, 1923), 407.
8. William Carey, quoted in Smith, *Life of William Carey*, 204.
9. Ibid., 206.
10. Robert, "Historical Trends."

11. Wendell Berry, "Strachan Donnelly Lecture on Restoration and Conservation," (speech, Prairie Festival, Land Institute, Salina, KS, September 25, 2010).

12. Jonathan Wilson-Hartgrove, *The Wisdom of Stability* (Brewster, MA: Paraclete, 2010), 83–84.

13. Ed Brown, email message to author, June 29, 2011.

14. William Carey, quoted in Smith, *Life of William Carey*, 173–74.

15. John Montgomery, quoted in Smith, *Life of William Carey*, 174–75.

16. William Carey, "Extract from a Letter of Dr. Carey, in India, to Mr. J. Cooper, of Wentworth, Yorkshire," *London Magazine*, August 15, 1823, 676.

17. "Invasive Species," Exec. Order No. 13112, February 3, 1999, http://www.invasivespeciesinfo.gov/laws/execorder.shtml (accessed October 4, 2011).

18. E. Stanley Jones, *The Christ of the Indian Road* (New York: Abingdon, 1925), 28.

19. Ibid., 51.

20. Ibid., 194.

4

PROFILE OF AN ENVIRONMENTAL MISSIONS FIELD

The Republic of "Acts17land" is an island nation stretched off the southwestern tip of India in the Indian Ocean. Its 310,000 inhabitants reside in twenty-six atolls made up of approximately 1,200 islands, but primarily on the capital island of "Capital Island." The two major industries are tourism and fishing. The average elevation is one meter above sea level. The population is Sunni Muslim.

The first survey trip I ever made as the founder of Eden Vigil was to a country that was thoroughly recognizable as a "traditional" (i.e., church planting) missions field. Due to such issues as coastal erosion, marine pollution, and overfishing—to name just a few of its ecological problems—it was also recognizable as an environmentalist's tableau. And so, as the argument of integration goes, it should therefore be recognizable as an *environmental missions field.*

This country also has one of the strictest security regimes I have ever encountered. Its status as a "closed" or "creative access" country makes it a good choice for a profile in this book, since I hope to demonstrate how an environmental approach can open closed borders and closed hearts, this being a part of the strategic legitimation of environmental missions. Nonetheless this nation's hair-trigger aversion to Christian missions presents certain difficulties in writing about it. I rarely if ever use its actual name in public. The geographically astute in my audience will be able to identify this nation based on the description I give above. Others can get online to track down the reference to this nation being number six on the 2013

❧ ENVIRONMENTAL MISSIONS ❦

World Watch List of most religiously repressive countries. The code name that I use for our religiously repressive island example of an environmental missions field is Acts17land, a name which, as I will explain, has special reference to God's purposes in both creation and in the securing of borders. (One additional security measure: this chapter will not include endnotes.)

Muslim, Repressive, Least Reached

In 2008, free elections ended thirty years of totalitarian military rule for Acts17land, but the constitutional reforms that allowed the elections also had specific religious provisions. Previously only the president was required to be a Muslim; now all citizens were under the requirement of Islamic adherence. On this basis, the nation claims to be "100 percent Muslim." Followers of Christ are secret. Luggage at the airport is searched for Bibles and for other "anti-Islamic" items.

Islam arrived in the twelfth century, perhaps from Morocco, and replaced the Ashokan Buddhist expansion that had overwhelmed their closest neighbor, Sri Lanka. The people are Sunni Muslims and, similar to much of the Islam practiced in the Indian subcontinent, there are many occurrences of *pir* (saint) worship. Women seem to have a great deal of freedom. Startlingly, Acts17land has one of the highest divorce rates, not only in the Muslim world but in the entire world. Non-Muslim tourists flock to the islands every year for the beautiful white sand beaches and colorful coral reefs, but each tour group is met at the airport and whisked away to one of the "resort islands" where the alcohol and seminudity add billions to the tax base without tempting those citizens who live on what are called "the inhabited islands," places for which foreigners need special permits to visit, let alone reside.

Acts17land was briefly a British protectorate for the sake of a Royal Air Force base on a leased southern island. Its most profound experience with colonialism, however, was with the Portuguese, an experience that, although brief, to this day affects the national attitude towards Christianity. In 1558, in order to secure their Indian Ocean trade route, a small Portuguese invasion army killed the ruling sultan. Their fifteen years of occupation were cruel and, according to modern retellings, included forced conversions to Christianity at the threat of execution. But then the Portuguese were deposed—slaughtered actually—as the result of a well-planned, well-executed nighttime raid. The leader of that raid has become Acts17land's national hero, their George Washington figure. The ring road around Capital Island is named in his honor. His tomb is located at the center of that island and is an object of *pir* worship. The presence of this hero's name keeps the story of liberation alive, so much so that every child on Acts17land grows up equating Christianity with greed and cruelty. The *Lonely Planet Guide* claims: "Nationals are devout Muslims. In some countries this might be considered incidental, but the national faith is the cornerstone of Acts17land's identity and it is defended passionately at all levels of society . . . There's no scope for religious dissent, but there's also almost no desire *to* dissent" (p. 26).

In the strangest story to come out of Acts17land recently, a South Indian schoolteacher was conducting her daily lessons in a schoolhouse on one of the remote inhabited islands. She was teaching the points of the compass—north, south, east, west. That evening the children went home and complained to their parents, "Ma'am is teaching the Christian cross." A mob of parents formed, and the teacher was transferred to a different island for her own safety. "Keeping the peace" seems to be the government's primary religious motivation. In other words, they are not *shari'a* ideologues in themselves, nor do they use religion to garner votes; instead the government's religious repression seems preventative. They are intent on placating a Wahhabi element that returned to Acts17land after Afghanistan's *mujahadeen* wars, and so the government tolerates nothing that will rile them up, and certainly not Western (akin to the Portuguese) conversionist missionaries.

Since, as the saying goes, necessity is the mother of invention, those seeking to bring the good news to Acts17land are among the most creative of creative access workers that I know. They face two great obstacles: (1) how to gain residence among the people, particularly in the outlying islands; and (2) how to minister under such intense public scrutiny.

ENVIRONMENTAL MISSIONS

Trashed, Resource Diminished, Inundated

Begin with felt need. Thus goes the advice not only for an evangelist but also for the worker seeking a creative access visa. In the case of Acts17land, one doesn't have to listen too hard. Their greatest felt need is openly announced whenever their president appears before a microphone at the United Nations. These islands, among the most beautiful of all God's creation, are in need of environmental defense.

Each island is quite small. Even Capital Island, which houses 103,000 people, is only two square kilometers in size. Trash disposal is inevitably a problem, particularly as the country imports more and more goods made of, or contained in, plastic and Styrofoam. The resort islands, leased by huge international hotel chains, are under the strictest of environmental regulations and have a vested interest in keeping their beaches pristine. But trash on the inhabited islands often just gets thrown into the lagoon and, like most marine waste, washes back up on shore. As for Capital Island, their trash gets barged a few kilometers away to a nearby "Rubbish Island," where the landfill is so filled to capacity that the actual island grows out into the ocean by one square meter a day.

Skipjack tuna and yellowfin tuna have been major food crops and exports. Fishing is Acts17land's second leading industry. Due to the threat of overfishing, use of nets has been outlawed so that the fishing fleet is made up of medium-sized boats where individual fishermen—up to twenty abreast—use pole and line to hook each fish and fling it on board. But other countries, using big, industrial purse seine nets, occasionally intrude illegally in the Indian Ocean. And overfishing of other species, particularly of grouper, has disrupted the food chain to additionally threaten tuna populations. On land, since the soil is comprised largely of crushed coral, almost all agriculture is in the form of small homestead gardens. Rice, Acts17land's staple, is imported. UNICEF reports that nearly 17 percent of Acts17land's children are underweight and up to 19 percent suffer from stunting or low height-to-age ratio, largely due to a limited commitment to breastfeeding, but beyond that, "lack of a proper diet has meant that more than a quarter of [Acts17land's] children between six months to five years old are anaemic, and nearly 60 percent of children suffer from iron deficiency" (www.unicef.org).

Tourists to Acts17land are attracted by its vibrant coral reefs, but these ecosystems have not been immune to the effects of ocean acidification and warming. When temperatures warm, zooxanthellae algae, which give coral its color, die off, leaving it "bleached." If the algae don't return, the coral dies. The exposed calcium carbonate becomes brittle, and the coral will break off, even as the result of wave action. Of all of Acts17land's environmental threats, however, none has received as much attention as the sea-level rise, which is the result of global climate change. The average elevation of the islands is one meter above sea level. What that means is that when the tsunami of 2004 hit, for certain islands, the wave washed completely over them and kept right on going. Sea-level rise can occur when the world's glaciers or land ice melts and that water or those sliding ice sheets are added to the oceans. Consequently, there are nightmare projections of what would occur if the West Antarctic ice shelf or the Greenland ice shelf (or half of both) would collapse; ocean levels would rise ten to twenty meters worldwide. But Acts17land is not having to wait on sci-fi scenarios. Water molecules expand with heat, and so thermal expansion of the oceans is already resulting in a sea-level rise, which is already causing coastal erosion. Whole islands are being eaten away, meter by meter. The presidents of Acts17land have appeared before the United Nations and have declared, "We are in danger of losing our homeland." In one highly publicized event, the president conducted a cabinet meeting underwater, all ministers fitted with scuba gear passing an SOS resolution from tables anchored to the ocean floor. The president surfaced in front of the TV cameras and told the press, "We are trying to send our message to let the world know what is happening and what . . . will happen to [Acts17land] if climate change is not checked. This is a challenging situation, and we want to see that everyone else is also occupied as much as we are and see that people actually do something about it."

ENVIRONMENTAL MISSIONS

Sincerity, Opportunity, Access

In 2009 the president of Acts17land announced that his country was making plans to be the first carbon-neutral nation in the world, and to do so before 2020. Vatican City, a much smaller country, will likely beat them to that honor, and Acts17land will also have troubling addressing the diesel fuel burned to power their boats. Nonetheless, what makes Acts17land's pronouncement so interesting is that it was issued not by a Scandinavian country, nor by California, nor by a US Democrat; it was issued by the president of a repressive Muslim country, and he did so on Al Jazeera television. So much for the stereotypes of environmentalism!

I once had an occasion to ask a World Bank official about Acts17land. The country was one of his clients. I asked him how he addresses the skepticism that accuses Acts17land of being just another small developing country that uses environmentalism as a ploy to redistribute wealth from the West. He told me, "There's two things to keep in mind. One is that [Acts17land] is actually a *donor* state to the UN." In other words, they receive enough income from tourism to pay their own way, thank you. When they do collaborate with foreign governments, they enter into true partnerships. Such was the case with the Japanese partnership that designed, manufactured, and placed *tetrapods*—concrete objects that disrupt wave action and preserve the coastline around Capital Island. "Secondly," the World Bank official said, "I knew [the current president] when he was in the opposition in parliament. Even back then he was talking about these things." So there is a sincere appeal that qualified engineers, biologists, and other environmental professionals might join forces with Acts17land and come to the aid of a country that is progressively trashed, resource diminished, and inundated. And since it is more than the resort islands that are under threat, access is more freely given to the inhabited islands.

I suppose the question can be legitimately asked: what makes Acts-17land different than any other closed country for which some particular tentmaking opportunities present themselves? Couldn't someone just take a job, which in this case just happens to be environmental, and conceive of himself or herself as a regular tentmaking missionary? Why would this worker self-identify in a new category, "environmental missionary"? I suspect the difference is in how that worker *enters* that job in that country and then how he or she *leaves* it. Acts17land is a small country—population of 310,000—compared to other least-reached Muslim people groups of Bangladeshi Shaikh (128 million) or Indonesian Java Pesisir Lor (34 million.) Acts17land does appear on the World Watch List of most religiously repressive nations but is tucked among the more dramatic cases of Afghanistan, Iraq, Somalia, and Yemen. In some ways its paradisiacal tropicality makes it hard to take seriously as a mission field. But Acts17land is the poster child of global climate change. Christian environmentalists want to be there, as to an epicenter. And they enter Acts17land through the bigger picture. Coastal erosion, by definition, will present itself as a local problem and might offer up a local tentmaking job. But the "job" of preventing coastal erosion is to address climate change. Tetrapods are a laudable measure, but a Band-Aid one. Acts17land needs true believers. When the president of Acts17land appeared before the UN General Assembly, he likened his country's critical status in the world to the defense of Poland against the Nazi threat of 1939. "If you thought that defending Poland was important," he declared, "defending [Acts17land] is important. If you can't save [Acts17land] today, you can't save yourself tomorrow." In the end though, his analogy is tragic, because no one thought of defending Poland in 1939. Those who clamored to do so were considered fanatical interventionists. I don't know how else to say it: environmental missionaries enter a people group as unapologetic environmentalists; Christian in their worldview, but as environmentalists nonetheless.

And when I refer to how an environmental missionary "leaves" a job in that country, I'm not referring to how he or she *exits*, which to date has usually been the result of a police order. Instead, I mean, how do they leave the state of that ecosystem: improved? more hopeful? A business visa to a closed country can simply mean access for a disinterested tentmaker. Even the most dedicated of businesspeople (operating in Business as Mission (BAM)), while hoping to make profits, hoping to employ people, hoping to proliferate contacts, isn't necessarily interested in doing his or her part to "save" the national economy or add to the GDP. Environmental missionaries are truly out to save the planet. Churches planted without trees planted, who is to lament that except the environmental missionary? Souls saved without soils saved is considered a job half done, if only to the heart and calling of an environmental missionary.

Acts Chapter 17

Today military and intelligence agencies of the world have computer programs that randomly spit out code names. But the best code names have some underlying meaning behind them. They serve to inspire and give courage and hope to the campaigners. Acts 17 contains Paul's sermon at the Areopagus. He told his audience,

> The God who made the world and everything in it is the Lord of heaven and earth and does not live in temples built by human hands. And he is not served by human hands, as if he needed anything. Rather, he himself gives everyone life and breath and everything else. From one man he made all the nations, that they should inhabit the whole earth; and he marked out their appointed times in history and the boundaries of their lands. God did this so that they would seek him and perhaps reach out for him and find him, though he is not far from any one of us. (Acts 17:24–27)

The nation that I have tried to so secretively profile in this chapter has established a Sovereign Wealth Fund. Every year it takes a portion of its great tourism earnings and deposits it in this contingency fund. They will use this fund, as the seas rise and as the opportunity presents itself, to purchase a new homeland for their people: maybe from India, maybe from Sri Lanka, maybe from Australia. It is the Creator God who made the Indian Ocean and who made the coral islands. He, we are told, marks out the boundaries of the earth's inhabitants. But Scripture says he appoints the nations and their boundaries for one primary purpose: "that they would seek him and perhaps reach out for him and find him." The long, slow rise of the thermal expansion of the oceans is a matter of *chronos* time for

❧ Profile of an Environmental Missions Field ❧

Acts17land (eight inches since 1870, accelerating more quickly today), but reaching this people group with the gospel is a matter of *kairos* time, a divinely appointed moment, deserving of a new category within missions.

5

OLD TESTAMENT BASIS: A MANDATE TO BLESS

Agabus, as a character in Scripture, is best known as the prophet who ties Paul's belt around his own hands and feet, testifying that the owner of that belt would be arrested in Jerusalem and handed over to the Gentiles (Acts 21:11). But Agabus' first appearance in Scripture is in Acts 11 when he meets up with Paul in Antioch and predicts through the Spirit that a severe famine is imminent. The disciples mobilize: "The disciples, as each one was able, decided to provide help for the brothers and sisters living in Judea. This they did, sending their gift to the elders by Barnabas and Saul" (vv. 29–30). A spiritual message, an environmental crisis, a mobilization of the church—for precisely these reasons, I often claim that Agabus is the church's first environmental missionary.

My audience smiles politely. They know I'm engaging a teaching device rather than making a primary argument for the biblical legitimation of environmental missions. To claim that Agabus is the first environmental missionary sounds as cute as saying that Noah was the world's first wildlife conservationist, a claim I've nonetheless heard on more than one occasion. But at some point, to the extent that God's people should mobilize during times of resource scarcity for the sake of the poor, and to the extent that God's people do have stewardship for the flourishing of the animal kingdom (Gen 1:22), these are more than just amusing allusions. For example, to call Adam "the first gardener" is, as we will see, to say something profound about humanity's very reason for being, about our very bearing of God's image. The better-known story of Agabus—the belt-related prophecy in Acts 21—is really just an anecdote in the narrative of Paul's later years. The less-remembered story—mobilizing for famine in Acts 11—is the background for the passages in 1 Corinthians 16 and 2 Corinthians 8–9, passages that provide so much of the church's theology of giving.

Of course, no mention in the pages of Scripture is ever made of photovoltaic solar panels, just as there is no reference to drilling in the Arctic National Wildlife Refuge nor to regulating sulfur dioxide emissions for the sake of combating acid rain. But this lack of specificity is a good thing, at least for those who refuse to be lazy and distant in their approach to Scripture. We might think it would be easy if Scripture had said, "Thou shalt not blow the tops off mountains in order to get to the coal seams below." As the New Covenant instructs us, however, we are forced to build our specificity into a specific person: the Holy Spirit of the triune God—not "What did these words say?" but rather "What is *he* saying?" We are forced to burrow down to the specific essence of a command: love thy neighbor, do justly, love mercy, walk humbly. Once down deep enough, we discover that commands are but virtues; we get to *do* what in fact we *are* and are becoming in Christ Jesus. A common party game is to speculate: "If you were dropped in a forest with nothing but a bottle of water and a knife, could you survive?" I would argue that if you were dropped in an old-growth forest equipped with nothing but the command "Love thy neighbor," you would have all you need to protect that forest from clear-cutting, even if there wasn't another human being within a hundred miles, or a hundred years.

Environmental missions has the added task of building not only a theology of creation care but also its missiology. In other words, is there a biblical basis for the *integration* of creation care and missions? Our analogy to medical missions may prove helpful here. Medical missions did not achieve its legitimacy by trying to claim that Dr. Luke, accompanying Paul on his later journeys, is a biblical appearance of the first medical missionary. There's no evidence that Luke practiced a single leech-worth of medicine while on his travels. For that matter, references to physicians in both the Old Testament and the New are few, and none provide "either moral guidance or a favorable view of physicians." While "both Testaments abound

with healing and resurrections," as one medical ethicist writes, "none were ascribed to physicians or medicine, but rather all were acts of God through His appointed agents."[1] So medical missions finds its biblical legitimation by first developing a general theology of care for the human body, something easily evident in God's "appointed agents," including Jesus Christ. That theology of care then has an encounter with the theology of missions. This in turn is followed by some mediation of the two, a mediation that is best done in the life of Christ and in the gospel. This then is the dynamic you'll see unfold in this book for the biblical basis of environmental missions: (1) the development of a theology that has been underdeveloped to date, in our case a theology of creation care; (2) an encounter with a robust theology of missions, perhaps a first-time encounter; and (3) a mediation between the two, found primarily in Christ Jesus, the Creator, Sustainer, and Redeemer of all creation. At the end of each of the next three chapters, I will present an Environmental Missions Model in diagram form, which by chapter 8 will not only summarize the theology of environmental missions but indicate how we practically apply that theology.

This current chapter is about the Old Testament and will look at three passages (the first three chapters of Genesis actually). With only three passages, our theological goal is obviously not comprehensiveness, but certainly comprehension.

Genesis 1: God Created That Which Was Good

"In the beginning, God created the heavens and the earth." The only way to make Genesis 1:1 simpler is to strip it down to its subject and its verb: "God created." Creation implies ownership. "The earth is the Lord's, and everything in it, the world, and all who live in it; for he founded it on the seas and established it on the waters" (Ps 24:1,2). Theologian John Stott writes, "For the earth belongs to God by creation and to us by delegation."[2]

Complexity is going to want to rush straight to the conjunction ("and") in Stott's statement in order to speculate about what delegation to us humans might mean. We too will go there, to discuss what it means for humanity to have dominion in creation, but it pays to linger over the phrase "the earth belongs to God by creation." A mutually accusatory debate argues whether environmentalism should be earth-centric or anthropocentric. Both sides are wrong. The gentle answer from Genesis 1 is that environmentalism should be theocentric. Even when the *Cape Town Commitment* introduces its Action section in order to spur us on to human action, it begins with a gentle tug on the reins, as if to say, "Slow down, simplify, think God first":

> All human beings are to be stewards of the rich abundance of God's good creation. We are authorized to exercise godly dominion in using it for the sake of human welfare and needs, for example in farming, fishing, mining, energy generation, engineering, construction, trade, medicine. As we do so, we are also commanded to care for the earth and all its creatures, because the earth belongs to God, not to us. We do this for the sake of the Lord Jesus Christ who is the creator, owner, sustainer, redeemer and heir of all creation.[3]

Here are four basic observations from Genesis 1:1–25, the world before Adam and Eve:

1. God created all of it: flora, fauna, and ecosystems.

2. God reflects on his creation and calls each thing good.

3. God created not only creatures (plants, birds, cattle, etc.) but also natural processes (seed bearing, cycles of day and night, etc.).

4. God's blessing has a view toward the flourishing of his creation: "God blessed them [fish and birds] and said, 'Be fruitful and increase'" (1:22).

Part of the respect that we show to others is the way we treat their possessions. The reason I take off my muddy boots at the door of my neighbor's house is not because his carpeting is particularly beautiful nor because it represents some burning bush to which I should confer reverence. No, if there is any burning bush in my neighbor's house, it is in his image-bearing soul, and so the main reason I avoid soiling my neighbor's carpeting is

because I respect him. Because God is worthy of our worship, at the very least we seek to avoid the disrespect of trashing his creation. But the lover of God knows that engaging creation care can be a proactive means of worshiping and praising the Creator and Owner. In chapter 11, on the topic of prayer, I'll argue that environmental missionaries are well positioned to be among the most worshipful of all of God's laborers.

After each occurrence of God's creation, we read the pronouncement "And God saw that it was good." The Hebrew word for "good" is *tobh*. It is a basic word (i.e., not given to much complexity). It means an intrinsic goodness, a sense that God's handiwork turned out exactly as he intended. Long before the sun provided warmth on human skin, it was good. Long before the first fish was filleted and roasted on the grill, it was good, swimming as it was among the ocean's multitude. There is a seventh occurrence of the pronouncement of goodness. It occurs on the sixth day after the creation of Adam, but this time God declares that it is "very good" (1:31). Some preachers claim that adding the modifier "very" to what is obviously a formulaic pronouncement signifies that humanity's goodness somehow surpasses all that has preceded it in creation. This may be true, but the phrase actually reads, "God saw all that he had made, and it was very good" (1:31). The "very goodness" is in the whole composite of creation with mankind, for sure, right smack in the middle of it.

God's pronouncement of goodness extends over the natural processes that are part of creation. The sun, moon, and stars are all part of a diurnal/nocturnal cycle that we now understand as orbital patterns. Plants and trees were created "bearing seed according to their kinds" (Gen 1:12). This is a fertility process. We might understand it in terms of relationships. God created a relationship between the birds and the sky, between the fish and the oceans, between one generation of a creature and its progeny. All of these relationships are good. This is important because, as we'll see soon, the Fall is the story of broken relationships as much as it is a story of broken goodness. Additionally, so many environmental problems are definable in terms of an attacked or distressed relationship. For example, biologist E. O. Wilson employs the acronym HIPPO to categorize the ways in which species go extinct: Habitat destruction, Invasive species, Pollution, Population pressure, and Overharvesting.[4] In each case, there is a relationship—to habitat, to other nonhuman species, to air and water, to *Homo sapiens*, to predation—that has been broken.

"God blessed them and said to them, "Be fruitful and increase in number; fill the earth" (1:28). We might recognize this verse as God's blessing over Adam and Eve, but actually it's not, or at least not yet. One day earlier, six verses earlier than for humanity, God blesses the animal kingdom—or at least birds and fish—by name: "God blessed them and said, 'Be fruitful and increase in number and fill the water in the seas, and let the birds increase on the earth'" (1:22). Then the next day, six verses later, God gives a similar blessing to Adam and Eve. God does add a very important addendum for humans: "Be fruitful and increase in number; fill the earth and subdue it. Rule over the fish in the sea and the birds in the sky and over every living creature that moves on the ground" (1:28). Certainly we are not to believe that the blessing over Adam abrogates the blessing over the animal kingdom, as if God is a fickle creator. Instead we understand humanity's dominion as extending over what God has declared to be blessed and good. In other words, we have a stewardship over the flourishing of the natural world. It is like we have been appointed first-chair violin in an orchestra. We have a responsibility to play our own instrument beautifully, but the rest of the orchestra, while watching the conductor, is also listening to the first violin. The orchestra is taking visual cues from the conductor and auditory cues from the first violin. At the conclusion of the symphony, the conductor takes the first bow, but then turns to the first violin that he or she might take the second bow.

Part of our labor for the glory of God is to see to it that flora and fauna are fruitful, that they increase, that they fill the earth. It's hard to argue that we have been particularly good stewards when over 70 percent of the world's fisheries are being fished at or above capacity. Whole fisheries—like cod or bluefin tuna—have collapsed.

> How many are your works, Lord!
> In wisdom you made them all;

the earth is full of your creatures.
There is the sea, vast and spacious,
    teeming with creatures beyond number—
    living things both large and small.
There the ships go to and fro,
    and Leviathan, which you
        formed to frolic there.
(Ps 104:24–26)

Whenever I read this great paean of worship to God, often called the "Nature Psalm," and whenever I consider how whale populations have collapsed in our world's oceans, I remind myself that however much God intended whales to provide oil, ambergris, and meat, he also intended them to frolic.

We also read in Genesis 1 that "God created mankind in his own image, in the image of God he created them; male and female he created them" (v. 27). We'll consider in the next section the command given to humanity to subdue and rule, along with the command to till and keep (Gen 2:15), but here I'll make one final point about chapter 1. There is no doubt that being created in the image of God makes all the difference in the world for humanity, but we image bearers are nonetheless embedded as creatures alongside other species in God's creation, and this too makes all the difference in the world. (As first violins, we might be auditory conductors and second in line to receive applause, but we are also seated among the orchestra, and in fact could not influence it if we weren't.) Our embeddedness is part of the "very goodness" of the total creation. The molecules of our bodies, according to the imagery of Genesis 2, are formed by the dust of *terra firma*. We may have been enlivened by "the breath of life" (2:7), but so was the animal kingdom (1:30). We might have a unique role in the ecosphere, by way of image and added command, but it is a role that is nonetheless interior to that ecosphere, not exterior.

The great Christian thinker Francis Schaeffer, in his book *Pollution and the Death of Man*, approaches this topic of who human beings are by first making a declaration about who God is. "So the Judaistic-Christian God is unique: He is infinite, and He is, at the same time, personal."[5] And so when God creates the universe, because he is infinite, there is a great chasm between himself and all created beings, including humans. But because he is also personal, God creates human beings in his image, and so the chasm is also between humanity and other created beings: animal, plant, and machine. ("Machine" is his term for nonliving created order: rocks, soil, water, etc.) Schaeffer uses the following diagram to illustrate the created order. The personal nature of the Creator is reflected on one side; the infinite nature is reflected on the other. The chasm on each side is placed at different places so as to emphasize associations: image-bearing man related to a personal God, and created man related to his fellow finite creatures.

The Personal-Infinite God

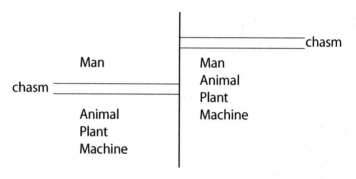

Diagram 1.[6]
Francis Schaeffer's diagram in *Pollution and the Death of Man* demonstrates that the personal and (simultaneously) infinite nature of the Creator means that we must account for both mankind's separation from *and* connection to the rest of creation.

We must maintain these two orientations of man simultaneously, every bit as much as we maintain the personal and the infinite nature of God. As Schaeffer writes,

> On a very different level, we are separated from that which is the "lower" form of creation, yet we are united to it. One must not choose; one must say both. I am separated from it [i.e.,

animal, plant, machine, "nature"] because I am made in the image of God; my integration point is upward, not downward; it is not turned back upon creation. Yet at the same time I am united to it because nature and man are both created by God.[7]

A great deal of Christian thought has gone into exploring the implications of how bearing God's image affects our approach to caring for creation, or whether we should care at all. And yet maintaining the two orientations of humanity simultaneously suggests that we should give equal exploration to the effect of our creatureliness. It was God's choice—unlike what he determined for the angels—to make us embodied beings and to embed us intricately in a web of natural relationships. We cannot fray even a single strand of the web without somehow skewing the whole and endangering our own node. It will be an argument for our New Testament chapters whether, as I heard one radio preacher say, we live on "a disposable planet," but it is at least in our genetic makeup as creatures to not foul the nest, to not pollute the watering hole while we do live here.

Genesis 2: God Confers Stewardship: "The Creation Mandate"

Genesis 1:28 and 2:15—be fruitful, multiply, subdue, rule, till, keep—is often called "the Creation Mandate." This is, of course, a label we've applied, similar to how the phrase "the Great Commission" embodies a set of disciple-making commands. At Eden Vigil we often say: environmental missions combines the Great Commission and the Creation Mandate in the Great Commandment, which is to love God and love others.

Much has been written about the verbs "subdue" (*kabash*) and "rule" (*radah*) of Genesis 1:28, verbs which theologian Chris Wright admits, "are strong words, with a sense of imposing of will upon another."[8] Before one examines these etymologies, we should recognize that the context of these imperatives is what God says first, a context of blessing and fruitfulness: "God blessed them and said to them, 'Be fruitful and increase in number; fill the earth.'" This blessing and command doesn't pit us against the natural world since, as we've seen, the same exact blessing and command was also given to nonhuman species (1:22). Sometimes we tragically position

God as the first Darwinian, as if he is but a boxing manager in the human's corner, cheering mankind on in the survival of the fittest, ignoring the punches we throw below the belt. The first imperatives in the Creation Mandate are not "subdue" and "rule," but rather "be fruitful," "multiply," "fill the earth."

To be fruitful and multiply, to fill the earth, certainly includes population growth of the human species. Numerical growth is in fact a standard mark of blessing: "A large population is a king's glory," according to Proverbs 14:28. Nonetheless, the emphasis of blessing and fruitfulness is not on demographic growth, but on what Christian philosophers refer to as "human flourishing." An unpruned grapevine can be said to have multiplied, but isn't necessarily fruitful. Cancers and landfills can also be understood in terms of multiplication. Another way to understand this first part of the Creation Mandate might be as follows: "Choose to be characterized by life rather than death," a choice very quickly violated by Adam and by his firstborn son, Cain. This admonishment is given voice in Moses' rousing appeal to the Israelites, verses that have become the basis for much of Jewish ethics:

> This day I call the heavens and the earth as witnesses against you that I have set before you life and death, blessings and curses. Now choose life, so that you and your children may live and that you may love the Lord your God, listen to his voice, and hold fast to him. For the Lord is your life, and he will give you many years in the land he swore to give to your fathers, Abraham, Isaac and Jacob. (Deut 30:19,20)

The word "subdue" (*kabash*) invokes images of wrestling holds or of policemen brandishing tazers, but the mandate comes before the Fall and the Curse, and thus there is no hint of antagonism in the air. Chris Wright claims: "The first word, 'subduing [the earth],' probably implies no more than the task of agriculture, though it now encompasses many other products of human ingenuity and effort."[9] We link the words "subdue" and "rule," but, textually, these commands are in two different sentences.

"Subdue" appears in the blessing: "Be fruitful and increase in number; fill the earth and subdue it" (1:28). We should more properly ask how subduing the earth relates to *filling* it, rather than ruling over it. "Subdue" is a strong word, but no word to fret over. Even the most radical environmentalist happily backpacking in a protected wilderness area, so long as she has a down-filled sleeping bag, a propane camp stove, and a bear bag with which to hang her food in a tree, is engaged in "subduing" that wilderness. In the end, subduing can mean more about increasing the capacity of the human rather than diminishing nature's. Choosing life for oneself does not necessarily mean choosing death for another, as if the Creation Mandate is a zero-sum game.

"The second word, 'rule over,' is more distinctive," Wright claims. "It describes a responsibility for human beings that is entrusted to no other species—the task of ruling or exercising dominion over the rest of creation. With this word, God is passing on to human hands a delegated form of God's own kingly authority over the whole of his creation."[10] The King James Version translates the Hebrew *radah* as "have dominion over," and this one term for kingly authority is how the question is normally engaged: what does it mean for humans to exercise *dominion* over creation? In our age, we are much more familiar with the term's cognates, such as "dominate" or "domineering," and less with its royal implications. The use of *radah* in Leviticus 25:43 and Ezekiel 34:4 does indicate that dominion can be exercised ruthlessly, harshly, and brutally, but these verses also indicate that neither should it be. In the end, our application of dominion must not only bow to Genesis 1's context of a life-giving blessing, but also to the context of how Scripture understands royal authority delegated to us from the King of kings. One Jewish scholar says of Genesis 1:28:

> This power, however, cannot include the license to exploit nature banefully for the following reasons: the human race is not inherently sovereign, but enjoys its dominion solely by the grace of God. Furthermore, the model of kingship here presupposed is Israelite, according to which, the monarch does not possess unrestrained power and authority, the limits of

his rule are carefully defined and circumscribed by divine law, so that kingship is to be exercised with responsibility and is subject to accountability.[11]

King David is a helpful example. As king, he had authority and power over Bathsheba and over her husband, Uriah (2 Sam 11:1–12:10). He was able to impose his will upon them. When David encountered an obstacle, namely, Uriah's honorable abstinence from his wife, David's authority extended even up to death, easily traceable through the command he gave to Joab to organize the battle that killed Uriah. David had authority, but as king he also had responsibility for Bathsheba and for Uriah. This was not only responsibility for their lives—why else did David send Joab out to battle Israel's enemies?—but also for their flourishing, even the flourishing of their marriage. What David did was wrong. When the prophet Nathan confronted David, he did so with a parable guaranteed to pierce through to David's core understanding of the authority and responsibility of dominion: he told a story that included a lamb. Long before David was a king, he was a shepherd. He had exercised dominion over a flock. When Nathan finally decried, "You are the [ruthless, harsh, brutal] man!" (2 Sam 12:7), David understood in a flash that he had treated Uriah (the poor man) in a way he would never have treated his flock of lambs. He had become, in literary terms, a grotesque, a violation of the image of God in which he had been created. Huw Spanner writes:

> This understanding [of the image of God] turns our supremacism upside-down, for if we resemble God in that we have dominion, we must be called to be "imitators of God" (Eph. 5:1) in the way we exercise it. Indeed, far from giving us a free hand on the earth, the *imago Dei* constrains us. We must be kings, not tyrants—if we become the latter we deny, and even destroy, the image in us.[12]

As an aside, I believe Nathan's confrontation of David also works as an environmental parable. Our modern sensibilities tend to interpret David's offense as a violation of property rights: the poor man who "had bought" the ewe lamb owned it in the same way that Uriah somehow owned Bathsheba. But property rights aren't the emotional thrust of Nathan's message, nor do they explain David's anger and his four-times-over punishment of the rich man. Besides, there seemed to be some mechanism, likely born out of serfdom, by which the rich man could take the poor man's lamb. I can just as easily imagine the rich man rolling his eyes at the lamb who "shared [the poor man's] food, drank from his cup and even slept in his arms. It was like a daughter to him" (2 Sam 12:3). "What sentimental bosh," the rich man thinks. Meanwhile he has a traveler who has come to visit, and the poor man's lamb is an underutilized asset, an untapped natural resource. He imposes imminent domain and puts the asset into use for the sake of what he considers to be a proper purpose. Yes, the rich man is selfish over his own hoardings, and that is his primary offense, but, then as now, it's the rationalizations that I find intriguing.

The remainder of the Creation Mandate is found in Genesis 2:15: "The Lord God took the man and put him in the Garden of Eden to work it and take care of it." Here the verbs—"work it [*âbad*] and take care of it [*samar*]," or "till and keep" as we've been saying—are not so much commands as they are a purpose clause, an answer to the question of why God placed man in the garden. One possible translation of *âbad* is "to serve," and so Cal DeWitt is fond of saying that *âbad* and *samar* can be translated "serve" and "protect," thus evoking the kindly mission emblazoned on the side of police cars, another example of divinely instituted dominion (Rom 13:1–4) as a blend of authority and responsibility. Apologist Cal Beisner notes, however, that while *âbad* can be translated as "serve," it is only appropriate for when one serves a person or persons. "When it is followed by the accusative of *things*," Beisner explains, "it is properly translated *to labor, work,* or *do work,* e.g., to till the ground, a vineyard, or a garden, or to work in flax."[13] In this way, *âbad* is similar to "subdue the earth," a more explicitly agricultural term. And agriculture is a rigorous, even violent, enterprise. Furrows are pierced, orchards are pruned, irrigation channels are diverted. Nothing is so central to all of agriculture as the seed, and of it we are told that unless it "falls to the ground and dies, it remains only a single

seed" (John 12:24). Nonetheless a seed is characterized by life and not by death, and our agriculture too is never violent for violence's sake, but rather to promote the flourishing that is our stewardship. Whatever harshness is in the word "to till" is easily modified by its companion, "take care."

As we've seen in the whole context of God's blessing over his creation, and in a biblical understanding of dominion, there is enough "till and keep" already in "subdue and rule" that any distinctions are superfluous. It's all one mandate, the essence of which is that human beings are not meant to keep themselves aloof from the creation in which they are embedded. We are to work the soil, getting it under our fingernails, partaking of its fruit, participating in its fruitfulness. Many theologians also call the Creation Mandate the Cultural Mandate. The Latin word for "keep" (*samar*) is *colere*, one source of the word "culture." But those who think of Genesis 1:28 and 2:15 as the Cultural Mandate have a tendency to too quickly disembody mankind and separate us from the soil. They give their attention to matters of law, education, and civil society, constructing elaborate -*isms*: Dominionism, Reconstructionism, Amillennialism, Neo-Calvinism. They forget that the word "culture" was an agricultural term even before the term "agriculture" appeared. (The mid-fifteenth-century origin of "culture" simply means "the tilling of land.") So even the Cultural Mandate, if one chooses to use that term, means that humanity is meant to mix in with the nature in which we are embedded, contributing to it whatever glorious properties we have as image bearers of God. Humanity is like a catalyst poured into a magic potion. We are amazed at the "very goodness" of the result. Or we are like a key ingredient added to a dish that simmers over the millennia, made more flavorful due to our influence. We get the added privilege of partaking with God of the end result.

Does this mean that human stewards are never to set aside any portion of the land for wilderness areas? In 1903 President Teddy Roosevelt stood on the rim of the Grand Canyon and declared to the people of Arizona: "Leave it as it is. You can not improve on it. The ages have been at work on it, and man can only mar it. What you can do is to keep it for your children, your children's children, and for all who come after you, as one

of the great sights which every American if he can travel at all should see."[14] Was Roosevelt speaking unbiblically? Sixty years later, Congress passed the Wilderness Act, which states: "A wilderness, in contrast with those areas where man and his own works dominate the landscape, is hereby recognized as an area where the earth and community of life are untrammeled by man, where man himself is a visitor who does not remain."[15] Is the very language of this legislation a violation of the Creation Mandate? And yet it is easy to see that Congress was in fact "exercising dominion" when they set aside this land, 9.1 million acres of national forest in their first designation. And wilderness areas protect and promote the flourishing of animal and plant species; that's part of our stewardship. And the Forest Service hopes that "man himself," while not remaining, will nonetheless be a visitor. (Right after college, I worked for a season near the West Elk Wilderness Area of Colorado. I was like the poor man in Nathan's parable. I loved it like a daughter.)

Genesis 3: Broken Relationships, by Sin and by Curse

John Stott writes in *The Radical Disciple*:

> The Bible tells us that in creation God established for human beings three fundamental relationships: first to himself, for he made them in his image; second to each other, for the human race was plural from the beginning; and third, to the good earth and its creatures over which he set them.
>
> Moreover, all three relationships were skewed by the Fall. Adam and Eve were banished from the presence of the Lord God in the garden, they blamed each other for what had happened, and the good earth was cursed on account of their disobedience.
>
> It stands to reason therefore that God's plan of restoration includes not only our reconciliation to God and to each other, but in some way the liberation of the groaning creation as well.[16]

❧ ENVIRONMENTAL MISSIONS ❧

Not surprisingly, due to Stott's influence in the Lausanne Movement, this is the same language as the *Cape Town Commitment*:

> The Bible declares God's redemptive purpose for *creation* itself. Integral mission means discerning, proclaiming, and living out, the biblical truth that the gospel is God's good news, through the cross and resurrection of Jesus Christ, for individual persons, *and* for society, *and* for creation. All three are broken and suffering because of sin; all three are included in the redeeming love and mission of God; all three must be part of the comprehensive mission of God's people.[17]

When I do presentations about the biblical basis of environmental missions, I employ an illustration that I have borrowed from Ed Brown. Ed identifies a fourth relationship: with *self.* I have four people from the audience construct cardboard boxes which, when folded, resemble dominoes. On the side of each box is written a relationship: with God, with self, with others, with creation. Each break of relationship is evidenced in the story of Genesis 3: (1) God: Adam rebels against God's commands and hides as God "was walking in the garden in the cool of the day" (3:8). (2) Self: Adam hides because he perceives himself as naked, his sense of self broken in a shame heretofore unknown. (3) Others: When questioned by God, Adam blames another, the one made "suitable for him" (2:18). The curse implies that husband and wife will struggle for position. The first generation of children in the world will know murder, brother against brother. (4) Creation: Creation is subjected to futility as a result: "Cursed is the ground because of you" (3:17). The illustration from Ed's teaching is predicated on the four broken relationships falling like dominoes, each in turn, and the order significant. Actually this is a psychological and sociological way of understanding the Fall; valid, I believe, but accepting it is only dependent on understanding that our broken relationship with God is first, and from it cascades all other tragedy: self, others, creation. I invite the four original box constructors to come up from the audience and hold their boxes on the stage floor in a row like dominoes. Meanwhile I have secretly

Old Testament Basis

substituted the first box—the God one—with an identical one filled with iron weights. When I invite the audience participant to tip over the first box, it crushes the other three and often flings the fourth box skidding across the stage. Such is the weight of our broken relationship with God.

A secular environmentalist might jam her fingers under the fourth fallen domino and try to lift it back up, to restore our broken relationship with creation. But she soon discovers that she is lifting it against the weight of the other three dominoes as well. Ed writes:

> We begin to understand why the environmental crisis is proving to be such a tough problem to solve. The stress we put on God's creation is caused in large part by our sinfulness as well as our sins. It is what we *are* that drives us to *do* what we do. Most of the solutions proposed for the environmental crisis are either technological (develop and implement "green" manufacturing) or regulatory (tax or prohibit what we don't want, subsidize what we do want). But neither technology nor regulation will solve a problem that originates in the human heart. We need changes in behavior. We need transformed lives. For it turns out that sin is far more than an academic question. Sin has consequences.[18]

Sometimes, though never as often as she hopes, the secular environmentalist may be successful. I would argue that success is an evidence of common grace. Jesus after all is the Creator, *Sustainer*, and Redeemer of all creation. Even then the great conservationist David Brower understood: "All our victories are temporary; all of our defeats are permanent." A canyon that Brower preserved from damming in one session of Congress was often all too easily lost in the next session. The lifting of the fourth domino will be unduly strenuous at best, and is ultimately impossible without God's full redemption of his broken world. Consequently the Apostle Paul writes of suffering, groaning, and hope in Romans 8:

> I consider that our present sufferings are not worth comparing with the glory that will be revealed in us. For the crea-

tion waits in eager expectation for the children of God to be revealed. For the creation was subjected to frustration, not by its own choice, but by the will of the one who subjected it, in hope that the creation itself will be liberated from its bondage to decay and brought into the freedom and glory of the children of God. (Rom 8:18–21)

Environmental missions engages head-on the debate in ministry circles over which of the four broken relationships should receive our first, or even our exclusive, attention. Some might biblically and logically argue that we must begin by addressing a person's broken relationship with God (i.e., evangelism first). Others who believe that they have no less of a commitment to evangelism might argue that as a strategy you begin with the fourth domino as a way of addressing felt need. Still others might say, "No, we must address each broken relationship simultaneously and holistically." My experience in India leads me to the opinion that a minister ends up addressing whatever broken relationship the Holy Spirit intends to drop in your lap at the moment. (For me, church planting seemed to develop a life of its own that never yielded itself to my best systematic planning.) Of course, the church has experience with ministers and ministries whose only concern is the first domino: "Get 'em saved!" Few evangelism-oriented missionaries would deny the importance of postconversion discipleship and church participation, but if they fail to supply their teams with other equipping gifts, if they provide no follow-up for converts, if they cultivate or demand no transformation in character, if they appoint unqualified leaders and move on too quickly, then they, in practice, have an evangelism-only model of ministry, and an equally limited view of redemption. The saved are more than just "brands snatched from the fire." Most missionaries, however, will attend to the next two fallen dominoes as well, though few seem to think about it in terms of restoring broken relationships with self and with others. We call it "growth in Christ," or discipleship or church planting. The message of the domino illustration is not just to get the person working on the fourth domino to consider the other three, but also to get the missionary working from the first domino to consider *all four*.

It is possible for the evangelist to create individual converts. It is possible for the church planter to create individual enclaves. But there is a fullness of Christ's redemption that extends to all creation, which commissions us to linger with those converts and congregations to work for the transformation of their communities and their world. This then is environmental missions: attending to all four broken relationships, through evangelism, discipleship, church planting, and creation care. What this likely means is amassing the team where the necessary expertise and gifting are present to address all four dominoes. Being in the body of Christ means we are never expected to be able to do all the work ourselves.

There is an argument against the fourth domino that has to do with causation and blame and the difference between the Fall and the Curse. It states that the first three dominoes were pushed down by the hand of humanity and are sin, but the fourth domino (fallen creation) was pushed down by the hand of God and is judgment. "The fall is man's sin, and the Curse is God's response to man's sin," writes Cal Beisner.[19] The implication is twofold: if humankind did not break it, we are under no obligation to fix it; and, if environmental distress is not the result of sin, there is no basis for creation care to be considered spiritual ministry. Beisner quotes Richard Young:

> It is clear from Scripture that nature was affected by the fall and that the curse on the ground marks a relational skewing between humanity and the earth. The problem is to comprehend the precise cause-effect relation . . . The wording [of Genesis 3:17, "Cursed is the ground because of you,"] is ambiguous. It could mean that the ground will produce poorly because of divine action or human abuse.[20]

Beisner, by his own admission, is an apologist trained in Western logic. Like most of the modern church, he owes a great deal of his understanding of cause and effect to Aristotle and David Hume. For most Western thinkers, sin and judgment are legal terms. But any missionary who has worked in a shame-based culture (as compared to a guilt-based one) knows that there is a complex dynamic to sin and judgment. Certain causal relationships may be obvious "in the heavenlies" or in the suppressed places of our soul, but full comprehension of them is denied to us, at least until, as per C. S. Lewis' rendering in *The Great Divorce*, we understand that while hell is an eternal reality, it is a place that the damned themselves have constructed sin by sin. Is there ever a judgment from God that somehow isn't a "natural consequence" of our own making? When God says to us, "Cursed is the ground because of you," humanity's best response is not to call David Hume to our defense, but rather, contritely whisper, "I'm sorry." For example, say you are driving your car recklessly above the speed limit and it careens off a tight corner. Your car is damaged and in need of repair. Thus the mechanic's bill represents a blow to your bank account. When your accountant (or more likely your spouse) asks, "Why is your bank account short?" you would have to explain, "Because, while speeding, I couldn't hold a curve, ran off the road, and blew a tire." But say that you are driving above the speed limit and a police officer pulls you over. He or she writes you a ticket you must pay. When your spouse asks about the shortfall in the bank account, you would be disingenuous in saying, "Traffic court took it." The judge may have exacted the money from you, but it was "because of you." What *about* you caused the judge to take it? Sin.

I've only given you a taste of the theology of creation care that emerges from the Old Testament. I've also given just a hint of creation care's encounter with a theology of missions. I will, however, circle back time and again to these topics throughout the book. In the next chapter, we'll look at the third component of building a biblical basis for environmental missions; namely, the mediation of creation care and missions in Christ Jesus. Francis Schaeffer says of humanity's condition:

> Man was divided from God, . . . separated from himself, . . . divided from other men . . . And then man is divided from nature, and nature is divided from nature. So there are these multiple divisions, and one day, when Christ comes back, there is going to be a complete healing of all of them, on the basis of the "blood of the Lamb."[21]

Strange that the corpuscles of our Savior are traceable through Mary's ovum to that moment when Jesus himself, as one with the triune God, called it all into being. Is it any wonder that we worship him?

The Environmental Missions Model

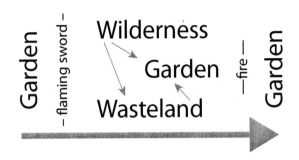

Diagram 2

This is the Environmental Missions Model. It is meant to summarize the theological chapters. By the end of chapter 8, I will have explained fully how the Gardens represent occasions where relationships (with God, self, others, and creation) have been made right; in the end, fully and for all eternity. The smaller arrows, as I will also explain, represent human action by which we can cooperate with what God is doing in and for creation, or by which we can work counter to his purposes. Here in this Old Testament chapter, the diagram begins on the left where Garden means the garden of Eden, what God alone has created, the place and period of our forefather's *shalom*, where we received our blessing and mandate. Fire on the left side of the diagram means banishment and is in the form of the flaming sword in the hand of the angel set at the eastern gate of the garden, "to guard the way to the tree of life" (Gen 3:24). Humanity can never look back for life. We must now search for a different tree on which hangs the fruit that gives life, and indeed we find one in each of the two subsequent gardens described in the next two chapters.

Adam and we his descendants now live in the Wilderness. This can be a troublesome word to use in the model. For environmentalists—like

Aldo Leopold, founder of the Wilderness Society, or like Cal DeWitt, or myself—wilderness has positive connotations. We consider it pristine, as close to what the garden had been as our fourfold brokenness can allow. For Cal Beisner, wilderness has negative connotations. He claims that even before our banishment, the wilderness existed as that part, "the rest of the Earth," that "has yet to be subdued and brought under godly dominion."[22] He argues that *subdue* and *rule* is what we do to wilderness; *till* and *keep* are for gardens. Wilderness must be approached harshly because it is a harsh place, not greatly removed from when the world was fully "without form (*tôhûw*) and void." Beisner points out that "*tôhûw* also connotes something contemptible in its emptiness, vanity, or confusion."[23] In the end the debate is moot for two reasons. First, because the Creation Mandate—bless, flourish, subdue, rule, till, and keep—is one mandate. Secondly, because, due to the flaming sword, we could have applied any word to wilderness. We could call it "here" or "now." It is essentially the backdrop of broken relationships into which Adam was exiled, into which Christ would incarnate, and in which we now minister.

The arrow which extends from Wilderness to Garden represents our work in the Creation Mandate. We are meant to touch the earth with the caring hands of godly dominion. As we've noted, sometimes this means preserving and protecting the land to the satisfaction of Leopold's and DeWitt's idea of wilderness. The arrow that proceeds from Wilderness to Wasteland represents our capacity to choose, not life, but death for our stewardship, but that's the subject for a later chapter. Finally, the word "Garden" is an appropriate term for the success of our godly efforts. Scripture itself keeps the garden of Eden alive as a metaphor (Isa 51; Ezek 31; 36; Joel 2). These references are more than just the invocation of a golden age from which we've fallen; they are a metaphor for the beauty that attends "right relationships." In the end, that's what the diagram means by Garden: relationships that can be made right in Christ Jesus, and that will have visible expression in this world and the one to come.

Old Testament Basis

NOTES

1. Jeffrey D. Pomerantz, "The Practice of Medicine and the First Commandment: General Considerations," *Journal of Biblical Ethics in Medicine* 1, no. 1 (2003): 21.
2. John Stott, *The Radical Disciple* (Downer's Grove, IL: InterVarsity Press, 2010), 51.
3. Third Lausanne Congress, *Cape Town Commitment*, II.B.6.
4. E. O. Wilson, *The Creation: An Appeal to Save Life on Earth* (New York: W. W. Norton & Company, 2006), 75.
5. Francis Schaeffer, *Pollution and the Death of Man: The Christian View of Ecology* (Wheaton: Tyndale, 1970), 48.
6. Ibid.
7. Ibid., 52.
8. Christopher J. H. Wright, *The Mission of God's People* (Grand Rapids: Zondervan, 2010), 50.
9. Ibid.
10. Ibid.
11. Nahum Sarna, *JPS Torah Commentary: Genesis* (Philadelphia: Jewish Publication Society, 1989), 12–13.
12. Huw Spanner, "Tyrants, Stewards—or Just Kings?," in *Animals on the Agenda: Questions about Animals for Theology and Ethics*, eds. Andrew Linzey and Dorothy Yamamoto (London: SCM, 1998), 222.
13. Calvin E. Beisner, *Where Garden Meets Wilderness* (Grand Rapids: Acton Institute, 1997), 15.
14. Theodore Roosevelt, "At Grand Canyon, Arizona, May 6, 1903," in *A Compilation of the Messages and Speeches of Theodore Roosevelt*, ed. Alfred Henry Lewis (Bureau of National Literature and Art, 1906), 327.
15. Wilderness Act of 1964, Pub. L. No. 88-577, 78 Stat. 890 (1964).
16. Stott, *Radical Disciple*, 49–50.
17. Third Lausanne Congress, *Cape Town Commitment*, I.7.A.
18. Edward R. Brown, *Our Father's World: Mobilizing the Church to Care for Creation* (Downer's Grove, IL: InterVarsity Press, 2006), 68–69.
19. Beisner, *Wilderness*, 19.
20. Richard Young, *Healing the Earth*, quoted in Beisner, *Wilderness*, 21.
21. Schaeffer, *Pollution*, 66.

22. Calvin E. Beisner, "Biblical Geography and the Dominion Mandate," *Cornwall Alliance Newsletter*, March 9, 2011.

23. Beisner, *Wilderness*, 116.

6

NEW TESTAMENT BASIS:
JESUS THE RECONCILER

The other day while driving back from the airport, my wife was listening to Christian talk radio. The conversation had moved, as it is wont to do, to "the liberal agenda" and had eventually landed on environmentalism. "Isn't it true," one commentator asked, "that the only example in the New Testament of Jesus interacting with nature is when he cursed the fig tree and made it wither?" Great! Jesus participates in deforestation.

Talk radio isn't conducive to careful biblical exegesis. At the least, we could have hoped for an interpretation of this passage (Matt 21:18–22; Mark 11:12–25) that would be either a recapitulation of what we just saw in Genesis 3, that even the fig tree is not exempt from the curse over the fruitlessness of Israel and its temple (Mark 11:15–17), or that this is a lead-in to Christ informing the disciples of the extent we share our dominion over nature with Christ through prayer (Mark 11:22–24). But the only answer necessary to the assertion that a withered fig tree is the sole example of Jesus interacting with nature is to say, "What? Haven't you heard of the *Incarnation?*"

Christ's multiplication of the fish and the loaves was surely more than a culinary miracle, just as the healing of the issue of blood was more than gynecological, or the calming of the sea more than meteorological. Christ's miracles certainly demonstrate his dominion over creation, and were no doubt enervating for a species, *Homo sapiens*, who had become proud of their own royal authority. Jesus, not interacting with creation?! He's the Creator! It's like the modern-day parable of the scientist who confronts

God by saying, "We humans have learned so much over the decades that now we too are able to create life," and so he challenges God to a contest: create a man from a pile of dust. Yet when the scientist reaches down to scoop up a handful of soil with which to begin his experiment, God says, "Hey, wait a minute, get your own dirt."

As N. T. Wright teaches, the miracles of Jesus aren't simply a set of trump cards to prove the divinity of this Nazarene. The miracles are portraits of what life in the kingdom looks like now that God has become king in and through Christ Jesus. What will life look like in the kingdom? Full bellies, sufficient wine for the wedding, resurrected loved ones, still waters, green pastures, unshadowed valleys, pigs that won't bear the brunt of our exorcisms, fig trees that are as fruitful as God's redeemed people. The talk radio commentators are free to ask, "Show me one instance of Jesus involved in the ministry of creation care." To which I'll answer, "Okay. He died on the Cross and rose again on the third day." The crucifixion and resurrection of Christ is the supreme act of creation care and the sole basis for the hope of environmental missions.

In the previous chapter, I introduced you to Dr. Cal Beisner, an apologist who would normally share the skepticism of our Christian talk radio host about the environmental enterprise. I'll refer to Beisner frequently throughout this book, primarily because he is an effective foil, "iron sharpening iron." There are occasions where we disagree quite emphatically. But when it comes to the work of the Cross, Beisner writes, "One theological issue on which evangelical environmentalists have contributed some excellent insights is the scope of redemption."[1] He claims,

> The effects of the atoning death, victorious resurrection, and triumphant ascension of Christ sweep over all creation, including man, animals, plants, and even the ground itself. They include the restoration of the image of God in the redeemed and through them—and by common grace even through many who are not redeemed—the restoration of knowledge, holiness, and creativity in working out the Cultural Mandate, including human multiplication, subduing and ruling the

earth, transforming the wilderness by cultivation into a garden, and guarding that garden against harm.[2]

When it comes to the Lord Jesus Christ's relationship to creation, the *Cape Town Commitment* piles up titles, the word "Lord" being just one of them. The Lord Jesus Christ is "creator, owner, sustainer, redeemer and heir of all creation."[3] In this chapter, we'll just consider the three titles included in our definition of environmental missions: that we labor with Christ, the Creator, Sustainer, and Redeemer of all creation. The gospel, we will see, is good news for creation as well.

Christ the Creator of All Creation

"In the beginning, *Elohim* created the heavens and the earth." As one of God's names, *Elohim* is a grammatical curiosity. When used with a singular verb, it's considered a singular noun; when used with a plural verb, a plural noun. So in the case of Genesis 1:26, we have: "Then *Elohim* said [singular verb], 'Let *us* make [plural verb] mankind in *our* image, in *our* likeness.'" This one verse gives non-Trinitarians fits. Of course, Moses as putative author of the Pentateuch should not be labeled a Trinitarian, but when God's people, now in Christ Jesus, look back on the first three chapters of Genesis, we see that the seed of the woman who would crush the head of the serpent was there all along. "In the beginning was the Word, and the Word was with God, and the Word was God. He was with God in the beginning. Through him all things were made; without him nothing was made that has been made" (John 1:1–3). The *Elohim* passages in Genesis 1 further reinforce an understanding of creation based on relationships, relationships which would quickly be broken by sin, but which would be restored through a promised offspring. In all things, our origins are in the fellowship of the Father, Son, and Holy Spirit, who have loved each other from eternity past, and who now invite (invites) us to share in that love.

The New Testament is crystal clear that Jesus the Nazarene is, and is a part of, the *Elohim* who created the heavens and the earth. You can trace not only Christ the Creator, but also Christ the Sustainer, and Christ the Redeemer through Colossians 1:15–20, and so I quote it here in full:

The Son is the image of the invisible God, the firstborn over all creation. For in him all things were created: things in heaven and on earth, visible and invisible, whether thrones or powers or rulers or authorities; all things have been created through him and for him. He is before all things, and in him all things hold together. And he is the head of the body, the church; he is the beginning and the firstborn from among the dead, so that in everything he might have the supremacy. For God was pleased to have all his fullness dwell in him, and through him to reconcile to himself all things, whether things on earth or things in heaven, by making peace through his blood, shed on the cross.

The thread is similarly traceable in the opening verses of Hebrews:

In the past God spoke to our ancestors through the prophets at many times and in various ways, but in these last days he has spoken to us by his Son, whom he appointed heir of all things, and through whom also he made the universe. The Son is the radiance of God's glory and the exact representation of his being, sustaining all things by his powerful word. After he had provided purification for sins, he sat down at the right hand of the Majesty in heaven. (Heb 1:1–3)

In Christ all things were created—through him and for him as well. With how we normally think of the God of the Old Testament, and with such great creation hymns as "This Is My Father's World," it is easy to ascribe the role of Creator primarily to the first person of the Trinity. To additionally think of Christ as the Creator has, in my opinion, four implications. First, it ascribes to Jesus all the worship for him, and respect for his possessions, that we described in the previous chapter. In some ways, and this is purely subjective, it brings creation care into the church age for me. Creation care is not just for the garden of Eden, nor just for Adam, who received the Creation Mandate. Instead I now look out on my ecosystem, which happens to be the tallgrass prairie of the Kansas Flint Hills, and I

think: "This belongs to Jesus." Christian creation care is (Christlike) care of a (Christ-owned) creation.

Secondly, Christ the Creator clarifies for us humanity's dominion over creation. If we are kings, well, Christ is the King of kings. What freedom we have is a freedom to follow his lead. In Ed Brown's new book, *When Heaven and Nature Sing*, he writes about the great nature (and dominion) Psalm, namely, Psalm 8:

> The beginning and end of Psalm 8 together affirm God's control and sovereignty over us, his people: "O Yahweh, you who are our absolute master and sovereign, how majestic is your name in all the earth . . ." (vs. 1,9). And the point is? Just this: Our authority over God's creation begins and ends with God's authority over us. We asked earlier whether we human beings have authority or dominion over God's world. We saw that this is the case both in Genesis 1 and in verses 6–8 of this psalm. What we are learning now is that our authority over God's creation is subordinate and subject to God's authority over us.[4]

We understand this authority localized in Christ Jesus, in the words of the Great Commission: "All authority in heaven and on earth has been given to me" (Matt 28:18), the very words that linger in our ears as we are launched into the church age. And it suggests a program for us: "Thy kingdom come, Thy will be done in earth, as it is in heaven" (Matt 6:10 KJV). (In fact, in his book, Ed argues that the Lord's Prayer is Psalm 8's New Testament correlate.) The kingdom of Christ was inaugurated at the Cross and the Resurrection. The kingdom of Christ will be consummated upon his Second Coming. In the meantime we announce his kingdom and implement what grace-laden parts of it we can, hoping not only for the kingdom's full consummation but also for a serious incursion of it right now, today. Surely restorative dominion over Christ's creation is part of the kingdom work of the church.

ENVIRONMENTAL MISSIONS

Thirdly, the second person of the Trinity's participation in the act of creation clarifies the *purpose* of creation. One radio preacher ended an antienvironmentalist sermon with this statement: "This planet is here for man to use, and as long as it is here God will sustain it for our use and our good and our joy and our praise to him. So don't worry about it. As Rick [apparently a friend] says, 'Step on the grass, shoot a deer, drill for oil.'"[5] It was a throw-away moment at the end of the sermon, and while I'm sure this preacher would defend what he said, I also suspect he wouldn't object if I rewrote his words: "This planet is here for Jesus to use, and as long as it is here God will sustain it for Christ's use and his good and his joy and for the praise of God's Son." So we do worry about caring for the planet, but only in the way that those who have found freedom in Christ alone step on the grass, shoot deer, or drill for oil when they can do so for the glory of Christ Jesus (1 Cor 10:31). Scripture is explicit: "All things have been created through him and *for* him" (Col 1:16, emphasis added).

A couple summers ago, I went for a solitary walk in the woods behind my parents' house. I happened upon a tiny lavender wildflower, which on closer examination was really a wonder of beauty. My parents are private people, so not too many people hike in their woods. Plus the lifecycle of this flower—whose glory withers and falls (1 Pet 1:24)—was short enough that in all likelihood I would be the only human being who would ever see this flower. Sure, Dad's cattle pastured up in these woods, but I would be the only creature who could exercise the capacity to know that this flower was beautiful. I prayed a prayer of gratitude. God, the giver of good gifts, had made me feel special indeed. But then I began to think: What if I had never wandered this path? Would the beauty of the flower have gone unnoticed? No. Lavender, scale, texture, movement in the breeze—there was never a moment—perhaps even within the foreknowledge of God—that God had failed to notice and enjoy that tiny flower. And then my thoughts turned to a larger scale. I love the imagery from the Hubble space telescope. The Swan Nebula, 5,500 light years away, colorized by the scientists as a leaping ocean of turquoise and rust, is my favorite. Of course we are seeing only one angle of this nebula. Maybe the "back side" is even more dramatic. And, in my mind, the great message of the Hubble photos is that beyond the furthest reaches of any of our spacecraft, or any possible future reach of human travel or sight, are wonders which humankind will never, ever see. If we'll never see them, then why did God bother to create them? "Thou art worthy, O Lord, to receive glory and honour and power: for thou hast created all things, and for thy pleasure they are and were created" (Rev 4:11 KJV). One of the reasons I didn't tear out the lavender wildflower is because I wanted God to continue to enjoy it after I had gone.

A final implication of promoting Christ the Creator is that, to the extent that we believe there is a unity to the ministry of Jesus, then we have our first hint of how the *Cape Town Commitment* relates creation care and the gospel:

> If Jesus is Lord of all the earth, we cannot separate our relationship to Christ from how we act in relation to the earth. For to proclaim the gospel that says "Jesus is Lord" is to proclaim the gospel that includes the earth, since Christ's Lordship is over all creation. Creation care is thus a gospel issue within the Lordship of Christ.[6]

We'll take this up in the discussion later as we consider Christ the Redeemer of all creation.

Christ the Sustainer of All Creation

The Psalmist in chapter 104 sings, "[The Lord] waters the mountains from his upper chambers; the land is satisfied by the fruit of his work. He makes grass grow for the cattle, and plants for people to cultivate—bringing forth food from the earth" (vv. 13,14). Furthermore,

> All creatures look to you
> to give them their food at the proper time.
> When you give it to them,
> they gather it up;
> when you open your hand,
> they are satisfied with good things.

When you hide your face,
> they are terrified;
when you take away their breath,
> they die and return to the dust.
When you send your Spirit,
> they are created,
> and you renew the face of the ground.
(Ps 104:27–30)

In the New Testament passages, we have already read that "in him all things hold together" (Col 1:17) and that Christ is "sustaining all things by his powerful word" (Heb 1:3).

Sustainer is more of a creedal title for Christ rather than a biblical one. Additionally, you'll find the term "Christ the Sustainer" more often in modern creeds than in ancient ones. For centuries, commentators on the ancient creeds have written about the Godhead's sustaining work. For example, here's how Martin Luther catechizes from the affirmation of the Apostles' Creed, "I believe in God, the Father almighty, creator of heaven and earth":

Q. What does this mean?

A. I believe that God created me, along with all creatures. He gave to me: body and soul, eyes, ears and all the other parts of my body, my mind and all my senses and preserves them as well. He gives me clothing and shoes, food and drink, house and land, wife and children, fields, animals and all I own. Every day He abundantly provides everything I need to nourish this body and life. He protects me against all danger, shields and defends me from all evil. He does all this because of His pure, fatherly and divine goodness and His mercy, not because I've earned it or deserved it. For all of this, I must thank Him, praise Him, serve Him and obey Him. Yes, this is true![7]

New Testament Basis

Nowadays, *Christ the Sustainer* has leapt from commentary on creed to language within the creedal statements itself. The *Cape Town Commitment* declares, "We are also commanded to care for the earth and all its creatures, because the earth belongs to God, not to us. We do this for the sake of the Lord Jesus Christ who is the creator, owner, sustainer, redeemer and heir of all creation."[8]

Some mainstream Christian celebrants have begun to refer to the Trinity as "Creator, Sustainer, and Redeemer," apparently in order to avoid the male references of "Father, Son, and Holy Spirit." Besides that controversy, this usage unfortunately confuses the triune personhood of the Godhead, since if we attribute one activity, like redemption, to one person, do we deny it to the others? Among the many dangers of this substitution is the decline into Sabellianism, a fourth-century heresy that taught that the Godhead is only one person who revealed himself in three successive modes, as Father (Creator), as Son (Redeemer), and as Spirit (Sustainer.) In Sabellianism, sustaining the creation is associated only with the Spirit, the third (mode) of the Godhead, not with Jesus.

In my prayers, I occasionally find myself addressing God as *Jehovah Jireh*, God my Provider. I suspect, if I examined my thoughts closely, I would conclude that I am really praying to God the Banker, or God the Financier, as what I am asking of God is *money*—money to pay my bills, including my grocery bill. I've commodified God's provision. But milk for my children's cereal neither originates from a carton nor from an ATM machine. I can trace the water that I drink, first through my tap, then through my municipal water bill, but ultimately to the God of whom it is said, "All creatures look to you to give them their food at the proper time" (Ps 104:27). In 2010, in Mozambique, the price of a loaf of bread spiked by 30 percent. Nearly three-quarters of the household budget in Mozambique is already being spent on food, so you can imagine the increased hunger and the outrage. Riots broke out in the capital of Maputo. Thirteen people died and hundreds more were wounded in the three-day protest. Perhaps Mozambican Christians stayed home quietly in their prayer closets during those three days, appealing to *Jehovah Jireh* for the funds needed to pay that day's prices in order to feed their families. However, few of them likely knew that their prayers to *Jehovah Jireh*, to Christ the Sustainer, should also have included petition for the Russian heat wave and global warming. In 2009 the Black Sea region of Russia contributed one-quarter of all international wheat exports, but in 2010, sustained record temperatures and wildfires, which at one point ignited at the rate of three hundred to four hundred new fires a day, forced the Russian government to announce a ban on all grain exports. Prices on the global market jumped. Since Mozambique imports 60 percent of its grain, the cost of bread was at the mercy of Russia's environmental troubles.[9]

As in Christ the Creator, I believe there are implications for understanding the second person of the Trinity's activity in our sustenance, as compared to just the first person (or the Sabellian third). The first implication has to do with Christ's power being theistically active on our behalf, as evidenced in the phrase: "The Son is the radiance of God's glory and the exact representation of his being, sustaining all things by his powerful word" (Heb 1:3). We often leave the theism/deism debate back in the period of the earth's creation. The deistic God is the one who created the universe, set it all in motion like the inner workings of a clock, but who then left the universe to its own devices. But theism by contrast is predicated not on what happened *then*, but on what is happening *now*. God has remained involved with his creation. He not only created the mountains, the grass, the people, but

> He waters the mountains from his upper chambers;
>   the land is satisfied by the fruit of his work.
> He makes grass grow for the cattle,
>   and plants for people to cultivate—
>   bringing forth food from the earth:
> wine that gladdens human hearts,
>   oil to make their faces shine,
>   and bread that sustains their hearts.
> (Ps 104:13–15)

Theism's crowning moment is not creation but rather the Incarnation—Immanuel, God is with us—and Jesus Immanuel is the one who now sustains all things by his powerful word. In a document released by the Cornwall Alliance, an organization of which Cal Beisner is director, the authors state: "Environmentalism sees Earth and its systems as the product of chance and therefore fragile, subject to easy and catastrophic disruption. The Biblical worldview sees Earth and its systems as robust, self-regulating, and self-correcting, not immune to harm but durable."[10] Christian environmentalists—of which I am one—do *not* see earth as a product of chance. Neither do we see the earth's system as deistically as Beisner's second sentence seems to imply. The question is not whether the earth is or is not fragile, but whether Jesus is. Any robustness, regulation, correction, and durability in our planet should be ascribed, with thanksgiving, to Christ the Sustainer. To give the Cornwall Alliance credit—being neither deists nor inadvertent earth worshipers—in their summary statement, they write that the earth is "the robust, resilient, self-regulating, and self-correcting product of God's wise design and powerful sustaining."[11] I simply wish that they would have led with the sustaining power of Christ, in which case they may have arrived at the same conclusion that so many other followers of Christ are beginning to arrive at, namely, that there is no greater environmentalist at work in the world today than Jesus Christ himself.

Additionally, Christ the Sustainer provides an answer for those who despair and say there is nothing we can do about the large, intractable problems of the environment. This is often said about climate change. Secular environmentalists say, "Why hope?" and skeptics say, "Why bother?" Of course there is something we can do: we can pray in the name of Christ, as he instructed us to. I for one pray about global climate change. I pray that the Lord would strengthen his carbon sinks (e.g., oceans and plant life, which absorb CO_2 from the atmosphere) and perhaps activate new ones. I pray that the Lord will activate negative feedback loops (perhaps some of them currently undiscovered), which would mitigate the positive feedback loops (e.g., methane clathrates, thawing peat bogs, etc.), which could make global warming worse. Scientists might find such prayers naive, but I'd also like to think they would be grateful to know that I pray for them and for engineers, that the Lord might inspire them to discover renewable energy solutions. When I pray, my prayers become a contribution to science beyond what any paltry Nobel Prize could recognize.

Christ the Redeemer of All Creation

"Christ Jesus came into the world to save sinners" (1 Tim 1:15). Such a clear statement about Christ's mission leads Chris Wright to ask a legitimate question: "For if our mission flows from the redeeming work of Christ and his cross, where does creation fit into that? Saving sinners, not saving whales or trees—is that not what we should concentrate on?" Wright answers his own questions this way: "Although it is gloriously true that sinners are saved through the cross of Christ, it is not actually the whole gospel or the whole achievement of the cross—not according to the New Testament itself."[12]

In the prayer of Ephesians 3:14–19 Paul prays that we might "grasp how wide and long and high and deep is the love of Christ." For those of us who live in a three-dimensional world, that's one dimension too many, and Paul does say that this love "surpasses knowledge" (v. 19). It will confound us. Since it is "the fullness of God" that Christ brings to our redemption, what hope do we have of ever accurately codifying, collectivizing, labeling, or understanding the fullness of his redemptive plan? Missionaries have been more generous than most in confronting the limitations that Christians might place on God's redeeming love. The Apostle Paul knew that God's offer of salvation could apply to the Gentiles too, and not just to the Jews. William Carey refused when told by Northern Europe's Christendom, "Young man, sit down! When God pleases to convert the heathen, he'll do it without consulting you or me." Zinzendorf and Brainerd reached out to black Africans or Native Americans, when portions of the church considered them soulless humanoids. We have preached that "there is a wideness to God's mercy," and so the gospel must go out beyond any border, boundary, or barrier created by

God or man. There are many dimensions of God's love, and we should not presume that we know them all.

Frankly, though, it's hard to imagine any of my colleagues following St. Francis of Assisi's example and preaching to the birds. "My little sisters the birds," he told them, "ye owe much to God, your Creator, and ye ought to sing his praise at all times and in all places . . . Beware, my little sisters, of the sin of ingratitude, and study always to give praise to God."[13] It's doubtful that such altar calls are what is meant in Mark 16:15 when the Lord said, "Go into all the world and preach the gospel to all creation." While noting that this "longer ending" of Mark's Gospel may not have been original text, Chris Wright does say, "It certainly reflects a truly biblical insight"; namely, that "the gospel of the death and resurrection of Jesus is indeed good news for the whole creation, as the author of Psalm 96 would doubtless have agreed."[14]

The gospel is good news for the whole creation. God's restorative mercy will extend even unto a new heaven and a new earth, all made possible because Jesus Christ was crucified and has risen again in a glorified body. Whatever preaching we do to creation is more in the form of a pronouncement over it. We can look over a decimated landscape and proclaim over it: "It will not always be this way. Jesus Christ, triumphant over sin and death, will return to restore all things. All will be made new. This is good news!" Of course the Psalmist in the song Wright alludes to did not hesitate to address nature as Francis did:

> Let the heavens rejoice, let the earth be glad;
> let the sea resound, and all that is in it.
> Let the fields be jubilant, and everything in them;
> let all the trees of the forest sing for joy.
> Let all creation rejoice before the Lord, for he comes,
> he comes to judge the earth.
> He will judge the world in righteousness
> and the peoples in his faithfulness. (Ps 96:11–13)

❧ ENVIRONMENTAL MISSIONS ❦

Christar, the church planting mission agency that sent Robynn and me to India, includes this declaration about God the Father in their Statement of Faith:

> We believe that God the Father loves the world and gave his Son to be its Savior. He is the Father of all who trust in Jesus Christ for their salvation. He is rightly passionate about His glory and desires and delights in the praise of His glory by the nations. His will is for man to firstly know, then worship, trust, love, and obey Him. His plan for fulfilling this purpose involves the restoration of creation and man to His original creation purpose and under the headship of Christ. God's completion of this plan includes the witness of His people in every age.[15]

The restoration theology behind this statement we have already read in Colossians 1: "For God was pleased to have all his fullness dwell in him, and through him to reconcile to himself all things, whether things on earth or things in heaven, by making peace through his blood, shed on the cross" (vv. 19–20). It is most fully developed in Romans, chapter 8:

> For the creation waits in eager expectation for the children of God to be revealed. For the creation was subjected to frustration, not by its own choice, but by the will of the one who subjected it, in hope that the creation itself will be liberated from its bondage to decay and brought into the freedom and glory of the children of God.
>
> We know that the whole creation has been groaning as in the pains of childbirth right up to the present time. Not only so, but we ourselves, who have the firstfruits of the Spirit, groan inwardly as we wait eagerly for our adoption to sonship, the redemption of our bodies. For in this hope we were saved. (Rom 8:19–24)

New Testament Basis

When the consultants gathered in Jamaica in October 2012 for the Lausanne Consultation on Creation Care and the Gospel, our original agenda had this task: "Goal #1: To come to an understanding of, and agreement on, how creation care is included in the gospel, God's plan of redemption through Jesus Christ." But we were quickly reminded that the *Cape Town Commitment* is very careful about its wording on this subject. It does not say that creation care *is* the gospel, or even a *part of* the gospel. It says that "creation care is . . . a gospel issue within the Lordship of Christ."[16] An issue is a topic for consideration, discussion, and action. *The Cape Town Commitment* is claiming that any consideration of "the whole gospel" must understand how the gospel is also good news for all of creation, how the broken relationship with creation is one of the fissures that redemption addresses. There is a second definition of the word "issue" that can be helpful. The word "issue" also commonly appears in a person's last will and testament, reference to the inheritance given to a person's progeny or "issue." The gospel, in this sense, "gives birth" to creation care. Creation care naturally emerges from following Christ as Lord and should be an essential component of our discipleship, as John Stott argues in his book *The Radical Disciple*:

> In pinpointing what (in my view) are several neglected aspects of radical discipleship, we must not suppose that these are limited to the personal and individual spheres. We should also be concerned with the wider perspective of our duties to God and our neighbor, part of which is the topic of . . . the care of our created environment.[17]

All of creation will share in the liberation, freedom, glory, redemption, and hope that have been purchased for us in Christ Jesus. That is part of the inheritance. Creation, in fact, seems afforded a universalism that is not granted in Scripture to human beings. In other words, gospel witness among humans must oftentimes take the form of persuasion (Acts 28:23; 2 Cor 5:11), and there are those who will refuse to believe and will face their eternal punishment in hell. This is the terror and the privilege of being the one creature created in the image of God! By contrast, while there is biblical evidence that there will be animals in the new heavens and earth (Isa 65:17–25), we have no assurance that our household pets—like my favorite black Lab, Koyla—will be among those gathered over yonder. Romans chapter 8 suggests that creation simply waits. And if it waits, what then, if anything, are humans expected to do for it by way of ministry? Bishop N. T. Wright writes:

> How do you answer someone who says, rightly, that the world will not be completely just and right until the new creation and who deduces, wrongly, that there is no point trying to bring justice to the world (or for that matter ecological health, another topic for which there is no space here) until that time?[18]

Wright advises us to "answer, from everything I have said so far: insist on inaugurated eschatology, on a radical transformation of the way we behave as a worldwide community, *anticipating* the eventual time when God will be all in all even though we all agree things won't be complete until then."[19] He further explains:

> And if people tell you that after all there isn't very much they can do, remember what the answer is. What would you say to someone who said, rightly, that God would make them completely holy in the resurrection and that they would never reach this state of complete holiness until then—and who then went on to say, wrongly, that therefore there was no point in even trying to live a holy life until that time? You would press for some form of inaugurated eschatology. You would insist that the new life of the Spirit, in obedience to the lordship of Jesus Christ, should produce radical transformation of behavior in the present life, *anticipating* the life to come even though we know we shall never be complete and whole until then. That is, actually, the lesson of Romans 6. Well, apply the same to Romans 8![20]

Creation waits, but it also groans. And so the environmental mission-
ary attends to the instances of that groaning, knowing that it is a groaning
"as in the pains of childbirth" (Rom 8:22); that is, a groaning produced as
much by hope and eager expectation as from pain. The environmental missionary also knows that creation's eager expectation is "for the children of
God to be revealed" (Rom 8:19), and thus inexorably linked to evangelism,
discipleship, and church planting among the *Homo sapiens* who share the
ecosystem. Romans 8:19 is in fact the inspiration, the theme verse, for our
ministry name, Eden Vigil. *Eden* refers to the "creation purpose" to which
all things will be restored. A *vigil* is a spiritual discipline; it is a self-imposed
period of active prayer and watchfulness. It waits on the Lord. A vigil will
often occur at night, through the dark hours, in this way evocative of the
hopelessness that many secular environmentalists feel about our current
ecological crisis. Our hope is in Christ and his coming, and is thus as sure
as the promises of God.

The New Testament and the Environmental Missions Model

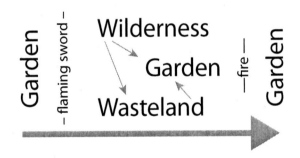

Diagram 2 (reproduced from page 71)

Not surprisingly, as is true of so many things, Jesus Christ fills the
Environmental Missions Model as the All-in-All, the Alpha and Omega.
He is the creator (Garden), sustainer (Garden), and redeemer (Garden) of
all creation. His cross stands as the tree of life in the middle of all things
and gives meaning to the "tree of life" as found in Eden (Gen 2:9) and in
the new Jerusalem (Rev 22:2). The bold arrow at the bottom of the model

represents the inexorability of his glory, all things being created for him and his purposes.

In the model, Wilderness represents the tableau of broken relationships from which humanity goes forth and exercises dominion, touching creation. The two arrows that proceed out of it, however, show that from the very beginning we have been presented with a choice: through our actions we can choose life or death. Joshua of the Old Testament knew about dominion and admonished his people: "Choose for yourselves this day whom you will serve" (Josh 24:15). Jesus looked out on the people he had created in his own image, on whom he had conferred regal stewardship, and admonished them in his day: "No one can serve two masters . . . You cannot serve both God and money" (Matt 6:24). Our current ecological crisis is evidence that in the face of the kindness of God, we often prefer mammon and our own version of the gods of Canaan. We are offered Garden in and through Christ Jesus, and instead we choose Wasteland. Jesus, in our model, forgives the arrow that renders his creation and his people dry and barren, what in chapter 9 I call the sin of unfaithful stewardship. By his grace, and through his Spirit, Jesus empowers us in the ministries (the arrows) that fulfill the Creation Mandate (from Wilderness to Garden) or that restore the woefully abused (from Wasteland to Garden).

NOTES

1. Calvin Beisner, *Where Garden Meets Wilderness* (Grand Rapids: Acton Institute, 1997), 23.
2. Ibid., 24–25.
3. Third Lausanne Congress, *Cape Town Commitment*, II.B.6.
4. Edward R. Brown, *When Heaven and Nature Sing* (South Hadley, MA: Doorlight, 2012), 41.
5. John MacArthur. "The End of the Universe, Part 1" (sermon, Grace Community Church, Sun Valley, CA, September 7, 2008), http://www.gty.org/resources/sermons/90-360/The-End-of-the-Universe-Part-1 (accessed February 8, 2013).
6. Third Lausanne Congress, *Cape Town Commitment*, I.7.A.
7. Martin Luther, "Small Catechism," Part Two: The Creed; I. The First Article: On Creation; quoted in Robert F. Lay, *Readings in Historical Theology: Primary Sources of the Christian Faith* (Grand Rapids: Kregel, 2009), 191.

New Testament Basis

8. Third Lausanne Congress, *Cape Town Commitment*, II.B.6.

9. Raj Patel, "Mozambique's Food Riots: The True Face of Global Warming," *The Guardian*, September 4, 2010, http://www.guardian.co.uk/commentis-free/2010/sep/05/mozambique-food-riots-patel (accessed February 11, 2013).

10. G. Cornelis van Kooten, E. Calvin Beisner, and Pete Geddes. *A Renewed Call to Truth, Prudence, and Protection of the Poor* (Burke, VA: Cornwall Alliance, n.d.), 3.

11. Ibid., 1.

12. Christopher J. H. Wright, *God's People*, 59.

13. Francis of Assisi, quoted in Elizabeth Goudge, *My God and My All: the Life of St. Francis of Assisi* (New York: Coward-McCann, 1959), 160.

14. Ibid., 60.

15. "Statement of Faith," Christar, http://www.christar.org/about/statement-of-faith.html (accessed July 15, 2013).

16. Third Lausanne Congress, *Cape Town Commitment*, I.7.A.

17. Stott, *Radical Disciple*, 49.

18. N. T. Wright, *Surprised by Hope* (New York: HarperCollins, 2008), 221.

19. Ibid.

20. Ibid.

ENVIRONMENTAL MISSIONS AND THE FUTURE OF CREATION

Romans 8:19 reads: "For the creation waits in eager expectation for the children of God to be revealed." The children of God are those who have been, by grace through faith in Christ, reconciled with God. The moment of their revelation is the time of the Lord's second coming. The revelation of the children of God is the fruit of not only Christ's atonement but of the work of the evangelist in obedience to the Great Commission. In turn, creation responds eagerly, expectantly. The gospel is good news for all creation. This verse suggests that an environmental missions perspective provides for creation care an eschatology, and therefore a hope. If this is true, then this is a profound gift indeed, because evangelical eschatology has been perceived—both from within and outside the church—as one of the biggest obstacles to the advancement of creation care.

Occasionally the question comes out this way: "Why should we bother with the planet when we are going to leave it someday soon and when it's all going to burn up anyway?" PBS commentator Bill Moyers, a graduate himself of Southwestern Baptist Theological Seminary, has consistently held out hope for evangelical activism, but seems just as consistently disappointed. In 2005 he published an essay, "Welcome to Doomsday," that blamed the doctrine of the Rapture for an evangelical ambivalence to the environment.

> Why care about the earth when the droughts, floods, famine,
> and pestilence brought by ecological collapse are signs of the

apocalypse foretold in the Bible? Why care about global climate change when you and yours will be rescued in the Rapture? Why bother to convert to alternative sources of energy and reduce dependence on oil from the volatile Middle East? Anyway, until Christ does return, the Lord will provide.[1]

What Moyers repeats with a tone of incredulity, I've heard others ask in all gentle sincerity. Part of Moyers' incredulity is that, as indicated in the title of his essay, some evangelicals seem to take joy in the news of droughts, floods, famine, climate change, and Middle East volatility. We take comfort in our rescue from the Tribulation without giving thought to those left behind. One secular environmentalist comments, "I'm scared to death. These radical evangelical Christians actually believe that the faster we destroy the earth and our environment, the faster the 'second coming of Christ' will happen."[2]

I'm a radical evangelical Christian, and I don't believe that way, which makes me think that what Moyers and secular environmentalists are responding to with fear, frustration, and ridicule is actually a gross caricature of evangelical eschatology. Consider what happened to James Watt, Secretary of the Interior under Ronald Reagan and, by accounts, a strong evangelical believer. Watt is remembered for authorizing the clear-cutting of millions of acres of forest on federal land, and for invoking the return of Christ as a rationale. He is reported to have said, "After the last tree is felled, Christ will come back." As it is, Watt never said this. Secretary Watt's actual testimony to Congress was: "I do not know how many future generations we can count on before the Lord returns, whatever it is we have to manage with a skill to leave the resources needed for future generations."[3] If I wanted to get picky, I could deconstruct what Watt said here, but received on its own terms, it sounds like a solidly evangelical statement of our stewardship of God's creation. Indeed, years later, responding to yet another reoccurrence of the misquotation, Watt wrote, "I never said it. Never believed it. Never even thought it. I know no Christian who believes or preaches such error. The Bible commands conservation—that we as Christians be careful stewards of the land and resources entrusted to us by the Creator."[4]

Admittedly, there is no one evangelical eschatology. Those who understand that Christians are "caught up" (Latin *rapio*) in 1 Thessalonians 4:17 will nonetheless argue whether this is pre-, mid-, or post-Tribulation. Some argue that the Rapture does not occur at all except as a welcoming party to greet the Lord in the air as he steps down upon the Mount of Olives in the one and final, eternally enduring appearance of his Second Coming. Bill Moyers considers the Rapture to be an aberrant theme in modern Evangelicalism. He describes it as "a fantastical theology concocted in the nineteenth century by two immigrant preachers who took disparate passages from the Bible and wove them with their own hallucinations into a narrative foretelling the return of Jesus and the end of the world."[5] (The two immigrant preachers are apparently John Nelson Darby and Charles Henry Mackintosh.) And yet advocates for an evangelical creation care do not need to agree with Moyers about Darby and Mackintosh. Neither do they need to insist on one version of evangelical eschatology in order to find a home for creation care. In fact, for the purpose of this chapter, let's use the most conservative eschatology we can find, such as that described by the dispensationalist James Quiggle in the footnote below.[a] Can creation care

---

[a] Arguing that dispensational eschatology is based on the "grammatical-historical interpretation" of Scripture, theologian James D. Quiggle describes the parameters we'll use for this chapter:

Let me very briefly summarize dispensational eschatology as concerns the end of the New Testament church age and the Davidic-Messianic kingdom (the 1,000 year or millennial kingdom). Christ will return at the end of the Tribulation period to destroy his enemies. He will then re-gather national ethnic Israel out of all the nations where God has dispersed them. National ethnic Israel will be saved at this time and restored to the land promised them in the Abrahamic and Palestinian covenants. Christ will rule for a thousand years on the throne promised in the Davidic covenant. The living saved (not the resurrected or raptured believers, these rule and reign with Christ; the living saved are those who

ENVIRONMENTAL MISSIONS

operate in an eschatology that has these familiar component parts: rapture, seven-year tribulation, second advent, one-thousand-year reign, Armageddon, resurrection, judgment, hell, destruction of earth, eternity in the new Jerusalem? I am comfortable with employing this eschatology; indeed it is the one with which I grew up, and the one I received in my missionary training at Bible college.

The Eschatology of Missions

The one end-times prophecy, bar none, that church planting missionaries seem to encounter most often in our work is Revelation 5:9, 10:

> And they sang a new song, saying: "You [Jesus] are worthy to take the scroll and to open its seals, because you were slain, and with your blood you purchased for God persons from every tribe and language and people and nation. You have

are alive at the end of the Tribulation period at Christ's second advent) will enter the millennial age. These believers will have children, who will be born sinners (just as people are born today), and must believe in Jesus as Savior to be saved. Jesus (or his regent) will reign from Jerusalem during the thousand years. Satan and his evil angels will be imprisoned (in the abyss, a spirit world prison, also known as the bottomless pit) for the thousand years. He will be let loose at the end of the thousand years and will stir up a human revolt against King Jesus. These rebels will be destroyed by fire coming down out of heaven from God. Satan and his evil angels will be put permanently into the Lake of Fire. The unsaved dead of all ages will be resurrected into corruptible bodies. There will be a judgment of these unsaved people, known as the Great White Throne judgment. The unsaved will be put permanently into the Lake of Fire. The current heavens and earth will be destroyed and God will make a new heaven and earth. God will place the New Jerusalem on the new earth. God and Jesus will be immediately present with believers, in the city, forever.

(James D. Quiggle, "A Brief Review of Dispensational Eschatology," First Baptist Church of Sparks, 2008, http://www.fbcsparks.org/library/Dispensational%20Eschatology.pdf [accessed May 10, 2013], 1.)

made them to be a kingdom and priests to serve our God, and they will reign on the earth."

The Apostle John's vision in heaven is not only of the throne, but of the "right hand" of him who sat upon it. In that hand is the scroll, which when opened will set in motion the end of all things, the summation of the Creation Mandate and of what has existed in the mind of God from all eternity. But John despairs because there is no one who is found worthy in all God's earthly and heavenly creation to walk up to the throne of God, receive the scroll from God's right hand, break the seals, and open it. Then an elder reassures him: "Do not weep! See, the Lion of the tribe of Judah, the Root of David, has triumphed. He is able to open the scroll and its seven seals" (Rev 5:1–5). There was a time when John, this "son of thunder," would have been surprised to have discovered a lamb when he was looking for a lion. "Then I saw a Lamb, looking as if it had been slain" (Rev 5:6). We want our future, like our creation care, like our ministries, to be leonine. And it is, but it is the mystery of the Cross that the Lion of Judah who has triumphed did so as the Lamb who was slain. This is the missionary's appeal to creation care: preach the cross of Christ. It is the basis for our hope of final victory.

The elders and heavenly inhabitants bow down before the Lamb and sing their song of his great worthiness. In that song it is like we missionaries too hear the reassurance given to John: "Do not weep! See, the Lion of the tribe of Judah, the Root of David, has triumphed."

The missionary endeavor is strenuous and dangerous. We may have our share of defeats, including the threat of a whole "failed" career. In the end, however, glory is guaranteed. We cannot lose! People from every tongue, tribe, and nation will join us in worship of the Lamb of God. John saw it and heard it. It's recorded in the pages of the Almighty's holy Word. The gates of hell will not prevail against the church. The unreached will be reached. The unengaged will be engaged, not just by missionary strategists but by the regenerating Holy Spirit himself. The lost will be found. And we get to participate in the whole glorious enterprise!

❧ ENVIRONMENTAL MISSIONS ❧

Environmental missionaries turn to their fellow creation care advocates and tell them, "Do not weep!" You feel the Crucifixion; remember the Resurrection. You see the slain Lamb; have faith that he is the triumphant Lion. Don't linger exclusively in the first three chapters of Genesis. The Creation Mandate is but the pointing of a finger: "There! Walk in that direction." Fix your eyes on the destination. Embrace the milestone of Romans 8, but pick up the study of Revelation 21 and 22. In the words of the dispensationalists, "God will make a new heaven and earth. God will place the New Jerusalem on the new earth. God and Jesus will be immediately present with believers, in the city, forever." Neither will we begrudge "the city." The Creation Mandate itself presupposes cities, and this one is the new Jerusalem, a city finally and fully under godly dominion, with all inhabitants in relationships of *shalom* with God, with themselves, with each other, and with the new earth. There is a river there, "the river of the water of life, as clear as crystal, flowing from the throne of God and of the Lamb" (Rev 22:1). Water that is as clear as crystal, imagine it! There is a tree there. "On each side of the river stood the tree of life, bearing twelve crops of fruit, yielding its fruit every month. And the leaves of the tree are for the healing of the nations. No longer will there be any curse" (Rev. 22:2,3). Jesus is coming back to planet Earth to save his people and restore his creation.

The Elements Will Be Destroyed by Fire

"But!" so the objection is raised, "Earth, unlike human followers of Christ, is destroyed, not saved, right?" What we see all around us, what creation care advocates appeal to us to treat tenderly is all going to be consumed by fire and be wholly replaced, right? There does seem to be more obvious continuity in how people are saved (literally, "made whole"). James Quiggle, our dispensationalist, classifies human beings who pass into the glory of eternity as the resurrected believers, the raptured believers, and the living saved (those converted during the Tribulation or the Millennium). There is continuity as the one believer passes into eternity through resurrection, the other through the Rapture and advent, and the third through some unexplained means. Of the heavens and the earth, however—although they bear the same name before and after, albeit one old and the other new—there does not seem to be that same sense of continuity, of a passing through. We have the one earth and then—in a flash of blaze—we have a different one. Quiggle writes, "The current heavens and earth will be destroyed and God will make a new heaven and earth." He is referring to 2 Peter 3:10–13:

> But the day of the Lord will come like a thief. The heavens will disappear with a roar; the elements will be destroyed by fire, and the earth and everything done in it will be laid bare. Since everything will be destroyed in this way, what kind of people ought you to be? You ought to live holy and godly lives as you look forward to the day of God and speed its coming. That day will bring about the destruction of the heavens by fire, and the elements will melt in the heat. But in keeping with his promise we are looking forward to a new heaven and a new earth, where righteousness dwells.

If the old house is completely torn down and hauled away, then what value has the old house for the new? If God is so quick to light a match to the old earth, then do we in fact, as I've already quoted from one radio preacher, live on a "disposable planet"? This then is the question: why should we care for the planet when it is all going to burn anyway?

There are any number of ways to answer that question that aren't directly related to the surety of a future conflagration. We care for the earth because God told us to, because we respect it as his, because it is a way of loving our neighbor who shares the planet, because—as James Watt seemed to answer—future generations before the conflagration still need to use it. There are also, however, some related answers. The main answer has to do with the transformed physicality of the resurrected, the raptured, or the "living saved." We must never forget that our bodies are as much a part of creation as any landscape or any species of flora or fauna. In our bodies, we have an example of the continuity of the old creation "passing through" but transformed into the new.

> Listen, I tell you a mystery: We will not all sleep, but we will all be changed—in a flash, in the twinkling of an eye, at the last trumpet. For the trumpet will sound, the dead will be raised imperishable, and we will be changed. For the perishable must clothe itself with the imperishable, and the mortal with immortality. (1 Cor 15:51–53)

It is easy to assume that it is the soul of the believer that now clothes itself (discontinuously) with a new imperishable, immortal body, echoing Paul's complaint that his body is like a tent whose canvas has become worn (2 Cor 5:1,4). But our souls are never described as perishable and mortal. It is more likely that our perishable and mortal physical bodies are the ones that put on imperishability and immortality. There is a sense in which they catch up with what Christ has already accomplished for our souls. "For while we are in this tent, we groan and are burdened"—an echo in our bodies of what Romans 8:19 says of all creation—

> because we do not wish to be unclothed but to be clothed instead with our heavenly dwelling, so that what is mortal may be swallowed up by life. Now the one who has fashioned us for this very purpose is God, who has given us the Spirit as a deposit [earnest], guaranteeing what is to come. (2 Cor 5:4,5)

We have only one truly reliable picture of what creation will mean in the new earth and how the old is somehow in continuity with the new. That picture is the body of the Lord Jesus Christ, the firstfruits of the Resurrection (1 Cor 15:20,23). Do you want to know what the second-fruits will look like? Consider the firstfruits. Jesus' body—the one to which Mary gave birth—was changed but still recognizable following the Resurrection. It acted in uncommon ways (e.g., able to walk through walls) and in common ways (e.g., able to ingest fish). We might say that it eliminated the need for the prefix in the word "supernatural." But the most startling thing is that Jesus was able to show Thomas and the disciples the scars in his hands and in his side. Those marks, more than anything else, are the evidence of the transformed continuity between the old creation that was Jesus' body and the new creation that is forever Jesus' body. Those scars are sure signs of Christ's ability to redeem the ugly and the abused and restore it to glory. We may find ourselves unsurprised when God places the new Jerusalem just on the other side of a redeemed and recognizable Kidron Valley. When the wind blows from the north, we may catch the redeemed scent of the cedars of Lebanon.

A second direct answer to the question of discontinuity and why we should care for a planet that is going to burn is that some theologians believe that while fire can be a destruction that leads to elimination, Scripture also describes a fire whose destruction is actually a purification. "Gold, silver, [and] costly stones" are as much natural substances as "wood, hay, or straw," but the latter burns up because it cannot withstand the judgment of fire: "their work will be shown for what it is, because the Day will bring it to light. It will be revealed with fire, and the fire will test the quality of each person's work" (1 Cor. 3:12,13). "The elements will be destroyed by fire, and the earth and everything done in it will be laid bare" (1 Pet 3:10). Other translations use the words "expose," "disclosed," or "discovered" for "laid bare"; it is the language of judgment, not as annihilation but as revelation. One commentator takes a scientific approach to consider the idea of the old heaven and old earth dissolving:

> The idea contained in the word "dissolved," is, properly, only the change which heat produces. Heat changes the forms of things; dissolves them into their elements; dissipates those which were solid by driving them off into gases, and produces new compounds, but it annihilates nothing. It could not be demonstrated from this phrase that the world would be annihilated by fire; it could be proved only that it will undergo important changes. So far as the action of fire is concerned, the form of the earth may pass away, and its aspect be changed; but unless the direct power which created it interposes to annihilate it, the matter which now composes it will still be in existence.[6]

ENVIRONMENTAL MISSIONS

This commentary is all the more remarkable because Albert Barnes wrote his famous *Notes on the New Testament* in 1832, when our knowledge of created matter was more rudimentary. Chris Wright claims of this passage in 1 Peter:

> The language of fire and destruction does not mean that the whole of creation will be *obliterated*. Rather, it is parallel to the same terms used to describe the way the sinful world was "destroyed" by water in the flood (2 Peter 3:6,7). What was destroyed in the flood was not the whole planet, but the world of sin and rebellion. Likewise, what will be destroyed in the final judgment is not the universe, but the sin and rebellion of humanity and the devastation they have caused. It will be a conflagration that purges and purifies, so that the new creation will be a place devoid of sin but filled with righteousness, because God himself will dwell there among his redeemed people (Rev. 21:1–4).[7]

The current earth on which we live is more than just an airport transit lounge. All evidence suggests that it is the raw material of glory itself. Every instance where we build gold, silver, and costly stones into the foundation of restored relationships with God, with self, with others, and with creation will survive the fires of judgment—the dross burnt off—and will pass through, as immortal and imperishable as the body of Jesus himself, the firstfruits of the Resurrection. But "listen, I tell you a mystery," as Paul himself admits (1 Cor 15:51), contemplating the resurrection of physical matter. In the end, trying to grasp the continuity between the old heavens and earth and the new may prevent us from seeing the most obvious message of all. There *will be* a new heavens and a new earth. We will not go through eternity as disembodied beings floating through an ether of a landscape. We will be apparently surrounded by rocks and trees, animals and scenery. This is certainly the witness of the latter half of Isaiah.

> You will go out in joy
>   and be led forth in peace;

the mountains and hills
will burst into song before you,
and all the trees of the field
will clap their hands.
Instead of the thornbush will grow the juniper,
and instead of briers the myrtle will grow.
This will be for the Lord's renown,
for an everlasting sign,
that will endure forever.
(Isa 55:12,13)

What this means is that "matter *matters.*" Human beings were created in it and will reside in it for all eternity. It will be different in the future, but then so will we. And God has declared his purposes for his material creation. He has made those purposes known in Genesis 1 and in Revelation 22. As followers of Christ we are to walk in those purposes.

Individuality and the End Times

Perhaps part of our difficulty in accepting a continuity of purpose between how we treat the old earth and how we anticipate the new has to do with the individuality of those who are saved. For example, I can believe that my Indian friend Raju's eternal destiny is at stake, and so I treat him well and I witness to him, and in his having believed the gospel, I have hope— *sure* in the promises of God, and *reasonable* in the evidence of Raju's new life—that I will see Raju in the new heavens and new earth of eternity. By contrast, although I loved my Labrador retriever dearly, although I gave him a name (Koyla) and felt his soulful affections, I never once thought Koyla's eternal destiny was at stake, nor do I have any expectation whatsoever that I will see his beloved wagging tail in the new Jerusalem. Similarly, should those creation care advocates restoring eroded trails on Longs Peak in Rocky Mountain National Park hope to enjoy that mountain in eternity? Will General Sherman—the grand old tree of Sequoia National Park—be somehow resurrected in the new earth, part of its redemption being a name change, all hint of ruthless violence obliterated? I cannot say, but it seems unlikely for Koyla, Longs Peak, or the General Sherman tree.

Admittedly, the promises of God for the salvation of human beings as well, while applied individually, are nonetheless offered generally. In other words, while the promise is sure that if Raju calls on the name of the Lord, he will be saved (Rom 10:13), heading into my first encounter with him there was no guarantee that Raju would actually believe. While the Apostle Paul prays in Roman 10:1 for the Israelites (generally) "that they may be saved," there is no recorded prayer in the New Testament for the salvation of so-and-so, a specific individual by name. The issue is that we must place our hope in the promises of God alone, and the promises of missionary eschatology are as general as the promises of creation care eschatology. There will be people from every tongue, tribe, and nation in heaven. Our steadfast hope is that people will indeed be saved and that salvation will be as far reaching as the missionary enterprise to which we are giving our lives.

I have a *steadfast* hope that I will see Indian Brahmins—that is, members of that people group—in heaven. I have a *reasonable* hope that I will see Raju, an individual Brahmin, in heaven. To my great heartache, I have no reasonable hope that I will see Golu there. He is the Hindu friend I mentioned in chapter 1 who died of cerebral malaria. The more I preached the gospel to him, the stronger a Hindu he seemed to become. But Golu's resistance to the gospel hope did not obviate my love for him; if anything, it intensified my love as I brought my heartache to God in grief and lament. Neither did a dashed hope release me from the Redeemer's command to love Golu, my neighbor. I know people who love individual landscapes or individual physical features of that landscape. I myself love the Kansas Flint Hills, that remaining portion of the American tallgrass prairie. I loved the old maple tree that was in the backyard of my parents' farmhouse. It blew down in a windstorm, and now even its stump is gone. I retrieved a portion of wood from that tree, from where it had split open at the trunk, and that piece of wood sits on my bookshelf. No doubt this is sentimentality, but it illustrates something about the nature of love; namely, that we know love generally by loving individually. As Dag Hammerskjold said, "It is more noble to give yourself completely to one individual than to labor diligently for the salvation of the masses."[8] I would not have loved people unless I had learned to love Golu. "Whoever claims to love God yet hates a brother or sister is a liar. For whoever does not love their brother and sister, whom they have seen, cannot love God, whom they have not seen" (1 John 4:20). Similarly, it is unlikely that we will love the world of God's creation, and work toward the restored relationships that will be the raw material of a restored eternity, unless we first learn to love a Koyla, a Longs Peak, a prairie, or one individual maple tree. Additionally, it can be a serious thing to abuse a stream like Humboldt Creek, which flows through my parent's farm, without giving thought to how Humboldt Creek is representative of all of God's masterpiece now and of all the streams that will be part of the new earth. Love begins somewhere.

Matthew 24: Enduring in Love

Matthew 24 is an important passage for evangelical eschatology. The traditional church planting missionary might read this passage and ask what is his or her responsibility in relation to the Lord's Second Coming. An evangelical environmentalist might speculate whether something like global warming isn't a "sign of the End Times." Both of them—or both of them integrated in an environmental missionary—should recognize that the point of this famous passage is: regardless of how the *eschaton* unfolds—and none of us can accurately foretell it—our responsibility is to endure in love. For the environmental missionary, it means to preach the gospel until the end, care for creation until the end, and do so with love.

Once, while I was a student at Moody Bible Institute, I sat in chapel and heard a famous missiologist quote from Matthew 24:14: "And this gospel of the kingdom will be preached in the whole world as a testimony to all nations, and then the end will come." His interpretation was that we missionaries had an eschatological mandate, that there is a (necessary) causal relationship between preaching to all nations and the coming of the end, and not just a sufficient cause. We needed to search out every last hitherto-unreached people group. When the last one is checked off the list—much like felling the last tree—then the Lord will come. In this way, we can quicken the Lord's return (2 Pet 3:12). My next class after chapel was systematic theology. A fellow student asked our professor, equally famous but as a theologian, whether what we had heard in chapel was true. I can still remember the smirk on the professor's face. "No," he said, "Not true." (What is a kid to believe?!)

When it comes to the End Times, what are believers responsible for? According to Matthew 24, we aren't responsible for much. We are not even responsible for the accurate identification of the Messiah. When the Son of Man comes, it will be in such power and glory that his identity will be unmistakable. The only imperative in this passage is that we "watch out that no one deceives you" (v. 4), an action as passive as an action can be and still be called an action. The paragraph of verses 9–14 is prophetically descriptive. Even the preaching of the gospel is seen as an event that *will* happen; it's not a commission in itself. (Similarly, while Matthew 28:18–20 is a commission, Acts 1:8 is not; Jesus is prophesying over his church that we will indeed be witnesses in Jerusalem, Judah, Samaria, and to the uttermost parts of the earth.) Nonetheless Matthew 24 does imply responsibility, even if it doesn't explicitly state it: we will be handed over to persecution, but we shouldn't fall away from the faith. The gospel will be preached to all nations, and so we should be faithful to take it to them. Both of these statements give no guarantee that you or I, nor any individual believer or church, will be among the number who don't fall away, or who don't fail the Great Commission. If I'm not careful, I might be among the faithless.

Matthew 24:12,13 reads: "Because of the increase of wickedness, the love of most will grow cold, but the one who stands firm to the end will be saved." Most commentaries agree that this is a reference to Christian disciples. R. T. France writes that the fact that "it is the disciple group itself which is under pressure, suggests that it means that 'the majority' (of the disciples) will cool off in their love, whether for God or for their fellow-men. It is a sombre picture of a church in decline."[9] A waning love in the church is as much a sign of the times as earthquakes and famines. Evangelicals might wish that this prophecy be applied to Greenpeace activists, liberal Democrats, Californians, Catholics, or mainstream Protestants, but there is no guarantee that we will not be among the majority of disciples whose love has grown cold. D. A. Carson writes, "Only those who endure—in love (v. 12) and despite persecution (vv. 9–11); cf. Rev 2:10)—will be saved (v. 13). They must 'stand firm' [endure] to the end' [sic]; individual responsibility persists to the end of life, but corporate responsibility to the final consummation."[10] The church's great responsibility in any end-times scenario is to endure, but more accurately, to endure in love.

I am not prepared to say whether specific environmental crises, like global warming, for example, are end-times events. At one point in *An Inconvenient Truth*, Al Gore says that the extreme weather events in 2005 in Europe (floods, mudslides, heat wave, etc.) produced photos that were like a "major walk through the book of Revelations." Most evangelical viewers of the movie snort at Gore's reference. The Tribulation will be much worse than a mudslide devastating a Swiss hamlet. And yet scientific statesman James Lovelock's worst apocalyptic vision of climate change predicts world population culled down to as low as 500 million desperate souls, huddled without civilization in the northern latitudes.[11] Many conservative "end-times" theorists, at least back in 2008, didn't hesitate to equate global warming with Matthew 24. RaptureReady.com webmaster Todd Strandberg explains why climate change made his list of the Signs of the Times:

> I used to think there was no real need for Christians to monitor the changes related to greenhouse gases. If it was going to take a couple hundred years for things to get serious, I assumed the nearness of the End Times would overshadow this problem. With the speed of climate change now seen as moving much faster, global warming could very well be a major factor in the plagues of the tribulation.[12]

Strandberg has since repudiated this view. Matthew 24, however, would encourage us to not waste precious time approaching climate change—or any other issue for that matter, environmental or otherwise—from the standpoint of "signs of the time." Approach it instead with love.

ENVIRONMENTAL MISSIONS

As Sir John Houghton told pastors at Wheaton about global warming: "We just need the will, the determination, and the love, and the Christian concern to take action on this sort of issue."[13] Worldwide, temperatures are on the increase: polar ice caps, ocean subsurface currents, the atmosphere, and the earth's crust. Everywhere, everything is getting warmer, except, it seems, for the temperature of our human hearts. Most biblical prophecy, including love's wane in Matthew 24:12,13, announces an inevitable event or condition. But in each case, the individual believer, just like the church in any given generation, can declare: "Heaven forbid! Not in my heart! Not on my watch!" That's the message of environmental missions: we will love.

If our own love is all we really have control over, then the same thing is true in our evangelism. The people who are those of every tongue, tribe, and nation in heaven are *not* there because of us. They are there because of the regeneration of the Holy Spirit. In the end our evangelism is simply a stewardship. Paul understood his ministry that way: "This, then, is how you ought to regard us: as servants of Christ and as those entrusted with the mysteries God has revealed. Now it is required that those who have been given a trust must prove faithful" (1 Cor 4:1,2). We have a stewardship of the gospel, just like we have a stewardship of creation. Stewardships are important because of the one who confers them. We will be judged on our faithfulness, and surely faithfulness is judged by how well we have loved.

The Two Prayers of the End Times

And so, to restate an initial question: can creation care operate in an eschatology that has these component parts: rapture, seven-year tribulation, second advent, thousand-year reign, Armageddon, resurrection, judgment, hell, destruction of earth, eternity in the new Jerusalem? Yes. If we've had difficulty in the past answering yes to that question, I believe the problem is that we have allowed our perspective on each of those component parts to become more anthropocentric than Christocentric. It is the same problem that I face when people suspiciously ask me whether I interpret the Creation Mandate as anthropocentric (i.e., leaning towards human priority) or ecocentric (i.e., leaning towards nature's flourishing). "Neither!" I tell them. "The Creation Mandate is Christocentric." The earth exists for Christ and his purposes. So do the End Times.

When Scripture refers to this period of the End Times, its emphasis is overwhelmingly upon a "coming" to planet Earth rather than an "escaping" from it. The word "rapture" does not appear in Scripture, but the word "coming" (*parousia*) does, and *parousia* is often used to refer to this entire period including the Rapture. Dispensational eschatologists may prefer to reserve the phrase "the second coming of Jesus Christ" for that precise moment following the seven-year Tribulation, but we call the entire period the Second Coming because the Lord's return is the main point of the whole enterprise. The Rapture, as an escape of a few faithful, is a fascinating concept; it lends itself to exciting filmmaking. But even in terms of a grammatical-historical time frame, the Rapture is a mere moment the length of a trumpet blast. It is followed by just a seven-year hiatus before the saints return with Christ to planet Earth to reign with him in his kingdom. What is a mere moment, or a seven-year absence, compared to a thousand years or compared to eternity in a new Jerusalem that has itself come to a new earth? The End Times is primarily about "coming," not about "escaping." Earth and its ecosystems are the landscape of the End Times. The new earth and its ecosystems are the landscape of eternity. More importantly, the question of why someone would *come* to somewhere is different than why someone would *escape* from it. This speaks to the matter of goals. *Why* is Jesus returning to earth? We have seen already: he is returning not only to save his people, but to restore his creation.

The fact that Jesus is that "someone who comes" is my second point, and it is a significant corrective to how popular evangelical culture often approaches the End Times. Eschatology is primarily about Jesus Christ, and not about you and me. It is about *Christ's* coming, not about *our* escaping. "Why care about global climate change when you and yours will be rescued in the Rapture?" Bill Moyers asks. I fear that we evangelicals have fed Moyers' cynicism and have provided impetus to those who would misquote James Watt. We must keep all things, including our eschatology,

Christocentric. True, the Rapture may be a great vindication for those who are Christians. True, we all wish to escape the Tribulation. But the End Times exist for God's glory and purposes. According to dispensational eschatologists, we raptured believers will rule and reign with Jesus in his millennial kingdom, but as we saw in the Creation Mandate, our dominion is always predicated on his. What is King Jesus planning to accomplish as his kingdom (fully) comes, his will is (finally) done, on earth as it is in heaven? Only when we discern those purposes can we then participate in them.

In all of Scripture I only see two prayers suggested as appropriate for the End Times. The first is *"Maranatha,"* "Come, Lord Jesus" (Rev 22:20). It is a prayer of joyful anticipation. It is also—we should admit it—a prayer of lament. *"Maranatha"* was the prayer that came to my lips last summer when I took my family on vacation to my favorite campsite of all time: Sugarloaf in the Arapaho National Forest of Colorado. The forest looked like a war zone. Pine beetle infestation—a documented projection of warming global temperatures—had killed the trees. For safety reasons, the Park Service could not leave these trees standing above the campsites. The ground was bare. Sugarloaf campground has a boardwalk painstakingly constructed out over the beaver ponds that connect the campground to the hillside to the east. In my opinion, that boardwalk is the greatest icon I have ever seen of the godly dominion enjoined on us in the Creation Mandate. Of human construction, the boardwalk allowed physically challenged people the chance to venture out over the marsh where they could fish for trout or perhaps gain a sighting of a cow moose and her calf. The boardwalk too had now been abandoned, parts of it fallen into the creek. We all piled out of the car into what was left of a landscape that I had loved. My wife glanced over at me. She asked if I wanted to be alone for a while. I went for a hike through the devastation and the prayer that I prayed was "Lord Jesus, come! Please come and restore all things, just as you have promised."

The second prayer of the End Times is almost a reply that God gives to our lament. In Jesus' parable of the widow pleading for relief, he says, "And will not God bring about justice for his chosen ones, who cry out to him day and night? Will he keep putting them off? I tell you, he will see that they get justice, and quickly. However, when the Son of Man comes, will he find faith on the earth?" (Luke 18:7,8). This second prayer, then, is "Lord, may I be found faithful." In light of Matthew 24, it is "Lord, please do not let my love grow cold." In the face of the Lord's future return, Scripture returns our attention to our present stewardship—to take up what we are responsible for *now*, to what is under our control *now*. This, we have seen, is a stewardship of the gospel, and a stewardship of God's creation.

In the next chapter we consider how to participate in the ways that the gospel is good news for the creation *now*. David, the Apostle Paul tells us in a sermon, "served God's purpose in his own generation, [and then] he fell asleep" (Acts 13:36). What does it mean for us, before we ourselves also fall asleep (or exit by rapture), to serve in our own generation the purposes of God in creation care and environmental missions?

Eschatology and the Environmental Missions Model

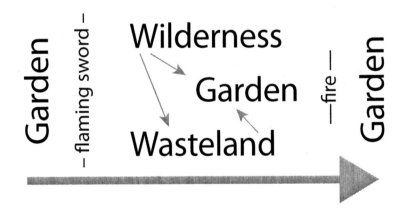

Diagram 2 (reproduced from page 71)

The eschatology of the Environmental Missions Model begins with a fire that purges without annihilating. Secular environmentalists fear that the evangelical doctrines of the Rapture and the Judgment act like a *deus ex machina*, an arbitrary god who descends into the amphitheater and says of whatever good humanity has done, whatever evil we have perpetrated, "Oh, never mind." The play is over. The theater is closed. But evangelicals understand that even the purging judgment of God is a grace purchased for us by the cross of Christ, since it is the sin in our existence that he considers dross, and not our existence itself. We are saved. And creation passes through with us—new heavens and a new earth.

In our model, the new heavens and the new earth of eternity also bear the name Garden, since all broken relationships have finally and fully been healed. The word "Eden" does not appear in the New Testament, although Peter quotes extensively from Joel 2 in his sermon at Pentecost, and the words "the garden of Eden" do appear in Joel's vision of "the day of the Lord" (2:3). The New International Version of the Bible released an updated edition in 2011. The old version (1984) uses the subtitle "The River of Life" to introduce chapter 22 of Revelation. The new edition, however, has changed the subtitle. The NIV 2011 now reads "Eden Restored." Subtitles of course are editorial devices and thus interpretative, but what an interpretation! Something in the last twenty-seven years of rereading Revelation 22 has led the NIV editors to believe the river of life in the new Jerusalem is what we have so long been waiting for: a restoration of Eden.

NOTES

1. Bill Moyers, *Welcome to Doomsday* (New York: New York Review of Books, 2006), 23.

2. Robert Wuthnow, *Be Very Afraid: The Cultural Response to Terrorism* (Oxford: Oxford University Press: 2010), 198.

3. James Watt, "The Religious Left's Lies," *The Washington Post*, May 21, 2005, http://www.washingtonpost.com/wp-dyn/content/article/2005/05/20/AR2005052001333.html (accessed July 15, 2013).

4. Ibid.

5. Moyers, *Welcome to Doomsday*, 23.

6. Albert Barnes, *Notes on the New Testament: James, Peter, John, and Jude* (Grand Rapids: Baker, 1972), 262.

7. Christopher J. H. Wright, *The Mission of God's People: A Biblical Theology of the Church's Mission* (Grand Rapids: Zondervan, 2010), 61.

8. Dag Hammarskjold, quoted in Kenneth Boa, *Conformed to His Image* (Grand Rapids: Zondervan, 2001), 369.

9. R. T. France, *The Gospel according to Matthew: An Introduction and Commentary* (Grand Rapids: Eerdmans, 1985), 905.

10. D. A. Carson, "Matthew," *Matthew, Mark, Luke,* vol. 8, Expositor's Bible Commentary, ed. Frank E. Gaebelein (Grand Rapids: Zondervan, 1984), 499.

11. James Lovelock, *The Revenge of Gaia* (New York: Basic Books, 2006).

12. Glenn Scherer, "Christian-right Views Are Swaying Politicians and Threatening the Environment," *Grist,* October 28, 2004, http://grist.org/politics/scherer-christian (accessed February 23, 2012).

13. John Houghton, "Sir John's Word to Pastors" (speech, Center for Applied Christian Ethics, Wheaton College, January 25, 2007), http://www.wheaton.edu/CACE/CACE-Audio-and-Video (accessed October 6, 2011).

8

PRAXIS: BIBLE IN ONE HAND, SHOVEL IN ANOTHER

One afternoon, during the time that I kept an office at our church, I looked up from my computer with a compelling urge to "do something." It was a beautiful spring day and I certainly wanted to be outside, but mostly I had grown tired on that afternoon of thinking and writing about creation care—cerebral work, similar to the last three theological chapters—and I wanted to do something practical and physical, something with discernible results, and something I could do right now. The only activity that seemed to meet my urgent criteria was to grab two trash bags from the custodial closet, go out to the road alongside the church, and begin picking up trash. It was a throwback to my days as a Cub Scout. The adult pack leaders made decisions for you, and back in the early 1970s, a childhood environmentalism was so simple: don't be a litterbug; give a hoot, don't pollute.

Because I don't often live outside my head, it wasn't long before my mind was racing as fast as the cars that zoomed by. What does picking up roadside rubbish *mean* as a ministry? Did picking up an aluminum beer can somehow embody the theology I had been studying? Is my little stint at highway cleanup more appropriately a spiritual discipline? Shouldn't I be back in the office, back on the clock, back to strategic and scaled-up activities?

Spiritual disciplines, of course, should not be despised. "Discipline, strictly speaking," Dallas Willard teaches us, "is activity carried on to prepare us indirectly for some activity other than itself. We do not practice the piano to practice the piano well, but to play it well."[1] Certainly this activity was exercising my humility. Except for adopt-a-highway civic groups, who picks up trash along the roadside anymore? Did the drivers of the passing cars think I was working off court-appointed community service hours? Did they think I was collecting aluminum cans to earn some spare change? Picking up trash also disciplined my sanctimony, a temptation to which environmentalists are notoriously prone. This wasn't my trash. There really is something outrageous about that moment when a person decides not to drop his or her garbage in the seat well of the car for disposal later in a trash can at home, but rather rolls down the window and tosses it out into the ditch. Some passersby honked their horns and gave me the thumbs up. One was a woman from our church. Being seen by these people made me feel good, but I knew their affirmation was just fueling my pride.

I also had to assess the grace that I showed myself. When it comes to good works, how much is enough? For example, I had two bags with me. In one I collected recyclables; in the other, trash to throw out. I thought: instead of putting it in the trash bag, should I have recycled that one plastic bottle, even though it was half-shredded and had been used as a spittoon? Or as I stood above a glass bottle that had shattered, just how many of the glass shards was I required to pick up? Having cleaned up a half-mile stretch of road, should I turn back to the church now, or continue on a bit? When it comes to creation care, enough rarely feels like enough. Finally, I also had to confront hope. This stretch of road would be trashed again, just give it a couple of weeks. In my Cub Scout days, environmentalism meant cleaning up litter in a park, but now our landfills are all full. Let today's local Cub Scout packs fill a thousand trash bags; we've got little room to put them.

Once in India, we picked a trashed man up out of a ditch, a human throwaway. He was lying naked in his own excrement, slowly dehydrating in the hot afternoon sun. He was crazy and couldn't speak. We took him to the ashram. Robynn washed the worst part of his soiling off of him. We gave him a T-shirt and a *lungi* to tie around his waist, and then loaded him back into the auto rickshaw and set off in search of a placement for him,

Praxis

finding it at the Ramakrishna Mission hospital. We made a donation for his upkeep, and I brought my barber in to shave the man's head and to cut the cockleburs out of his pubic hair. Judging from his circumcision, the man was a Muslim, so I gave him the Urdu name *Hazarat*, which means "lord." The name was a feeble attempt to restore dignity. What does it mean to recycle Hazarat? Humiliation, self-righteousness, perfectionism, and hopelessness—the personal spiritual rigors of picking Hazarat out of a ditch were not greatly different than my experience of cleaning along the highway. I could say that with Hazarat I wasn't greatly concerned about restoring the pristine condition of the roadside, but that's not exactly true. It troubled me greatly that our city, which I had grown to love, could leave a human being to die in the dust of the thoroughfare, regardless of how crazy or disgusting he might be. Something was ugly and broken and in need of restoration.

I know some fervent evangelists and some hard-working conservationists who would have little patience with the three theological chapters that preceded this one. With so much urgent need in the world, "Just roll up your sleeves and go do something about it," they tell us. And of course, they have a point: our theology should translate into practice. If this is a book about definitions, then an environmental missionary is someone who does . . . what, exactly? But the opposite sentiment is also true: our practice *must* have a theology. The Apostle Paul's eulogy for David was that he "had served God's purpose in his own generation" (Acts 13:36). Stewards begin their work with as thorough as possible an understanding of their stewardship, of their Master's purposes. Chris Wright makes the link between God's purposes and our labor:

> So our care for creation is motivated not solely by the fact that it was created by God and we were commanded to look after it, but also by the fact that it has been redeemed by Christ, and we are to erect signposts towards its ultimate destiny of complete restoration in Christ. God's redemptive mission includes creation. Our mission involves participating in that redemptive work as agents of good news to creation, as well as to people.[2]

✥ ENVIRONMENTAL MISSIONS ✥

In this chapter about translating theology into environmental missions, about "participating in that redemptive work as agents of good news" in practical ways, we will consider the four arrows in the Environmental Missions Model.

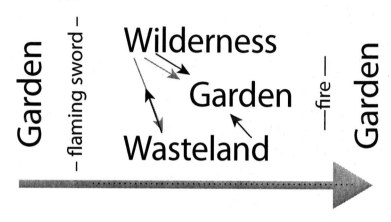

Diagram 3

You'll notice I've added a new component to the Environmental Missions Model: black arrows or dots that sit in relation to the grey arrows. The grey arrows that we've seen over the last three chapters represent movement and choices. For example, the bold, underlying arrow represents the inexorable movement of God's glory in and through creation: "For the earth will be filled with the knowledge of the glory of the Lord as the waters cover the sea" (Hab 2:14). The two grey arrows that proceed out from Wilderness represent the choice that humans make between reigning in obedience to God's dominion over us or conversely in obedience to our own lusts and greed. The newly added black arrows and dots represent the specific *work* of the environmental missionary in relation to divine or human choices, the praxis in relation to the theology. And so the arrow from Wilderness to Garden is a partnership in the mandate to bless and flourish, subdue and rule, till and keep. The arrow from Wasteland to Garden is the work of restoring that which has been abused. Another black arrow runs counter to the choice that sinful humanity makes to turn Wilderness into Wasteland and so represents the prophetic work of an environmental missionary. Finally, the black dots in the grey arrow of Christ's prevailing purposes represent the hope, trust, and prayer that are also an environmental missions labor. Each of these arrows includes the work of evangelism and discipleship. The environmental missionary has a Bible in one hand, a shovel in the other.

And so the structure of the remainder of this chapter will be simple: one section for each of the four arrows. Each section will begin with a sentence about the essence of the "work" that an environmental missionary does. Then I'll briefly draw a link between that work back to the theology of the previous chapters. Then I'll sketch as practical as possible a picture of what that environmental missions work can look like, even down to actual career titles. Finally, I'll discuss the role of evangelism, discipleship, and church planting in that particular labor.

From Wilderness to Garden

An environmental missionary works as the partner who pointedly builds sustainability, resilience, evangelism, and discipleship into the work of the Creation Mandate.

The *Cape Town Commitment*, in its Call to Action section, divides out the missional calling of Christian creation care. It states:

We encourage Christians worldwide to:

. . . Recognize and encourage the missional calling both of (i) Christians who engage in the proper use of the earth's resources for human need and welfare through agriculture, industry and medicine, and (ii) Christians who engage in the protection and restoration of the earth's habitats and species through conservation and advocacy.[3]

A similar division is made in the Confession of Faith section: "We support Christians whose particular missional calling is to environmental advocacy and action, as well as those committed to godly fulfillment of the mandate to provide for human welfare and needs by exercising responsible dominion and stewardship."[4] I once asked Chris Wright why the missional calling was split out in this particular way (e.g., (i) and (ii)), when no hint of that division was given in the preliminary Lausanne proceedings in Beirut (March 2010) that took up the topic of creation care. Wright replied that he wasn't greatly aware of the difference from Beirut, nor necessarily of a split in missional imperatives, but that, yes, a colleague had pointed out prior to Cape Town that not enough attention had been paid to biblical dominion or proper use.

Where Garden Meets Wilderness (the direction of our first arrow) is in fact the title of Cal Beisner's book, which itself is an argument for proper attention given to the unfolding of the Creation Mandate, the civilizing work of bringing that which has been "untouched by human hands" (a classic definition of wilderness) under the godly dominion that we've been called to exercise. The first arrow, to use the language of the *Cape Town Commitment*, is the godly fulfillment of the Creation Mandate through using the earth's resources in a proper fashion. This represents a "responsible dominion and stewardship." Wilderness, however, is not *tabula rasa*. One should not underestimate the amount of wasteland already built into the wilderness. Wilderness is the backdrop of broken relationships. Early in the Genesis history, Cain murders Abel, and the blood in the ground is described almost as a pollution that cries out, curses, and drives from the land (Gen 4:10,11). We can describe the first arrow—Wilderness to Garden—as positive movement, as building, but it is the type of construction that is always mindful of a cracked foundation, of less-than-perfect building materials.

Part of the work of environmental missions is the proper use of the earth's resources for the sake of human and nonhuman flourishing. And so you will find environmental missionaries working cross-culturally as farmers, engineers, scientists, technicians, etc., in the examples given of agriculture, industry, and medicine, etc. Of course Wright's realization and Beisner's argument is that you don't have to self-identify as an environmentalist in order to be a person who participates in the Creation Mandate.

Praxis

Consequently the black arrow of the environmental missionary is shown working in cooperation with the general grey arrow. For the sake of writing this chapter, I have in my hands a book in the Career Opportunities series, this one entitled "Career Opportunities in Conservation and the Environment."[5] Some readers will want to scan the footnote below to look for one of the sixty-five creative access platforms (CAP) or business-as-mission (BAM) opportunities that best serve their passions as an environmental missionary.[a] Many people would argue that this list is not exhaustive since the call today is for every profession to somehow "go green." As another

---

[a] (Arranged alphabetically by category): **Ecotourism:** Camp Cook, Camp Counselor, Camp Director, Resort Operator, Resort Planner, River Guide, Tour Guide, Travel Agent, Wilderness Guide; **Engineering:** Biological and Agricultural Engineers, Community Planner, Environmental Engineer, Geospatial Engineer, Mining and Geological Engineers, Surveying and Mapping Technician, Surveyor; **Farming and Fishing:** Agricultural Consultant, Commercial Beekeeper, Crop Farmer, Crop Scientist, Dairy Farmer, Farm Manager, Fisher, Fish Farmer, Livestock Farmer, Rural Appraiser; Forestry: Forester, Forestry Technician, Logger, Urban Forester; **Legal and Regulatory:** Environmental Attorney, Environmental Campaign Staff Worker, Environmental Compliance Specialist, Environmental Economist, Environmental Health Officer, Irrigation Auditor, Occupational Safety and Health Office, Park Manager; **Other:** Ground Maintenance Worker, Landscape Architect, Nature Photographer; **Outdoor/Environmental Education:** Ecological Restoration Instructor, Environmental Education Program Director, Environmental Science Professor, Environmental Science Teacher (High School), Field Education Coordinator, Field Teacher/Naturalist, Forestry and Conservation Science Professors, Marine Science Instructor, Outdoor Education Instructor, Recreation and Fitness Studies Professor, Recreation Planner, Recreation Worker; Scientific: Atmospheric Scientist, Chemical Laboratory Technician, Environmental Chemist, Environment Technician, Geoscientist, Marine Biologist, Marine Science Technician, Oceanographer, Plant Scientist, Range Manager, Soil Scientist, Veterinarian, Wetland Scientist, Wildlife Rehabilitator, Wildlife Scientist. (Paul R. Greenland and AnnaMarie L. Sheldon, *Career Opportunities in Conservation and the Environment* [New York: Checkmark Books, 2008], vii-viii.)

exercise in writing this chapter, I went through this list myself to see how many CAPs and BAMs I could put a face and name to from my twenty years of involvement in overseas missions. In other words, these would be self-identified missionaries sent cross-culturally, often through traditional mission agencies. I was surprised at the number. I know trek guides in the Himalayan mountains; soil scientists in Orissa, India; and fish farmers in Kenya. I have met environmental professors who teach in Haitian colleges, wildlife conservationists who patrol Central African game preserves, and beekeepers who export their honey from Pakistan to the UAE. In China alone, I have known waste managers, flood managers, and a young lady from Pennsylvania who teaches what she calls "environmental art."

Of course few of these acquintances over the years would have identi-fied themselves as "environmental missionaries," and so it's the purpose of this chapter to ask a question that remains in this section: what do environmental missionaries bring to the work of laboring alongside oth-ers in fulfilling the Creation Mandate? There are two answers. First, we bring a particular concern with building sustainability and resilience into the positive construction from Wilderness to Garden. We know without sustainability and resilience the inevitable result will be an overshoot into Wasteland. "What use is a sawmill without a forest?" asks ecological econ-omist Herman Daly.[6] While it undergoes continual dispute and pleas for revision, the Brundtland Commission's (UN) definition of sustainability remains the place where all workers begin: "Sustainable development is the development that meets the needs of the present without compromising the ability of future generations to meet their own needs."[7] Resilience is defined as "the capacity of a system, enterprise, or a person to maintain its core purpose and integrity in the face of dramatically changed circum-stances."[8] Climate change, with its extreme weather events, has catapulted resilience to the forefront of the creation care agenda. More and more of moving forward in the future is going to require some bouncing back. And that means that someone must be at work now building that capacity into our systems, enterprises, and people.

Praxis

Evangelism, discipleship, and church planting (including cross-cultural frontier missions) have particular resonance in the Creation Mandate. In Genesis 9:1, God repeats for Noah what he said to Adam: "Then God blessed Noah and his sons, saying to them, 'Be fruitful and increase in number and fill the earth.'" The next event in Scripture where God pronounces a blessing over a human is that of Abram, a blessing of fruitfulness that concludes with the statement: "and all peoples on earth will be blessed through you" (Gen 12:2,3). The seed of Abraham, we know, is the Lord Jesus Christ: "He redeemed us in order that the blessing given to Abraham might come to the Gentiles through Christ Jesus, so that by faith we might receive the promise of the Spirit" (Gal 3:14). Ralph Winter recounts the story of when theologian Walter Kaiser told him, "Well, you can call Genesis 12:1–3 the Great Commission if you want." Winter reflects: "And this element in the Perspectives course is one of the biggest jolts which especially seminary students get when they take the Perspectives course. The idea that the Great Commission is the backbone of the whole Bible— not just one of the teachings of the NT—is a major shift in perspective, a frontier yet to be crossed for most Christians."[9] If the Garden in our model represents the full blooming of right relationships, then peace with God through faith in Jesus Christ means that evangelism must be one of the core enterprises of the entire Creation Mandate. In addition to the blessings in Genesis 12, the idea of wilderness as space waiting to be touched by the human hand of godly dominion has significance for missions among unreached or unengaged people groups. Paul's ambition was to "preach the gospel where Christ was not known, so that I would not be building on someone else's foundation. Rather, as it is written: 'Those who were not told about him will see, and those who have not heard will understand'" (Rom 15:20,21). Paul's quoting of Isaiah 52:15 is another allusion to the Bible's Great Commission backbone, as well as a reference to the preaching of the gospel to all people groups prophesied in Matthew 24.

There is interesting synergy between resilience and evangelism/discipleship, which even secular research studies are beginning to notice. Andrew Zolli in his book *Resilience: Why Things Bounce Back* argues that systems are most resilient when populated by resilient people living in resilient communities. Resilient people are those who have developed certain beliefs and habits. For example, of beliefs, Zolli writes:

> Social psychologists refer to this as *hardiness*, a system of thought based, broadly, on three main tenets: (1) the belief that one can find a meaningful purpose in life, (2) the belief that one can influence one's surroundings and the outcome of events, and (3) the belief that positive and negative experiences will lead to learning and growth. Considering this, it should come as no surprise that people of faith also report greater degrees of resilience.[10]

Regarding habits, Zolli gives a nod to Buddhist meditation, but habits for us can be understood as prayer and the practice of the other Christian spiritual disciplines.[11] And then communities, the other component of the resilience equation, are made resilient through trust and cooperation.[12] How is this any different than the function of a healthy church? So if an environmental missionary wants to build resilience in her work of the Creation Mandate, the best thing she can do is preach the gospel, make disciples, and surround them with a healthy local, indigenous church.

(Counter to) From Wilderness to Wasteland

An environmental missionary works, by prophetic action and by preaching the cross of Christ, to oppose the sin that would destroy the environment.

The *Cape Town Commitment* loads up its call to action with adjectives: use of the earth's resources must be *proper*; dominion and stewardship must be *responsible*; fulfillment of the Creation Mandate must be *godly*. Such qualifiers indicate that there is an exercise of dominion that can be improper, irresponsible, and ungodly. Indeed, we can sin. The Tower of Babel is an interesting case study to follow early on the Creation Mandate. Taken on its own, it should have qualified as a civilizing enterprise. Using brick and tar (rather than stone and mortar) seems like a human innovation. And the builders seem as skilled in their construction as Jubal was in music (Gen 4:21), Nimrod was in his hunting (Gen 10:9), or Noah in his shipbuilding. It's hard to put a finger on the tower builders' actual transgression, but judging from the words of God, it seems to be a usurpation of the Creation Mandate for their own human purposes: "If as one people speaking the same language they have begun to do this," God says, "then nothing they plan to do will be impossible for them. Come, let us go down and confuse . . ." (Gen 11:6,7).

The next chapter will look specifically at the topic of sin and God's creation. In this chapter we simply take note that the black arrow of the environmental missionary's labor runs in opposition to that sin. Practically speaking, this takes the form of prophetic action and preaching the gospel of repentance. The *Cape Town Commitment*, employing adjectives for various types of ministries, is fond of the word "urgent." But it labels only two ministries both "urgent and prophetic." Creation care is one. (HIV/AIDS ministry is the other.) Prophetic action is not new for missionaries. Witness William Carey's confrontation of the practice of *suttee* (widow burning), or his opposition to the murder and suicide of the *thuggi* and *Juggernaut* cults. But prophetic action that employs political activism and a stand against injustice may feel new to modern evangelical missionaries (see chapter 12). If we train ourselves according to the Old Testament model of a prophet, then we'll know that prophecy often means standing up in opposition to a false god, calling people instead to the worship of the only true and living God. The *Cape Town Commitment* identifies our particular opponent as the toxic idolatry of consumerism: "Such love for God's creation demands that we repent of our part in the destruction, waste and pollution of the earth's resources and our collusion in the toxic idolatry of consumerism. Instead, we commit ourselves to urgent and prophetic ecological responsibility."[13]

In 2005 Sister Dorothy Stang, a Catholic nun from Ohio, was found murdered in Pará, Brazil. She was age seventy-three, and she died with a Bible in her hand. Sr. Dorothy was a defender of a trans-Amazon development project that was designed to generate jobs for the Anapu people through creation of a fruit processing industry, construction of two small five-hundred-kilowatt hydroelectric power plants, and reforestation in degraded areas. However, "according to Reuters [news agency], loggers, ranchers, and large farmers have been strong opponents of the project and of Stang."[14] One of these opponents has since been convicted of hiring the two assassins who murdered her. People call Sr. Dorothy a "rainforest martyr." Is that silly? But what if we said she was a martyr for the Anapu people? What if we said she was a martyr for the Bible she held in her hand when she died?

Peter Harris himself traces the founding of the organization A Rocha in part to the legal investigation and protest that attended the draining of a marshland near their home in Vila Verde, Portugal:

> As we watched what happened on the marsh, and later at the many other sites along the coast, we became increasingly aware that some of the forces that cause such environmental destruction are not morally or spiritually neutral. "The earth is defiled by its people; they have disobeyed the laws, violated the statues and broken the everlasting covenant. Therefore a curse consumes the earth," says the prophet Isaiah [24:5,6], drawing the explicit connection between that particular form of abuse and rebellion against God.[15]

Harris' response to this sin was to establish a Christian presence near the marshlands in the form of a field study center. (See Peter Harris' profile in appendix 3 for a discussion of how evangelism fits in with the ministry of A Rocha.) In addition to prophetic action, the gospel of Jesus Christ once again proves itself to be good news for all of creation, and evangelism shows that it cannot be divided out from the church's best, most effective environmental action. We preach a gospel of repentance made possible by the kindness of God (Rom 2:4) in Christ Jesus. Environmental missionaries confront the sinful action that would turn wilderness into wasteland by helping change the sinful hearts bent on that destruction.

Praxis

From Wasteland to Garden

An environmental missionary works to restore to rightness the relationships found in broken ecosystems and among the broken people who live there.

Cal DeWitt writes,

> Creation's garden abundantly yields blessed fruits, sustainably supporting us and all life in its God-declared goodness. We "disciples of the first Adam" have made the choice to extract more and yet more of the fruits of creation—even at the expense of destroying creation's protective provisions and blessed fruitfulness.[16]

The full meaning of this statement isn't evident unless one knows of another DeWitt phrase: "We must be disciples of the Last Adam, not of the First Adam." In other words, "As disciples of the one by whom 'all things were made,' and through whom 'all things hold together,' we participate in undoing the work of the First Adam, bringing restoration and reconciliation to *all things*."[17] So for DeWitt, creation care often involves an "undoing," or a "returning to." But this is not a naive return, as Beisner alleges, to some imagined garden of Eden, which is in fact locked away in our model by a flaming sword. If anything, it is a return to the Creation Mandate as it has now been redeemed in the Second Adam. It is a gracious and merciful second chance before the Second Coming. The Cape Town Commitment describes those who do this work as "Christians who engage in the protection and restoration of the earth's habitats and species through conservation and advocacy."[18]

If the denotation of "wilderness" means "untouched by human hands," then twenty-first-century humankind has a dilemma: there is ostensibly no more wilderness. There is no scrap of land that has not somehow been touched by a human. One of the most famous garbage dumps on earth is at Camp 4 just below the summit of Mount Everest. Nowadays, expeditions are organized solely for the purpose of bringing the pile of discarded oxygen canisters back down the mountain. The world's largest garbage dump is the "Great Pacific Garbage Patch," a gyre in the North Pacific that collects plastic and styrofoam from Asia's east coast and North America's west coast. It floats in one big circle the size of Texas. The ocean floor is no longer untouched, not when BP's Deepwater Horizon, before its explosion and spill, was able to drill a mile below the surface of the Gulf Coast. But it is air pollution and global climate change that has ecologists reevaluating their understanding of wilderness. Earth's atmosphere knows no boundaries. Sulfur dioxide emissions from coal-fired power plants in the American Northeast resulted in acid rain that killed trees and fish in remote Northern Ontario. Chlorofluorocarbons from aerosol cans used anywhere in the world helped thin the ozone layer and open a hole above Antarctica. Scientists have for a long time traced smog in California that originates in China. Global climate change is the most startling story of "wilderness" passing from the scene. The first measurable effects of climate change have touched many of our most engrained icons of wilderness. In 2012 NASA reported that the Arctic ice cap shrunk to its lowest level in the history of satellite data. Over the past three decades, it has shrunk 13 percent each decade in its minimum summer coverage while simultaneously continuing to thin. The famous Northwest Passage, which inspired and stymied such explorers as Lord Franklin, has now opened. Countries are now competing for rights to drill for oil on the Arctic shelf.

We might call this "Creation Mandate overshoot." We set out to make a garden, and on countless occasions we were certainly successful. To say that there is no more wilderness does not mean that everything is like the wasteland depicted in the Disney Pixar movie *Wall-E*, no square inch of the ground left uncovered by scrap metal. But in other cases we overshot. We went from wilderness to garden to wasteland. Or maybe we didn't remain vigilant or far searching enough. The causes of wilderness' disappearance in the examples I just gave all seem inadvertent. For example, the invention of aerosol deodorant was certainly a good act of dominion over nature, but we were unaware of the effect of chlorofluorocarbons on the ozone layer. However, if the world's governments had failed to back the

Montreal Protocol in 1987 that began the phase out of CFCs, then that would have been an example of the arrow moving directly from wilderness to wasteland, deserving of an environmental missionary's prophetic opposition. As it is, overshooting, even inadvertently, past garden into wasteland seems similar to having exorcised one demon, but then living to see it return with seven more demons ("more wicked than itself") to invade a space we once thought we had faithfully "swept clean and put in order" (Matt 12:43–45).

Restoration ecology has been one of Cal DeWitt's research interests at the University of Wisconsin for many decades. The town of Dunn, just south of Madison, has benefited from his practical leadership in its many acres of restored prairie and wetlands. In one article published in the *Christian Scholar's Review*, DeWitt quotes a paper in *BioScience* (2002), which recognized that "the global extent of the human footprint suggests that humans are stewards of nature, whether we like it or not," and another in *Science* magazine (1997), which concludes: "Humanity's dominance of Earth means that we cannot escape responsibility for managing the planet." The evidence is indisputable, DeWitt argues: "We find the whole Earth under human domination. We are the first to see our planet thus and it is dawning on us that this necessarily makes us its stewards," whether we ever initially heeded the words of the Creation Mandate or not. In this "time of domination," when we more than ever need to "transform our management into stewardship," DeWitt lists the three tasks that we can claim as the black arrow of labor for the environmental missionary: "(1) preservation of biospheric systems that are working quite well, (2) application of the physician's art and science at setting the conditions for restoration and healing of whatever we have abused and degraded, and (3) making peace with creation and its creatures in deliberate and determined reconciliation."[19] Among missionaries that I already know, an example of the first task of preservation are the marine protection units that are being established in Kenya and other places in the Indian Ocean. These MPUs allow fish populations to sustainably regenerate their numbers even in the surrounding unprotected waters. An example of the second task of restoration is the vetiver grass plantings in Papua, Indonesia, which prevent erosion and allow native species to reestablish themselves. An example of the third task—often called "reconcilation ecology"[b]—is the installation of solar panels in villages in the Sunderban region of West Bengal. These panels provide light at night which prevent tigers from wandering into the villages, thus protecting both the villagers (from man-eaters) and the tigers (from revenge killings). This last example is not from missionaries, but it could be, or should be; according to the Joshua Project, Christians make up only 0.007 percent of West Bengal's Southern 24 Parganas district.

When DeWitt employs the word "reconciliation" in addition to restoration—"We participate in undoing the work of the First Adam, bringing restoration and reconciliation to all things"—he points the way to the role of evangelism and discipleship in the work of the environmental missionary. The organizing principle for our ministry that the Apostle Paul uses in his second letter to the Corinthians, when he explains what remains after Christ's death and resurrection for us to do—and that is the topic of this

---

[b] The new field of ecology that bears the name "reconciliation ecology" has De-Witt's blessing: "In pursuing this work of biospheric stewardship, ecologists and environmental scientists must continue their progression in research from reservation ecology [i.e., setting aside natural land] and restoration ecology [i.e., returning some developed land to a more natural state] on to reconciliation ecology." The term was coined by Michael Rosenzweig and is defined as "the science of inventing, establishing, and maintaining new habitats to conserve species diversity in places where people live, work, or play" (Michael J. Rosenzweig, *Win-Win Ecology: How the Earth's Species Can Survive in the Midst of Human Enterprise* [Oxford: Oxford University Press, 2003], 7). The premise is that conservationists concerned with the loss of biodiversity must come to grips with the fact that 7 billion *Homo sapiens* are not going to be, nor should they be, excised from the biosphere. Win-Win is "sharing our habitats deliberately with other species." Stated this way, it sounds like the Creation Mandate, and again shows that the work of the environmental missionary is *not* that of restoring the earth to the first Garden in our model, but rather to the second in anticipation of the third and final Garden.

chapter: what is it that environmental missionaries *do?*—is contained in a single word, *reconciliation*:

> Therefore, if anyone is in Christ, the new creation has come: The old has gone, the new is here! All this is from God, who reconciled us to himself through Christ and gave us the ministry of reconciliation: that God was reconciling the world to himself in Christ, not counting people's sins against them. And he has committed to us the message of reconciliation. We are therefore Christ's ambassadors, as though God were making his appeal through us. We implore you on Christ's behalf: Be reconciled to God. God made him who had no sin to be sin for us, so that in him we might become the righteousness of God. (2 Cor 5:17–21)

Many of us are used to the King James rendering of this passage which reads in verse 17 as "If anyone is in Christ, *he is a new creature*" (emphasis added). But commentator Richard Hays says that the phrase is more explosive than that, "a burst of wonder" that proclaims: "If anyone is in Christ . . . *New Creation!*" Hays explains the effect:

> The background of this text is Isaiah 65:17, where Israel's God declares: "For I am about to create new heavens and a new earth; the former things shall not be remembered or come to mind." So Paul is proclaiming the transformation of the world, and summoning us to see all things made new in light of that transformation. Note: "God was reconciling *the world* to himself" (2 Corinthians 5:19). Not just individuals. The frame of reference is cosmic and corporate. Paul is not just saying, "Look at me, my sins have been forgiven, and so I'm now a new creature." He is saying that the whole world is being made new by the cross and resurrection and that all our relationships have to be re-evaluated in light of that transformation.[20]

The context of environmental missions ends up, surprisingly, to not be creation at all, but rather "new creation," and not just "new creatures,"

but the whole new context that human beings find themselves in now that Jesus Christ has risen from the dead. Evangelism and discipleship are at the core of an environmental missionary's restorative work. We are Christ's ambassadors. He has committed to us the message of reconciliation.

From Garden to Garden to Garden

An environmental missionary works at developing hope as an expertise and labors in prayer that God's kingdom come, God's will be done on earth; that is, in its ecosystems and among all who dwell in them.

"Hope is a duty." A duty, in turn, is something you do, a labor, a task. This phrase is in circulation among secular environmentalists, including the well-known David Orr from Oberlin College, who uses a variation of it as a title for his collection of essays: "Hope Is an Imperative." The origin of the phrase, however, seems attributable to Cardinal Suenens, Archbishop of Brussels, who was once asked, "Why are you a man of hope, despite the confusion in which we find ourselves today?" He replied that we must

be ready to expect the unexpected from God. The ways of Providence are by nature surprising. We are not prisoners of determinism nor of the sombre prognostications of sociologists. God is here, near us, unforeseeable and loving. I am a man of hope not for human reasons nor from natural optimism; but because I believe the Holy Spirit is at work in the Church and in the world, even when His name remains unheard . . . The long history of the Church is filled with the wonders of the Holy Spirit. Think only of the prophets and saints who, in times of darkness, have discovered a spring of grace and shed beams of light on our paths. I believe in the surprises of the Holy Spirit . . . To hope is a duty, not a luxury. To hope is not to dream, but to turn dreams into reality. Happy are those who dream dreams and are ready to pay the price to make them come true.[21]

Praxis

To repeat Cal DeWitt: "As disciples of the one by whom 'all things were made,' and through whom 'all things hold together,' we participate in undoing the work of the First Adam, bringing restoration and reconciliation to *all things*."[22] To repeat Chris Wright: "Our mission involves participating in that redemptive work as agents of good news to creation, as well as to people."[23] If the work of hope is to turn dreams into reality, then that turning is but a "participation" alongside the One in whom we have placed our hope. For that reason, in the Environmental Missions Model, the work of the environmental missionary is not portrayed as another black arrow but as a series of black dots, swept along in the mighty work of Christ, persevering with longsuffering trust until the new heavens and the new earth are finally revealed. But Cardinal Suenens is right: hope does exact a price. It is work.

Perseverance is a practical application of hope. So is prayer. We will discuss in chapter 11 the prayers of environmental missions, and prayer is a labor, a work, a discipline, a doing. To conclude this section and chapter, I'll simply let N. T. Wright summarize the theological legitimation of environmental missions in Christ Jesus and, in the process, describe the whole basis of our hard-working labor and our hopeful praying:

> The resurrection is all about Jesus as the *prototype* of the new creation. The ascension is all about Jesus as the *ruler* of the new creation as it breaks into the world of the old. The second coming is all about Jesus as the *coming Lord and judge* who will transform the entire creation. And, in between the resurrection and ascension, on the one hand, and the second coming, on the other, Jesus is the one who sends the Holy Spirit, his own Spirit, into the lives of his followers, so that he himself is powerfully present with them and in them, guiding them, directing them, and above all enabling them to bear witness to him as the world's true Lord and work to make that sovereign rule a reality.[24]

NOTES

1. Dallas Willard, *The Spirit of the Disciplines* (San Francisco: HarperSanFrancisco, 1988), 120.

2. Christopher J. H. Wright, *God's People*, 61.

3. Third Lausanne Congress, *Cape Town Commitment*, II.B.6.46.

4. Ibid., I.7.A.

5. Paul R. Greenland and AnnaMarie L. Sheldon, *Career Opportunities in Conservation and the Environment* (New York: Checkmark Books, 2008).

6. Herman E. Daly and John B. Cobb Jr., *For the Common Good: Redirecting the Economy toward Community, the Environment, and a Sustainable Future* (Boston: Beacon, 1989).

7. United Nations General Assembly, "Report of the World Commission on Environment and Development: Our Common Future," 1987, http://www.un-documents.net/our-common-future.pdf (accessed July 15, 2013).

8. Andrew Zolli and Ann Marie Healy, *Resilience: Why Things Bounce Back* (New York: Free Press, 2012), 7.

9. Ralph D. Winter, "Twelve Frontiers of Perspective," in *Foundations of the World Christian Movement: A Larger Perspective; Course Reader*, eds. Ralph D. Winter and Beth Snodderly (Pasadena: Institute of International Studies, 2008), 313.

10. Zolli and Healy, *Resilience*, 128.

11. Ibid., 132-43.

12. Ibid., 143.

13. Third Lausanne Congress, *Cape Town Commitment*, I.7.A.

14. "American Nun Murdered in Brazil," *Wikinews*, February 15, 2005, http://en.wikinews.org/wiki/American_nun_murdered_in_Brazil (accessed July 16, 2013).

15. Peter Harris, *Under the Bright Wings* (Vancouver, Canada: Regent College Publishing, 1993), 53.

16. Calvin B. DeWitt, *Earth-wise: A Biblical Response to Environmental Issues* (Grand Rapids: CRC Publications, 1994), 35.

17. Calvin B. DeWitt, "Creation's Environmental Challenge to Evangelical Christianity," in *The Care of Creation*, ed. R. J. Berry (Downer's Grove, IL: InterVarsity Press, 2000), 66.

18. Third Lausanne Congress, *Cape Town Commitment*, II.B.6.C.46.

Praxis

19. Calvin B. DeWitt, "Biogeographic and Trophic Restructuring of the Biosphere: The State of the Earth under Human Domination," *Christian Scholar's Review* 32 (2003): 363.

20. Richard Hays, "The Word of Reconciliation" (sermon, Duke Center for Reconciliation, Durham, NC, June 1, 2010), http://www.faithandleadership.com/sermons/the-word-reconciliation (accessed May 26, 2012).

21. Cardinal Suenens, quoted in Noel J. Tobin, "15th Sunday in OT: Hope," Catholic Diocese of Geraldton, http://www.geraldtondiocese.org.au/index.php?option=com_content&view=article&id=172:15th-sunday-in-ot-hope&catid=13:year-a&Itemid=51 (accessed May 15, 2013).

22. DeWitt, "Creation's Environmental Challenge," 66.

23. Christopher J. H. Wright, *God's People*, 61.

24. N. T. Wright, *Simply Jesus* (San Francisco: HarperOne, 2011), 194.

9

SIN AS UNFAITHFUL STEWARDSHIP

Here are two little-known facts about the marvelous creation hymn "How Great Thou Art": First, it was a missionary—Stuart K. Hine, a British Methodist—who brought the hymn back from the Ukraine and translated it into the English version we sing today. Secondly, after its first publication in 1949, Hine offered additional verses. One of the new verses hints at the possibility of what we might call "environmental sin," a mixture, according to Hine, of ingratitude, defilement, foolishness, and pride, which ultimately reviles the holy name of God. In the end, though, like any category of sin, it is not outside the grace of God for forgiveness.

> O when I see ungrateful man defiling
> This bounteous earth, God's gifts so good and great;
> In foolish pride, God's holy Name reviling,
> And yet, in grace, His wrath and judgment wait.[1]

Is there such a thing as environmental sin? My wife had an interesting moment one Wednesday morning during Ladies' Bible Study. Her group was working through a workbook on the Minor Prophets authored by a famous contemporary teacher. They were asked to "list the sins" found in the second chapter of Habakkuk. It was a fairly easy task: "woe to him" who steals, extorts, profits unjustly, murders, gets others drunk, worships idols, etc. When the workbook reiterated these sins, Robynn piped up, "Hey, wait a second. They totally skipped over one." Verse 17 reads, "You cut down the forests of Lebanon. Now you will be cut down. You destroyed the wild animals, so now their terror will be yours" (NLT). Admittedly, Robynn was reading from the New Living Translation. The NIV is more obscure: "The violence you have done to Lebanon will overwhelm you, and your destruction of animals will terrify you."[a] In the case of the second chapter of Habakkuk, neither modern English language translators nor popular Bible study leaders are predisposed to look for the possible existence of environmental sin. The point isn't lost on biblical scholars, however. John Watts, professor of Old Testament from Serampore College—yes, William Carey's university—writes:

> The atrocities of war return to burden the conqueror. The magnificent forests of Lebanon were cut by the Assyrians (Isa. 37:24) and again by the Babylonians (Isa. 14:8). The trees made excellent timber for large buildings, but the forests were destroyed in the process. The prophet is sensitive to the loss of wild life (*beasts*) as well. The lines of verse 8 are repeated, linking the guilt to *violence done* to God's *land* and to his *city*.[2]

The answer to the question of whether such a category as environmental sin exists will invariably depend on how one frames the question. Is it possible to sin against a tree or a stream? Is it possible to sin against a West Virginia mountaintop or an Amazonian forest? Couldn't we easily stand before God and make a reasonable argument that our actions fit within the proscribed limits of "dominion," which he himself gave us? One common

---

[a] The NLT translators, finding no antecedent in the text for the country of Lebanon, equate Lebanon with "the mountain region," the Hebrew word *behemôt* as a by-form of *bamôt* (peaks). Commentator Francis Andersen would likely commend the NLT translators for doing their homework: "The reference to Lebanon has a plausible explanation in the activities of Nebuchadnezzar in taking cedar from Lebanon for his building projects. This is alluded to in [Isaiah] 14:8, where the cedars are relieved when the King of Babylon stops chopping them down: 'Yes, the fir-trees rejoice over you, and the cedars of Lebanon: since you have been laid low, no feller has come up against us.'" (Francis I. Andersen, *Habakkuk,* The Anchor Bible (New York: Doubleday, 2001), 251.

way of developing an environmental hamartiology is to understand it in terms of justice. In other words, to trace our actions—say, the felling of a tree—and find the person or community or people group on whom that tree toppled—economically, socially, healthwise, I mean. Environmental injustice is often difficult to trace. We may have to traverse hundreds of square miles of soil, water, air, or atmosphere between cause and effect, action and harm. "Since love is work," psychiatrist M. Scott Peck once famously said, "the essence of nonlove is laziness."[3] If the end result of the hard work of tracing causality is personal culpability, then we can understand why so few people in our churches take up the labors of justice. It's just easier not to know. "Rescue those who are unjustly sentenced to die; save them as they stagger to their death. Don't excuse yourself by saying, 'Look, we didn't know.' For God understands all hearts, and he sees you. He who guards your soul knows you knew. He will repay all people as their actions deserve" (Prov 24:11,12 NLT). I am convinced that, like Solomon has concluded, we possess more actionable knowledge about injustice than we care to admit. In other words, God often overcomes our laziness and brings knowledge about the effects of our actions to us without arduous investigation on our part. Why? Because he is a just God and he truly wants to lift up the oppressed. Bringing knowledge to the church is just one of the ways he loves the poor, needy, and powerless. It is also one of the ways that he loves us. He who did not leave us dead in our transgressions and sin, will not leave us alive but wallowing in them. He confidently moves us toward a vision of all Christians transformed to the image of Jesus Christ, the suffering servant who acts justly, loves mercy, and walks humbly with his God.

North American evangelicals are unfortunately in a period of being greatly leery of calls to justice. We've been conditioned by prevailing politics and economics to fear that "justice" is just a code word for "the redistribution of wealth," and redistribution from the hard-working worthy to the chronically undeserving. The same credo of "personal responsibility" that we demand in our politics, we demand of our doctrine of sin. Sin is a personal transgression of a fixed absolute. A farmer who poisons his wife by slipping arsenic in her morning coffee is different than the farmer who poisons her through the overapplication of herbicide on their fields. In the latter case, she's a victim of cancer, not the victim of a murderer. And motive is also an important part of understanding sin as personal transgression. Our unfortunate farmer may have loved his wife dearly; he was simply trying to increase corn yields and maintain the profitability of a struggling operation.

Discussions of sin are inherently problematic inquiries. For one, God has placed himself as judge over all such matters and brooks no appellate court made up of you or me. In addition, the blood of Christ has paid for our sins once for all and has ushered in a righteousness that is apart from the law. And yet environmental missionaries are called to preach a gospel of repentance and forgiveness from sin. We disciple congregations in their freedom from sin, purchased for them by Christ Jesus. And as one of the arrows in the Environmental Missions Model indicates, we are called to oppose sin and act against it prophetically. Problematic or not, environmental missions as a new category within missions will invariably take its own fresh look at sin. In our inquiry, we are greatly assisted by two early missionaries to Southern Africa who, even more than William Carey (or Agabus of Acts 11), can lay claim to being the Protestant church's "first environmental missionaries." For all of Carey's botanical achievements, it was Robert Moffat who won the moniker "God's gardener," having worked as a professional gardener in England before leaving for Africa in 1817. Moffat was followed by Dr. John Croumbie Brown, described as "initially a missionary and subsequently a university teacher, botanist, state scientist and propagandist of conservation." The conservation movement in fact first emerged in colonial settings and only later arrived in Europe. Many consider these Scottish missionaries and their colleagues to be the forerunners of modern conservationism. One scholar calls Brown "the single most influential voice in the formation of a colonial and North American discourse on forestry, irrigation, range management, and on the environmental impact of settlement."[4] Moffat and Brown's influence on our perspective of sin is an approach that looks at the entire panorama of sin—and not just so-called environmental ones—against the backdrop of unfaithful stewardship.

Drought was the context for the great blossoming of Moffat, Brown, and conservationist theory. In 1821–23, 1845–47, and 1862–63, the whole of Southern Africa was parched and given little reprieve to revive.

> The droughts also stimulated the emergence of significant new ways in which colonial scientists and intellectuals began to interpret relationships between environmental change and human activity. They assigned blame for ecological degradation and sought, for the first time, to introduce conservation measures intended to inhibit artificially induced climate change. The most important feature of the European scientific response to drought episodes in Southern Africa after 1820 was the emergence of a "desiccationist" theory linking the removal of vegetations to rainfall decline and then to regional or global climatic desiccation.[5]

When it is written of Moffat and Brown that "they assigned blame for ecological degradation," that obviously means one thing in scientific circles, and quite another in missionary ones. Blame for a scientist can simply mean *causation*, and so desiccationist theory is a major breakthrough, identifying that devegetation of a region can contribute to drought. Blame for a missionary, however, especially of the strict Calvinist variety, will invariably invoke the category of sin and judgment. What makes Moffat and Brown distinctive is that we see in them the beginnings of a full-blown integration of theology and environmental service. Moffat rooted his creation care in a theology of judgment. Brown began with a more beatific vision.

When Moffat encountered the drought north of the Orange River, his biographer claimed he was "no ethnographer or social observer, zealous to relate what he saw and heard." Rather, "his business was to move about with disapproval of nakedness, theft, feasting and witchcraft, to convince people of their state as sinners and 'to preach the unsearchable riches of Christ among the heathen.'[6] Moffat himself wrote of his travels:

> As an inhabited country it is scarcely possible to conceive of one more destitute and miserable; and it is impossible to traverse its extensive plains, its rugged, undulating surface, and to descend to the beds of its waterless rivers, without viewing it as emphatically "a land of droughts," bearing the heavy curse of
>
> Man's first obedience, and the fruit
> Of that forbidden tree, whose mortal taste
> Brought death into the world, and all our woe.[7]

Moffat's quoting of Milton's *Paradise Lost* is significant in that it links the African drought to original sin. Some say that Moffat was forced into an apologetic by native rainmakers who blamed the white man for the drought. "The charge brought against us by the rainmaker," Moffat writes, "was by every passing cloud and blast from the torrid zone brought fresh to our minds . . . and they thought that having teachers of strange doctrines among them such as their forefathers never knew, the country would be burnt up."[8] Moffat's apologetic strategy was to identify a golden age of abundant rainfall—as he did, not only in biblical chronology but also in Tswana oral tradition—and then pose the question: when did this pluvial age exist (and end): immediately before the Europeans arrived, or before the Tswana began their destructive environmental practices? To prove causation, Moffat turned to Alexander von Humboldt's theories of the desiccating effects of deforestation found in the recently published *Personal Narrative of Travels to Equinoctial Regions of the New Continent 1799–1804*. In doing so, Moffat brought—perhaps truly for one of the first times in the history of modern missions—science into the employ of power encounter. Scholar Richard Grove writes, "The situation was, moreover, one in which superiority in the interpretation of environmental processes became a symbol or a test of the superiority or truth of the Christian religion."[9]

Drought, particularly in an active Christian theology of the Old Testament, has long been considered a sign of judgment:

❧ Sin as Unfaithful Stewardship ❧

However, if you do not obey the Lord your God . . . The Lord
will strike you with wasting disease, with fever and inflam-
mation, with scorching heat and drought, with blight and
mildew, which will plague you until you perish. The sky over
your head will be bronze, the ground beneath you iron. The
Lord will turn the rain of your country into dust and pow-
der; it will come down from the skies until you are destroyed.
(Deut 28:15,22–24)

Sin such as rampant fornication need not be directly related to the
judgment (e.g., drought), but as surely as sin results in judgment, so fornication might be blamed for drought. Moffat's argument could well be
considered an innovation. Drought (a judgment) is a natural result of cut-
ting the forests and burning the veldt. By claiming that devegetation is a
sin that contributes to judgment, Moffat introduces a middle term and
embraces a theology of natural consequences. Underlying whatever natural
processes von Humboldt and others may discover is a natural law and a
moral law, which are inexorably linked. For however much Moffat might
also decry "nakedness, theft, feasting and witchcraft," it is all part of the
Tswana's "state as sinners," a state wherein they have turned their back on
the Creator and his ways. Such a sinful state will bear damning consequences both in this age and the next.

In his survey of the destruction, Moffat touched on numerous topics
including the extirpation of wildlife like the hippo, the elephant, and the gi-
raffe. Among plant species, he had a particular interest in the *Acacia giraffea*.

When the natives remove from that district, which may be
only after a few years, the minor species of the acacia soon
grows but the *Acacia giraffea* requires an age to become a tree,
and many ages must pass before they attain the dimension of
their predecessors. The wood, when old, is dark red, rough-
grained and exceedingly hard and heavy; after being dried for
years, when thrown into water it sinks like lead. In the course
of my journeys I have met with trunks of enormous size

which, if the time were calculated necessary for their growth, as well as for their decay, *we might be led to conclude that they sprung up immediately after the flood*, if not before then.[10]

It is Richard Grove who italicizes that final phrase and considers it "most revealing of Moffat's inflexible and preconceived environmental religion." Grove observes:

> Not only were the Tswana destructive, [Moffat] considered, but they had caused permanent damage to a tree dating back to the time of the biblical flood, and conceivably before it. The theme, then, concerns the destroyers of the trees in the "neglected Garden," possibly the Garden of Eden. The destructiveness of the Tswana is thus directly equated with the transgression which led to the Flood and not only that, but with the continuing transgression which has brought about the drought and the arid landscape of divine retribution. The implication was that those who were responsible for such transgression could not be trusted with the "garden," as its continued despoliation served to prove.[11]

This last statement—the implication that the Tswana cannot be trusted with their own land—speaks volumes about colonialistic mentality and explains some of the ongoing controversy behind the setting aside of the Matopo National Park in what was then Rhodesia—a cause for which John Croumbie Brown was active. But the implications of Moffat's thinking are even more far reaching. Fallen humankind has been proven untrustworthy. None of us are worthy of the confidence that God placed in us at the time of the Creation Mandate. We are failed stewards; that is, sinners.

John Croumbie Brown's experience of Africa, and his spiritual experience of it, began not with destruction but with beauty. In 1844 the London Missionary Society transferred Brown from Russia to Cape Town. One of his first labors was the translation of a travel text by two French Protestant missionaries, T. Arbousset and F. Daumas. Brown was captivated by the imaginative language of the travelers, a language that probably owed more to the French Romantic tradition than it did to scientific rationalism. Of the landscape to the northeast of the colony of the Cape of Good Hope, Arbousset and Daumas wrote, "Never before had we experienced a sweeter, more ecstatic joy than we did when, with the bible in our hands and our prayers on our lips, we turned towards the outlet from that mountain . . . to gaze on the work of God and the magnificent vestment with which he had clothed creation."[12]

When Brown went on his own tour a year later, his own experience was decidedly different. Once, he stumbled upon the bones of oxen that had perished eighty-four miles from the nearest water source. He also witnessed the debilitating effects of flash flooding. In each case, his reflections still seemed to originate from the Edenic vision of Arbousset and Daumas, in the same way that Cain's exile to the land of Nod draws its coordinates from the garden, that is, *east* of Eden. "All that was wanting," a colleague of Brown's theorized about the region of the Karoo, "to convert that wilderness into a smiling garden was speeding away to swell the rivers into dangerous torrents, and carrying along with it some of the most fertile soil of the country."[13] And thus we have the hints of soil erosion as a metaphor for sin, and conservation as a metaphor for conversion.

Brown's missionary career, officially defined, would end in 1848 when he returned to Scotland and took a pastorate in Aberdeen, where he also studied botany at King's College, being awarded an L.L.D. degree in 1858. When he returned to South Africa in 1862, it would be as the officially designated "colonial botanist," the second person ever to hold the post. When he translated Arbousset and Daumas (1846), he could not as yet imagine the integration of missionary activity and environmental service. In fact, in his preface to the translation, he wrote that the proper duties of a missionary included "finding unknown tribes, contacting their chiefs, locating suitable land for mission stations, and extending Christianity and civilization." These pursuits he called "sacred purposes and nobler objects."[14] Nonetheless he argued that scientific activities such as geography, ethnology, and natural science could certainly contribute to missionary work, making it a point to praise how Arbousset and Daumas used sci-

ence to further the work of the Paris Missionary Society. Before his departure from Cape Town, Brown published a second book, *Pastoral Discourses*
(1847), a collection of his sermons preached at the Union Church. The
sermons reveal a transformation in his thinking, a rather obvious attempt
to achieve a greater integration than what he could confess in his preface
of Arbousset and Daumas. To understand environmental degradation in
the context of Christian theology would equip Brown to return to South
Africa as a government botanist, but no less a missionary. He never left the
missions community, and in fact was famous for mobilizing missionaries
(including missionary wives and missionary kids) for the sake of collecting and recording species. He was once accused of misuse of government
funds because, while out on tours, he would preach on Sundays in whatever local church was at hand. Regardless of the ongoing connections to
missionaries, according to Richard Grove, "the sermons found in Brown's
Pastoral Discourses of 1847 continued to serve as the religious basis of his
environmental mission for the next 40 years."[15] In other words, even when
Brown was most obviously "colonial botanist," he remained an environmental missionary.

By his own account, when Brown left the colony in 1848 at
the end of his first visit his mind was filled with images of
desiccation and death. Moreover the very starkness of the
contrast between a drought landscape and the idyllic landscape conjured in the *Narrative* served to reinforce Arbousset's
"promised land" as a symbol of environmental salvation in the
mind of Brown. The strength of this image, coupled with the
ferocity of the drought, which awoke associations of the worst
Old Testament disasters in his mind, ensured that Brown's
religious mission would become primarily an environmental one. The vigour of this new mission cannot be underes-
timated. As a self-appointed messenger of the environmental
"word" the erstwhile Congregationalist missionary was later
to publish a whole set of environmental gospels; over sixteen
books on water, climate and forest conservation.[16]

❧ Sin as Unfaithful Stewardship ❧

These sixteen books were world-changing texts, some referenced before the Royal Geographic Society, and Richard Grove can conceive of them in no other terms than as "environmental gospels."

Brown's environmental gospel, as revealed in *Pastoral Discourses*, is rooted in individual conversion. "He [Jesus Christ] knew what was in man," the Reverend Brown preached, "and not by national decrees, but by individual conversions, did he seek to reform the world."[17] The converted individual would first endeavor to preach the gospel—laity as well as clergy, from the pulpit as well as in the world—resulting in more converted individuals. But converted individuals would also engage in good works, of which creation care is an example. By Sermon VIII, based on Isaiah 32:13–15, Brown has a vision of creation care greater than just an example of love. Isaiah declares,

> Upon the land of my people shall come up thorns and briars; yea, upon all the houses of joy in the joyous city: because the palaces shall be forsaken; the multitude of the city shall be left; the forts and towers shall be for dens for ever, a joy of wild asses, a pasture of flocks; until the spirit be poured upon us from on high, and the wilderness be a fruitful field, and the fruitful field be counted for a forest. (Isa 32:13–15 KJV)

When Brown equates the condition of the Karoo to the state of Jerusalem under siege by Sennacherib (the reference of the Isaiah passage), he identifies the same causation: the land was devastated as a result of human sin. When God's moral order is violated, the social and the natural order also suffer. The only means of restoration is that "the [S]pirit be poured upon us from on high." Brown concludes,

> If, then, I were asked what I consider the means most likely to bring under cultivation the vast uncultivated deserts of this land, the waste-howling wilderness stretching away from this point to the far north, I would reply at once: The spread of pure religion; "then shall the earth yield her increase; and God, even our [own] God, shall bless us" [Ps 67:6 KJV].[18]

In Brown's calculations, the opposite of pure religion was superstition and vice. "The tendency of the former is to enervate, the tendency of the latter to extirpate, a people, the tendency of both, to devastate a land."[19] In this way, Brown was willing to implicate white colonial farmers as well as blacks. Much later as a biologist, in official reports filed in 1863 and 1873, and even quoting Moffat in the 1873 report, Brown drew some ire when he defended the Tswana and condemned the Europeans:

> That the heathen in their ignorance have acted as described need not surprise us; but what better has been the course pursued by the more civilized? Is it not the case that the history of civilized man in his colonization of new countries has been in every age substantially this—he has found the country a wilderness; he has cut down trees, and he has left it a desert?[20]

As the years progressed, Brown began to differ from Moffat in his use of Old Testament references to droughts and floods. Brown saw them as natural events that existed as historical data but for which causation was only sketchily assigned. He would be as careful in his theological conclusions as he was in his scientific ones. Brown's primary interest was in how contemporary science could assign causation, which then demanded a societal response. Repent and do right! Drought in a particular region, which could be identified as the natural consequence of the greed of a particular people group, demanded a full-scale conversionist and conservationist response: preach the gospel and plant trees. He thus had more latitude to target European settlers with their misguided farming practices in his preaching. It may be easier to assign moral retribution for the sin of overt paganism, but to be caught red-handed in one's own environmentally destructive greed can be equally as convicting.

We can look, as Moffat and Brown suggest, at the entire panorama of sin—and not just so-called environmental ones—against the backdrop of failed or unfaithful stewardship. The context in which Adam took the fruit from his wife's hand and sunk his teeth into it is varied. There is the context of innocent, undefiled beauty, or paradise, as we say. There is the context of relationship: the as-of-yet-unoffended God walking leisurely in the garden with the man and the woman. There is also the context of regulation and injunction or law: "You must not eat from the tree of the knowledge of good and evil" (Gen 2:17). But this injunction doesn't appear until the latter half of the second chapter of Genesis. Neither is it the full sentence, which begins: "The Lord God took the man and put him in the Garden of Eden to work it and take care of it. And the Lord God commanded the man, 'You are free to eat from any tree in the garden'" (Gen 2:15–16). Thus the context of humanity's original sin is equally, and emphatically, a context of stewardship. Adam was enjoined to take care of everything in the garden including—get this—the tree of the knowledge of good and evil. Why do we often picture this tree as set aside on some isolated grassy hilltop, off-limits to Adam's tender care? Or why do we picture it as snake infested, the serpent slithering through its seductive branches, vaguely sinister and threatening. In our imaginations we can easily suppose that this one lone tree does not take part in God's pronouncement of "goodness" over the garden. It is a painted lady. Unlike its good cousin, this tree is Cain to the tree of life's Abel.

Much is made of the serpent's distortion of God's words: "Did God really say, 'You must not eat from any tree in the garden'?" (3:1). Eve corrects him, but only partially. About the tree in the middle of the garden, she adds, "and you must not touch it" (3:3). The tree of the knowledge of good and evil was a part of Adam's stewardship. We don't know what caring for a garden looked like for Adam. We are more familiar with the "sweat of our brows" brand of stewardship, which includes cutworms, pH imbalance, and marauding raccoons. I think that we imagine Adam's stewardship to be one of perpetual harvest. Regardless, however much Adam touched and tended the other foliage of the garden, the tree of the knowledge of good and evil seems also to be in his care. We could even say that Adam had stewardship of the *fruit* of this tree. His stewardship of the fruit, however, was defined as "Don't eat it." To take one step back into the conceptual, it also seems legitimate to say that Adam had a stewardship over the injunction of God, the words of God's mouth, the dictates of God's will: "You must not eat from the tree of the knowledge of good and evil." Adam was expected to tend to this injunction, honoring and loving it, just as fully as he was to honor Eve or any plant or animal in his care. In other words, part of the beauty and the goodness that God spoke into the garden is the beauty of obedience. Obedience to God is an integral part of human flourishing. It shines as luminously as any sunset Adam may have seen. It is as brilliantly crystalline as any brook from which he may have drunk. Adam is a steward of trees, of fruit, of obedience.

In Matthew 21, Jesus tells two parables involving a vineyard. In the first, the father tells two sons to go work in it. One son says he will, but doesn't. In the second parable, the owner of the vineyard has entrusted his land to some renters. When he sends for his share of the harvest, as per the terms of the lease, the tenants kill three of the owner's servants before finally killing the owner's own son. In the first parable, the sin might be identified as hypocrisy, sloth, and rebellion. In the second case, the sin is greed, murder, and by interpretation, murder of the Son of God. In both cases, however, the context is the stewardship of a vineyard from which the workers enjoyed the fruit, without actually owning the vineyard. When Jesus explains the parables to the Pharisees who were listening, he declares (also in the language of cause and effect), "Therefore I tell you that the kingdom of God will be taken away from you and given to a people who will produce its fruit" (Matt 21:43). We have a stewardship to produce the proper fruit of the kingdom. For whatever else greed, sloth, rebellion, and murder may be, they are additionally violations of our stewardship. Brown looked to Old Testament accounts of drought and flood looking for the historical data from which he could identify cause and effect, sin and its retributive natural consequences. The Curse as described in the third chapter of Genesis has all the marks of a stewardship that has disastrously failed. Think of any stewardship you might have—of a bank account, a project, your children. When you violate the stewardship of obedience to God's word and will as applied to your finances, work, or parenting, doesn't pain, conflict, thorns, thistles, sweat, dust, and death *naturally* ensue? To violate our stewardship is a sin; to endure the consequences is our judgment.

❧ Sin as Unfaithful Stewardship ❧

If the New Testament church can no longer look to the stringencies of Deuteronomy or the imprecations of the Psalms or the invectives of the prophets, we still have the book of Revelation, however imagistically ambiguous, to help inform our understanding of judgment. In the eleventh chapter of Revelation, the seventh trumpet sounds out the culmination of all judgment. The twenty-four elders, flat on their faces, declare: "The time has come for judging the dead, and for rewarding your servants the prophets and your people who revere your name, both great and small—and for destroying those who destroy the earth" (Rev 11:18). And so, the Lord will destroy those who destroy the earth. The Greek word for "earth" is fairly consistent in its usage: earth, planet Earth, ground, land, and soil. While we are obviously judged for what has transpired on the soil, we are nonetheless judged for the soil itself. The phrase "those who destroy the earth" has an interesting grammatical feature. It lapses into the present tense. In other words, "the destroying of the earth" seems to be characteristic of the period of the seventh trumpet. What if this is not just a description of sin, but rather of judgment, and of judgment as the natural consequence of the accumulated sins of mankind, the full and final failure of our stewardship given in the garden? Verse 19 follows: "Then God's temple in heaven was opened, and within his temple was seen the ark of his covenant. And there came flashes of lightning, rumblings, peals of thunder, an earthquake and a severe hailstorm." The seven bowl judgments that ensue are horrific. Each remarkably seems to lend itself to natural, scientific interpretations easier than what some "End Times" theorists have construed for earlier images. My point, though, is this: we are quick to point to God's retributive destruction of the earth in Revelation. Things seem to "rain down from heaven," as if heaven were a place with a set of coordinates proximate to our physical planet. But what if even the destruction of the planet is simply a God-governed culmination of natural consequences of which the inhabitants of the earth are our own agents? The earth will experience a resurrection. "Then I saw 'a new heaven and a new earth,'" John writes, "for the first heaven and the first earth had passed away" (Rev 21:1). The historical pattern—foreshadowed in Genesis, fully realized in Christ, purchased for us by Christ, experienced by the church—is that crucifixion precedes resurrection. Who is to say that the crucifixion of the earth isn't also accomplished as was Christ's: "by God's deliberate plan and foreknowledge; and you, with the help of wicked men, put him to death by nailing him to the cross" (Acts 2:23)?

Paul once admonished the Corinthians: "Do not go on passing judgment before the time, but wait until the Lord comes who will both bring to light the things hidden in the darkness and disclose the motives of men's hearts" (1 Cor 4:5 NASB). To what judgment was Paul referring? It was the judgment over stewardship: "In this case, moreover, it is required of stewards that one be found trustworthy" (v. 2 NASB). There is such a thing as environmental sin. It might be best understood as unfaithful stewardship. God will hold us accountable. However, environmental missionaries preach a gospel that—praise be to our Savior!—is sufficient for whatever offense we might throw at God, any injustice toward another, any violation of our stewardship, or any destruction of God's creation.

NOTES

1. Stuart K. Hine, *Not You, but God: A Testimony to God's Faithfulness,* 1st ed. (S.K. Hine, 1953).
2. John D. W. Watts, *The Books of Joel, Obadiah, Jonah, Nahum, Habakkuk and Zephaniah* (Cambridge: Cambridge University Press, 1975), 141.
3. M. Scott Peck, *The Road Less Traveled* (New York: Touchstone, 1978), 130.
4. Richard Grove, quoted in Richard Darr, "Protestant Missions and Earthkeeping in Southern Africa 1817–2000" (PhD diss., Boston University School of Theology, 2005), 81.
5. Richard Grove, "Scottish Missionaries, Evangelical Discourses and the Origins of Conservation Thinking in Southern Africa 1820–1900," *Journal of Southern African Studies* 15 (1989): 164.
6. C. Northcott, quoted in ibid., 166.
7. Robert Moffat, *Missionary Labours and Scenes in Southern Africa* (London: John Snow,1842), 66.
8. Ibid., 329.
9. Grove, "Scottish Missionaries," 168.

10. R. Moffat, quoted in ibid.
11. Grove, "Scottish Missionaries," 170.
12. T. Arbousset and F. Daumas, *Narrative of an exploratory tour to the north-east of the colony of the Cape of Good Hope*, trans. J. C. Brown (Cape Town: Saul Solomon and Co., 1846), 22-23.
13. Dr. Rubidge, "Irrigation and Tree-planting," in *The Cape and Its People*, ed. Roderick Noble (Cape Town: J. C. Juta, 1869), 350.
14. John Croumbie Brown, "Preface" in T. Arbousset and F. Daumas.
15. Grove, quoted in Darr, "Protestant Missions," 97.
16. Grove, "Scottish Missionaries," 175.
17. John Croumbie Brown, *Pastoral Discourses* (Cape Town: Saul Solomon and Co., 1847), 66-7.
18. Ibid., 95.
19. Ibid., 96.
20. John Croumbie Brown, *Management of Crown Forests at the Cape of Good Hope Under the Old Regime and Under the New* (Edinburgh: Oliver and Boyd, 1887), 96.

10

THE ENVIRONMENTAL MISSIONARY'S GOSPEL: A NEW STORY FOR A NEW MAN

When we launched our new ministry Eden Vigil, I think my children wanted to affirm this transition in our lives, so they did so in a way that had meaning for them. On Father's Day one year, even before the release of the popular movie, they bought me a stuffed animal, the Lorax. If you're not already aware, the Lorax is the title character of Dr. Seuss' book, the walrus-mustachioed speaker for the trees.

> He was shortish. And oldish.
> And brownish. And mossy.
> And he spoke with a voice
> that was sharpish and bossy.
>
> "Mister!" he said with a sawdusty sneeze,
> "I am the Lorax. I speak for the trees.
> I speak for the trees, for the trees have no tongues.
> And I'm asking you, sir, at the top of my lungs"—
> he was very upset as he shouted and puffed—
> "What's that THING you've made out of my
> Truffula tuft?"[1]

Environmentalists, following the lead of the Lorax, "speak for the trees"; environmental missionaries additionally speak for *the* Tree; that is, for the Cross on which our Savior died, the basis for the restoration of his creation. The speech of environmentalists is often characterized, fairly or not, as "sharpish and bossy." Very upset, they shout and puff at the top of

their lungs. It is the Once-ler whom the Lorax is addressing in the quotation above. The Once-ler manufactures "thneeds," devastates the Truffula forest, and accuses the Lorax: "All you do is yap-yap and say, 'Bad! Bad! Bad! Bad!'" Surely environmental missionaries are not simply Christian counterparts to these yap-yap-yappers. If the gospel is good news for the whole of creation, then our message is Good! Good! Good! Good!, redolent of God's original pronouncement over his handiwork. The nature of the message that environmental missionaries preach (Bible in one hand) to accompany the work that they do of creation care (shovel in another) is essentially the new story of a new Man. Specifically, it is a gospel that can be characterized in four ways: a gospel of forgiveness, of new life, of rest, and of Christ crucified.

We Need a New Story of a New Man

In the case of *The Lorax*, there are two narrators. The book begins with a young boy who wanders to the far end of town where the Grickle-grass grows. He wants to know, "What was the Lorax? And why was it there? And why was it lifted and taken somewhere?" And so the boy seeks out the old recluse, the Once-ler, and pays fifteen cents to hear the story. The Once-ler then takes over as narrator. It's hard to find meaning in the silly names that Dr. Seuss gives to most of his characters, but the Once-ler's name is a moniker that gets to the essence of sustainability long before sustainability was even a concept. A Truffula forest, like an old-growth stand of timber, is apparently something you use *once*, and *once* is defined as the arc of *my* own career, *my* own lifetime. The Once-ler says, "I meant no harm," and at one point is genuinely sad about the effect of his industry, but he's a slave to the dictate "Business is business! / And business must grow," and finally his patience with the Lorax comes to an end:

> And then I got mad.
> I got terribly mad.
> I yelled at the Lorax, "Now listen here, Dad!
> All you do is yap-yap and say, 'Bad! Bad! Bad! Bad!'
> Well, I have my rights, sir, and I'm telling you

❧ The Environmental Missionary's Gospel ❧

I intend to go on doing just what I do!
And, for your information, you Lorax, I'm figgering
On biggering
and BIGGERING
and BIGGERING
and BIGGERING."[2]

It is possible for those of us living in a free society, making our livelihood on a free market, to be slaves to our own rights. We are subject to what the novelist Walker Percy calls "the great suck of self."[3] We exert our rights, exercise our rights, defend our rights, protect our rights, and demand our rights. But in the end, our rights can exercise us. In my very first missions class at Moody Bible Institute, we were required to read a 1957 book by Mabel Williamson, veteran of the China Inland Mission: *Have We No Rights?: A Frank Discussion of the "Rights" of Missionaries*. Everything about this book—even to the author's name—seems old-fashioned. This is a pity. Mabel was an abolitionist for those enslaved to the great suck of Self, as is Jesus an abolitionist, the subject of her last chapter entitled "He Had No Rights."

In the Seuss book, the font size of BIGGERING in the text grows so large as to even overpower the illustrations. But at that very moment the Once-ler and the Lorax hear a loud "whack," which even the Once-ler describes as a "sickening smack." The very last Truffula tree of all has been chopped down. The Once-ler retreats into reclusion and spends the remainder of his polluted days contemplating the one single word the Lorax leaves behind, engraved on a stone: "Unless." He has become not manufacturer, but monastic. He addresses the young boy:

> "But now," says the Once-ler,
> "Now that you're here,
> the word of the Lorax seems perfectly clear.
> UNLESS someone like you
> cares a whole awful lot, nothing is going to get better.
> It's not.

"SO . . . Catch!" calls the Once-ler.
He lets something fall.
"It's a Truffula Seed.
It's the last one of all!
You're in charge of the last of the Truffula Seeds.
And Truffula Trees are what everyone needs.
Plant a new Truffula. Treat it with care.
Give it clean water. And feed it fresh air.
Grow a forest. Protect it from axes that hack.
Then the Lorax
and all of his friends
may come back."[4]

The Once-ler is a changed man. He is . . . converted.

At the end of *The Lorax*, the narration, like the last Truffula seed, is handed back to the boy. "You're in charge of the last of the Truffula Seeds," the Once-ler tells him. The boy is also in charge of where the story goes from there. Unlike the character in the animated movie, the way Dr. Seuss drew the illustrations in his book, we never catch a full-on glimpse of the Once-ler. His yellow eyes peer out through the slats of his window. We see only his long, green, hairy arms. Nonetheless we see enough of the Once-ler to know that he is a different creature than the boy, who is recognizable as a boy. The boy is a normal boy, drawn in the wide-eyed, pug-nosed style of Seuss. In other words, the boy is a human and not a Once-ler. Therein lies the hope for the Truffula trees.

As regards a modern environmental crisis, theologian Sallie McFague writes:

> Global warming is not just another important issue that human beings need to deal with; rather, it is the demand that we *live differently.* We cannot solve it, deal with it, given our current anthropology. It is not simply an issue of management; rather, it demands a paradigm shift in *who we think we are.*[5]

We need a new Man.

❧ The Environmental Missionary's Gospel ❧

Conservationist Scott Russell Sanders is less interested in a new Man than in a new story that the new narrator of *The Lorax* might tell. We have had an old story, Sanders says, wherein we are urged by biggering advertisers to

> grab whatever we can, to indulge our appetites without regard for the needs of community, without gratitude to the people whose labor supports us, without concern for future generations, without acknowledging that we share the earth with millions of other species or that we draw every drop of our sustenance from nature.[6]

And so he writes:

> We need an alternative story, one that appeals to our generosity and compassion rather than our selfishness. We need a story that measures wealth not by the amount of money held in private hands nor by the stock market index but by the condition of the commons. We need a story that links the health of individuals to the health of communities, a story that reminds us we inhabit not merely a house or a city or a nation but a planet. Rather than defining us as consumers, this new story would define us as conservers; rather than cultivating narcissism, it would inspire neighborliness; rather than exhorting us to chase after fashions, it would invite us to find joy in everyday blessings—in the voice of a child or a bird, in music and books, in gardening and strolling, in sharing food and talk. To live by such a story, we need not be sages nor saints; we need simply be awake to the real sources of the good life.[7]

I wish that I could tell Sanders, with the same urgency that Paul brought to Felix or Agrippa, that we have such an alternative story. It is the gospel whereby we do become saints. It is the story of Jesus Christ crucified, dead, and buried for the remission of our sins. It is the story of Jesus risen from the grave, bringing with him a newness of life, which refashions humanity into new creatures where generosity, compassion, and neighborliness are at the core of our being, and *shalom* is the air we breathe. In his writings, Sanders exhibits ample familiarity with the gospel as it was preached to him since childhood in his native Tennessee and Indiana. He seems disappointed with it. It isn't the alternative story he was looking for. I wish he would respond as one of the disciples did to Jesus once in his disappointment: "Lord, to whom shall we go? You have the words of eternal life" (John 6:68). Sanders is seeking "the real sources of the good life" and is missing the real source of life, who is himself good.

Missionaries are conditioned—usually through the school of hard knocks—to entrust all listeners to the Holy Spirit. Our best human efforts at persuasion are incapable of speaking to the deep places of Felix's or Agrippa's heart where only the Holy Spirit whispers and woos. But we are also trained to constantly reevaluate our telling of the gospel. Did we preach the good news with all biblical accuracy? Did we preach with cultural relevance? Did our sermon come from a loving and prayerful portion of our hearts? Maybe the story that Scott Russell Sanders heard from Christians wasn't the *real* gospel at all or, in the words of the *Cape Town Commitment*, wasn't the *whole* gospel. If so, Sanders is right: we do need an alternative story, but only in the sense of an alternative to the partial gospel that has too often been preached. We need to preach of a full redemption in Christ that extends to all broken relationships: with God, with self, with others, and with creation. We preach a new story of becoming new creatures in Christ Jesus.

Cal Beisner once said in an interview, "Where environmentalists start off as fundamentally mistaken is their vision of human beings. They see human beings as, primarily, consumers and polluters. Whereas the Bible teaches that humans, who are made in God's image, are producers and stewards."[8] Beisner is right; human beings are not, primarily, consumers and polluters. Like the boy in Dr. Seuss' story, one of the reasons we can end up differently than the Once-ler is because we *start off* essentially different than the Once-ler. We are created in the image of God. Quotations from Cal Beisner have been an effective foil in previous chapters of this book, and I would like to use his quotation here as well to organize this chapter, examining mankind as consumer, polluter, producer, and steward. Beisner does say of our vision of humanity: "Obviously, it's not automatic. There needs to be education and moral commitment, and those things are furthered in my understanding through people being reconciled to God through the atoning work of Christ on the Cross and their faith in Him."[9] Consequently I wish to apply "education and moral commitment" as well as the gospel of reconciliation to our vision of humanity. What we will discover is that while we are not primarily consumers and polluters, neither are we primarily producers and stewards; there is more to humanity than anything that can be labeled. Additionally, while being created in the image of God also informs *all* our identities—including as a consumer—being *re-created* in the image of Jesus Christ (through the gospel) changes all that we've imagined about humanity. All of this informs the message of the environmental missionary.

Human Beings as Polluters and Stewards: The Gospel of Forgiveness and New Life

I'll combine these two points and discuss them briefly in a single section, largely because they have been adequately developed earlier in this book. While human beings are not primarily polluters, it is a necessary component of our biology that we produce waste products. This is inherent in every breath we inhale and exhale. We've conceptualized this fact in the laws of thermodynamics; we've identified it most graphically in our own digestive systems. Waste need not equal pollution, as an entire industry—waste management—has proven. But it's precisely that word "management" that draws the line between waste and pollution, and then additionally between life-giving obedience and sin. In other words, because of how we and this world were created, wise waste management is inherent in the command given to us to bless, flourish, subdue, rule, till, and keep. Mismanagement is unfaithful stewardship. Pollution is most obviously sin when we dump our waste in our neighbor's backyard, or when we steal from the "commonwealth" by failing to pay for externalities. Externality refers to the effect of an economic transaction on some third party, in which that party played no part in the decision, nor is compensated for the cost, in the event of a "negative" externality. The laws of a municipality may grant a particular industry certain free-of-charge "dumping" rights, but if that industry refuses to pay for the cancer treatments of the local residents (or grouses about Medicaid and Medicare), that's theft. They stole from the health of their neighbors to keep their own costs down.

In 2011 Good Friday and Earth Day fell on the same date, April 22. I can understand the umbrage that some Christians took in how creation care advocates took advantage of the coincidence. Quoting EEN's reference to the *Cape Town Commitment*'s call to repentance, Jan Markell wrote in a blog:

> I, however, do applaud the Evangelical Environmental Network for their statement, saying that, "Since sin is the root cause of our environmental and social crises, there is ultimately no answer to these problems apart from Christ and what He did on the cross." I am not in agreement with their belief that Earth Day and Good Friday go together, as Good Friday should cause us to only reflect on the suffering Savior who died that man might have eternal life. The nails in His hands had nothing to do with healing the planet, as more liberal outfits stated last week.[10]

And later Markell says,

> Again, we repent from sin, not from what we might have done to the planet. There is no more appropriate week during the year to get right with God than Easter week. Repenting from the damage we have done to the environment on Good Friday is misplaced passion. Statements like the one above further reveal how the world has entered into the church.[11]

Actually I would argue that such calls for repentance on April 22, 2011, show not how much the world has entered the church but, inversely, how little the church has entered the world. We preach a gospel that not only saves us from sin, but also saves us from endless squabbles about what does or does not constitute sin. Leave the debate to the Pharisees. Even if they end up proving that healing on the Sabbath is a sin, then we would still require a Savior to save us from that sin. Even if they convince Jesus that calling a brother "Raca" is not the same as murder, that doesn't make them any more righteous in a moral economy where the shed blood of Christ is all that matters. This is one of the (safer) ways that I apply the famous story of Martin Luther advising a fretful Melanchthon to "go, and sin boldly." In Christ, I have a genuine desire to do it right. I can be paralyzed by whether some course of action I'm contemplating might be sin. I might be genuinely confused. But in the end, isn't the cross of Christ sufficient for whatever I might do? Similarly, whenever I am ready to denounce something that I am still uncertain is sin, it is a good biblical reminder that I'm called to preach salvation, not condemnation. Why might Beisner or Markell be so reluctant to allow for a new category of sin—polluting—when the scope of Christ's forgiveness is so vast as to make the category moot? It's like the United Nations convening an international forum on smallpox. Let the scientists submit all the papers they wish, the last certified case of smallpox from the three-thousand-year ordeal of the disease was in 1977 in Somalia. New cases of smallpox do pop up, but Edward Jenner's vaccine can never be "undiscovered." Thank God that the W.H.O. undertook the worldwide project of eradication 150 years after Jenner's discovery.[12] The sanctity of Good Friday is not preserved because we protect it from Earth Day. The glory of Good Friday is its ability to address whatever Saint Patty's Day, Valentines Day, Halloween, or any other commemoration like Earth Day might throw at it.

"All human beings are to be stewards of the rich abundance of God's good creation," the *Cape Town Commitment* declares.[13] In an essay that makes a tour of environmental word usage, Scott Russell Sanders comments, "Some conservationists have shied away from describing their work as *stewardship*, because of the word's religious connotations."[14] I had never thought that Christians had so effectively laid claim to the word, but apparently so. Sanders' explanation of the religious basis for our gravitating to the word "stewardship" is encouraging in its accuracy. He writes:

In the Bible, stewards look after property on behalf of a master—and the ultimate master of all property is God. As the Psalmist says: "The earth is the Lord's and the fullness thereof, the world and those who dwell therein; for he has founded it upon the seas, and established it upon the rivers" (Psalm 24:1,2 ESV). In the biblical view, a steward is one who takes care of Creation out of love and respect for the Creator.[15]

The word "steward" in the English Bible appears often in the Old Testament, in descriptions of the household workings of the patriarchs and the kings. In translations of the New Testament, the word is a favorite of the older renderings such as the King James Version or the New American Standard Bible. The NIV and the New Living Translation feel the need to unpack the noun, and so we say "the person who has been entrusted" or "the person who is put in charge as a manager." First Corinthians 4:1,2 is our home base on this word—"Let a man regard us in this manner, as servants of Christ and stewards of the mysteries of God. In this case, moreover, it is required of stewards that one be found trustworthy" (NASB).

All humans are stewards—as Beisner's quotation states, and as the *Cape Town Commitment* affirms—but not all stewards are trustworthy. In other words, it's not enough to simply say that humans are stewards. All humans are stewards, but without Christ the record of our stewardship gravitates toward the "acts of the flesh" as listed in Galatians 5:19–21. By contrast, faithfulness is a component in the "fruit of the Spirit" (Gal 5:22). And so environmental missionaries preach to stewards the gospel of new life, of the fruitful indwelling of the Holy Spirit, which in the words of Galatians 5, is freedom, love, and life. How can a steward hope to be a life-giving blessing to creation if he or she remains dead and enslaved to trespass and sin?

Human Beings Are Producers, but Not Primarily Producers: The Gospel of Rest

"As the late Julian Simon used to put it," so Beisner continues in his argument,

"Every mouth that is born into this world is accompanied by two hands and, far more importantly, a mind." Those two hands and a mind are capable of producing far more than that mouth can consume. That's why, over the past several hundred years, each generation has also been wealthier on a per capita basis. We produce more wealth than we can consume. And that's a good thing.[16]

Obviously, this productivity, as Beisner previously said, is "not automatic." We should likely factor in those generations who were part of the age of cheap oil. The work that the energy in one gallon of gasoline can accomplish is equivalent to five hundred hours of human work output. Human beings do not *produce* oil; we discover it, we pump it, we refine it. Of course this processing of fossil fuel is a remarkable accomplishment of two hands and a mind, but the cheap-oil generations unduly skew the average. Fossil fuel also confuses our measurement of consumption. We consume gasoline in order to produce some other items that we then label "wealth," but our definition of wealth is woefully restricted, and we fail to count the totality of the things we consume in our production of it. Economists, calculating Gross Domestic Product, ignore externalities, which include the fertility of our topsoil, the health of our children, or the potability of our drinking water. If economists would ever allow for a qualitative definition of wealth, and if they would begin to count externalities, we might discover that we've crossed a historical threshold and that it is no longer true for our generation that we produce more wealth than we can consume.

Nonetheless it is true: human beings do possess two hands and a mind. God's creativity is part of our imaging him. We are producers. Philosophers like Hannah Arendt have proposed a term, *homo faber*—man the maker, man the producer. The term seems to have its origin in a speech given by Appius Claudius Caecus (340–273 BC): "*Homo faber suae quisque fortunae*" ("Every man is the artifex of his destiny"). An artifex is a craftsman or artisan. One scholar, quoting Arendt, has credited John Locke and his labor theory of value with making it "now possible to regard man as *homo faber*, an idea which 'followed its course when Adam Smith asserted that labor was the source of all wealth and found its climax in Marx's "system of labor," where labor became the source of all productivity and the expression of the very humanity of man."[17] Admittedly, the ability to produce is a wonderful thing, and no doubt is fitting for one made, as Beisner notes, in God's image. But the problem with the emergence of *homo faber*, as these quotations indicate, is his ability to squeeze out both creation and the Creator.

> Artificial tools allow man to inhabit a world of his own making, a world that can be modified and enriched indefinitely. In such a world, man's intelligence is devoted to action, and action is inventive. The definition of man as *homo faber* thus acquires the dignity that was typical of homo sapiens, for making is no longer opposed to knowing.[18]

We can imagine Adam standing at the edge of the garden, gazing out over the wilderness, and proclaiming, *"Homo faber suae quisque fortunae."* The rest is history.

The environmental missionary preaches to man the producer a gospel of sabbath rest in Christ Jesus. This is not an appeal for a strict forty-hour work week—that we should close down our factories and our offices, our stores and our boutiques for the weekend—though that may be an implication of sabbath. Sabbath means more than just forgoing the making of money one day a week. Ever since the seventh day of creation, much has been written, debated, and screwed up about the Sabbath as a day. Numerous references in the Torah have expanded on God's pronouncement in Genesis 2:2,3, codifying the Sabbath for the Hebrews. But much less has been considered, even by the Israelites, about the sabbath year (every seven) and the Year of Jubilee (every seven times seven). The sabbath year was pretty straightforward:

> The Lord said to Moses at Mount Sinai, "Speak to the Israelites and say to them: 'When you enter the land I am going to give you, the land itself must observe a sabbath to the Lord. For six years sow your fields, and for six years prune your

vineyards and gather their crops. But in the seventh year the land is to have a year of sabbath rest, a sabbath to the Lord. Do not sow your fields or prune your vineyards. Do not reap what grows of itself or harvest the grapes of your untended vines. The land is to have a year of rest. Whatever the land yields during the sabbath year will be food for you—for yourself, your male and female servants, and the hired worker and temporary resident who live among you, as well as for your livestock and the wild animals in your land. Whatever the land produces may be eaten.'" (Lev 25:1–7)

Cal DeWitt considers the "Sabbath Principle" to be an important component of creation care. As befits an ecologist like DeWitt, he promotes the principle primarily as a respectful way to give rest to the land, like a modern farmer who wisely keeps a rotating portion of his fields fallow. "Christ clearly teaches that the Sabbath is made for the ones served by it—not the other way around. Thus, the Sabbath year protected the land from relentless exploitation, helped the land rejuvenate, and helped it get things together again—a time of rest and restoration."[19] But the sabbath year is also meant to be a profound object lesson to the Israelites. It challenges them to consider on what—and on whom—they truly depend for production. The last sentence—"Whatever the land produces may be eaten"—is written in such passive tenses as to render *homo faber* a mere bystander. The land has its own work to do. It is not merely object (to be plowed), but subject (to do production). It is a humbling thing to be fed food that we did not cultivate nor pay for. It is a humbling thing to be fed by something that we consider "dirt." And the sabbath year suggests that the Lord has his own relationship with the land that he has created. It almost seems like every seven years he wants to revisit those five days of creation before Adam appeared on the scene. What could it mean for the Lord, who cannot grow weary, to "rest" on the seventh day? What is the "holiness" in which the Sabbath is kept, except the Lord's own good pleasure? This too is humbling to *homo faber*. Doesn't the Lord know that the land is just dirt meant for *our* use?

The Year of Jubilee adds a whole other dimension to the cycle of sabbath years. In the fiftieth year (or forty-ninth; commentators are uncertain), the same pattern of deferring to the Lord and the land's productivity is observed, but additionally, all lost property is restored to the original owners, all slaves (human property) are set free. The Year of Jubilee actually acts as a marker for a whole system of redemption operative in any given year. "Even if someone is not redeemed in any of these ways, they and their children are to be released in the Year of Jubilee, for the Israelites belong to me as servants. They are my servants, whom I brought out of Egypt. I am the Lord your God" (Lev 25:54,55). If the sabbath year challenges the Israelites' sense of themselves as producers, the Year of Jubilee additionally challenges their sense of themselves as property owners. God owns the land. God owns us. God owns the richest landlord as well as the landless slave. Repeatedly throughout Leviticus 25, the Israelites are encouraged to remember: they were slaves in Egypt and it was God who, first, redeemed them and then, secondly, gave them the land of Canaan. They have no rights to, or in, the land which God himself has not graciously given them. "Remember that you were slaves in Egypt and that the Lord your God brought you out of there with a mighty hand and an outstretched arm. Therefore the Lord your God has commanded you to observe the Sabbath day" (Deut 5:15). Any rights they might have are usufructary.

The sabbath year and the Year of Jubilee are not heard of in the Old Testament much beyond Leviticus 25. One reason is that there is no evidence that the Israelites ever—repeat, ever—observed the sabbath years. How serious was God about his sabbath commands? It is generally considered (according to Leviticus 26:35 and 2 Chronicles 36:21) that the seventy years of exile in Babylon is predicated on the desecrated sabbaths, one year in captivity for every sabbath year unobserved. "The land enjoyed its sabbath rests; all the time of its desolation it rested, until the seventy years were completed in fulfillment of the word of the Lord spoken by Jeremiah" (2 Chr 36:21). While the Israelites were in exile, the fields of Palestine were no doubt plowed, planted, and harvested by those who remained in the land. So the sabbath rest that the land enjoyed seems to mean more than just land kept fallow. It is the judgment on a nation (*hebrew faber*) who from the banks of the Jordan had looked over into the Promised Land and declared quietly in their hearts, "Every man is the artifex of his destiny." They were wrong.

It is therefore natural that the writer of the book of Hebrews would couch the gospel in terms of sabbath rest. It is also natural, considering the history of the Jews, that the writer would include so many warnings: don't fall short of it, don't fail to enter the promised rest.

> Therefore, since the promise of entering his rest still stands, let us be careful that none of you be found to have fallen short of it. For we also have had the good news proclaimed to us, just as they did; but the message they heard was of no value to them, because they did not share the faith of those who obeyed. Now we who have believed enter that rest, just as God has said, "So I declared on oath in my anger, 'They shall never enter my rest.'"

> And yet his works have been finished since the creation of the world. For somewhere he has spoken about the seventh day in these words: "On the seventh day God rested from all his works." And again in the passage above he says, "They shall never enter my rest."

> Therefore since it still remains for some to enter that rest, and since those who formerly had the good news proclaimed to them did not go in because of their disobedience, God again set a certain day, calling it "Today." This he did when a long time later he spoke through David, as in the passage already quoted: "Today, if you hear his voice, do not harden your hearts."

> For if Joshua had given them rest, God would not have spoken later about another day. There remains, then, a Sabbath-rest for the people of God; for anyone who enters God's rest also rests from their works, just as God did from his. Let

us, therefore, make every effort to enter that rest, so that no one will perish by following their example of disobedience. (Heb 4:1–11)

This passage also includes verses 12 and 13, which indicate that it is an attitude of the heart that is behind the disobedience of failure to enter into the sabbath rest of Christ. The gospel is a humbling thing. As faithless individuals, we thought that the good works we had produced were sufficient to save our souls. As a species, our thoughts were grander. We've been fruitful and multiplied. We've subdued the earth and exercised dominion. Surely human beings in our awesome productivity have attained our own salvation? Woefully, no. What we think are textile mills producing skeins and skeins of precious silk are nothing but warehouses of filthy rags. What we think are acres upon acre of orchards producing cleverly transgenic fruit are nothing but windswept hillsides of shriveled leaves (Isa 64:6). And it is humbling to wear and to eat what is offered up in the stead of our production. We put on the person of Jesus the crucified. We eat the flesh and drink the blood of Jesus the defeated. Our culture, as well as the undiscipled portion of our souls, continues to respond to Jesus the way that the Israelites of Amos' time responded to the Sabbath, saying, "When will the New Moon be over that we may sell grain, and the Sabbath be ended that we may market wheat?" (Amos 8:5). A platitudinous teacher like Jesus might be good for a Sunday morning, but there's no reason why the great work of the world can't recommence at 1 p.m. on a Sunday afternoon.

The gospel of Jesus Christ, like the sabbath years, humbles those who think they are productive landlords, but it redeems those who understand that they are landless slaves. The gospel is thus the good news of jubilee, of freedom. It is good news to the workaholic, who is afraid to let up lest his world fall apart. It is good news to the producer whose sense of personal worth is enslaved to her net worth. It is good news to the moral person crushed by her inability to be good enough. It is good news to the prodigal who returns to sign on as part of his father's crew, but is welcomed back as a son. Environmental missionaries preach to the Gentiles the boundless riches of Christ . . . His intent was that now, through the church, the manifold wisdom of God should be made known to the rulers and authorities in the heavenly realms, according to his eternal purpose that he accomplished in Christ Jesus our Lord. In him and through faith in him we may approach God with freedom and confidence. (Eph 3:8–12)

Jesus has accomplished it. It is finished. Jesus the producer is enough.

Human Beings Are Not Primarily Consumers, but They Do Consume: The Gospel of Christ Crucified

Beisner claims that human beings are not primarily consumers, but considering our daily need for the intake of food, water, and oxygen, consumption does seem rather primary. Man does live by bread; just not by bread alone. But, of course, the point that Jesus made about bread alone is really what Beisner meant. While it is true that we are embodied beings and will be for eternity, there is more to us than our stomachs. Metabolism is not our spirituality. However, the fact that Jesus and the apostles (as well as the Old Testament writers) continually harp on this point indicates that there are strong temptations afoot in this world for us to confer lordship on our appetites. "For, as I have often told you before and now tell you again even with tears," Paul writes, "many live as enemies of the cross of Christ. Their destiny is destruction, their god is their stomach, and their glory is in their shame. Their mind is set on earthly things" (Phil 3:18,19).

Whereas Beisner thinks that environmentalists start off fundamentally mistaken by seeing human beings as primarily consumers, I would argue to the contrary. Creation care advocates are among the loudest voices proclaiming, "You are *not* primarily a consumer! You've been duped! You've been brainwashed! There is more to life than stuff!" It's hard to make our voice heard, not only above the rumblings of the flesh and the whispers of the devil, but also above an advertising industry funded at the rate of 141 billion dollars annually.[20] If human beings are also producers, then it is also true that producers—particularly that unredeemed breed who have made gods of their own stomachs—would rather multiply consumers and kill off other producers (i.e., their competitors). They have a vested interest in their fellow human beings understanding themselves as consumers—thorough-going, regular, ready to believe anything, ready to pay top dollar. "But our citizenship is in heaven," Paul continues as he writes. "And we eagerly await a Savior from there, the Lord Jesus Christ, who, by the power that enables him to bring everything under his control, will transform our lowly bodies so that they will be like his glorious body" (Phil 3:20,21).

"The gospel challenges the idolatry of rampant consumerism," the *Cape Town Commitment* declares.[21] It's not consumers that environmental missionaries are concerned for, but consumerists. It doesn't seem a fundamental mistake to think that consumerism has *become* the vision for a twenty-first-century humanity. Interestingly, most dictionaries carry three definitions of *consumerism*. The first seems positive: consumerism is "the movement seeking to protect and inform consumers by requiring such practices as honest packaging and advertising, product guarantees, and im-proved safety standards." The second definition seems neutral: "the theory that a progressively greater consumption of goods is economically benefi-cial." And the third seems negative: "attachment to materialistic values or possessions."[22] The problem with the neutral definition—a conviction that consumerism is sound economic theory—is the temptation to undercut the positive regulation of the first definition and to excuse the materialistic attachment of the third. In 1992 President George H. W. Bush traveled to the Earth Summit held in Rio de Janeiro. Upon his return, he submit-ted the UN Framework Convention on Climate Change to the Senate for advice and consent. Upon ratification, the senior President Bush signed it, but he seems to have planted the seeds of the UNFCCC's own destruction when he famously and defiantly declared at Rio, "The American way of life is not negotiable." That precise phrase was subsequently picked up by Dick Cheney, the junior Bush's vice-president, and now is more often attributed to him. It is used whenever American access to crude oil supplies is in jeopardy, such as in Iraq. Whatever is meant by "the American way of life," it seems inexorably linked to goods and services. In 1955, retailing analyst

❧ The Environmental Missionary's Gospel ❧

Victor LeBow saw the trajectory of the US economy. LeBow's comments are often abbreviated, but here's how the quotation appears originally in *The Journal of Retailing*:

> Our enormously productive economy demands that we make consumption our way of life, that we convert the buying and use of goods into rituals, that we seek our spiritual satisfactions, our ego satisfactions, in consumption. The measure of social status, of social acceptance, of prestige, is now to be found in our consumption patterns. The very meaning and significance of our lives is today expressed in consumption terms. The greater the pressures upon the individual to conform to safe and accepted social standards, the more does he tend to express his aspirations and his individuality in terms of what he wears, drives, eats—his home, his car, his patterns of food serving, his hobbies.
>
> These commodities and services must be offered to the consumer with a special urgency. We require not only "forced draft" consumption but "expensive" consumption. We need things consumed, burned up, worn out, replaced and discarded at an ever-accelerating rate. We need to have people eat, drink, dress, ride, live, with ever more complicated and, therefore, constantly more expensive consumption.[23]

There is some debate over whether LeBow was speaking prescriptively, or just descriptively, about the US economy. Either way seems unsettling. And, of course, consumerism is in no sense limited to the USA. While I have been both to the Mall of America (Minneapolis) and the West Edmonton Mall (Alberta), I have never felt more overwhelmed than in my visits to malls in Hong Kong or in Noida, a suburb of New Delhi. These malls may have had less square footage, but both the press of humanity and the whirlwind of disposable income being disposed of were unnerving.

Understanding consumerism as a religion, or shopping as a spiritual satisfaction, is not far-fetched. Ephesians 5:5 says of the greedy person,

"such a person is an idolater." Colossians 3:5 says that greed "amounts to idolatry" (NASB). Idolatry is a real religious option for modern man, and we pursue it through greed. The *Cape Town Commitment* reserves some of its strongest language when it calls the church to "walk in distinctiveness, as God's new humanity":

> The people of God either walk in the way of the Lord, or walk in the ways of other gods. The Bible shows that God's greatest problem is not just with the nations of the world, but with the people he has created and called to be the means of blessing the nations. And the biggest obstacle to fulfilling that mission is idolatry among God's own people. For if we are called to bring the nations to worship the only true and living God, we fail miserably if we ourselves are running after the false gods of the people around us. When there is no distinction in conduct between Christians and non-Christians—for example in the practice of corruption and greed, or sexual promiscuity, or rate of divorce, or relapse to pre-Christian religious practice, or attitudes towards people of other races, or consumerist lifestyles, or social prejudice—then the world is right to wonder if our Christianity makes any difference at all. Our message carries no authenticity to a watching world.[24]

Once, as part of a post-Christmas break, our family traveled from India over to the UAE. There too we visited shopping malls. We consumed. We consumed some goodies that we couldn't get back in our Indian city. At one point in one mall, we found ourselves face-to-face with a wintery window display. The stylized snowflakes should have seemed as incongruous to us as the ski slope housed indoors at a neighboring mall in Dubai, but the display didn't seem out of place in a shopping center during the Christmas season. We read the big lettering of the theme: "The Spirit of . . . Shopping." Maybe we were expecting it to say "The Spirit of Christmas" or the spirit of joy, or peace, or family. There are certain Christmas clichés, but this store in the mall was not going to allow itself to be misquoted.

❧ The Environmental Missionary's Gospel ❧

Shopping is a spirit, and they were its priests. We may have felt the same discord in our spirit as Scott Russell Sanders did when, as he recounts: "I noticed a billboard featuring a young woman in a strapless green dress, holding a red spike-heel shoe in one hand, resting her chin in the other had, her eyes and lacquered lips expressing a combination of boredom and disdain, and below her picture the caption: 'I am what I shop.'"[25]

The message of the gospel is that we can find not only our righteousness but also our identity in Christ Jesus. Beisner's quotation, as it stands, would lead us to believe that producers and stewards are a vision of humanity rooted in being created in God's image, but that human beings as consumers are not necessarily so. The fact of the matter is, according to Scripture, God too is a consumer. Let me restate that: Scripture calls God a consumer. The important question of course is, what kind of consumer is God? If, as the *Cape Town Commitment* claims, "the gospel challenges the idolatry of rampant consumerism," then that challenge will come in the form by which idolatry has always been challenged: by biblically clarifying our image of the one true and living God.

In Leviticus 9 Aaron prepares three types of offering and lays them on an altar before the Lord. The scene is visceral, with references to kidneys, the lobes of the liver, and the fat of the breasts. When Aaron and Moses come out of the tent of meeting to bless the people, we read, "The glory of the Lord appeared to all the people. Then fire came out from before the Lord and consumed the burnt offering and the portions of fat on the altar; and when all the people saw it, they shouted and fell on their faces" (Lev 9:23,24 NASB). Now we are not to believe that the Lord ingested the offering, or that it added anything to his being, but nonetheless the word "consume" is used to describe what happened. One chapter later, we have the scene repeated, "And fire came out from the presence of the Lord and consumed them" (Lev 10:2 NASB), but this time it is the errant sons of Aaron, Nadab and Abihu, who are consumed. They had offered a "strange fire" before the Lord's altar, one which "He had not commanded them" (Lev 10:1 NASB). God's consumption is invariably linked to a fire that comes from his presence. It is a literal fire, as the Israelites had more than one occasion to witness, but its deeper meaning is in the wrath and jealousy of the Almighty. "For a fire is kindled in My anger, and burns to the lowest part of Sheol, and consumes the earth with its yield, and sets on fire the foundations of the mountains" (Deut 32:22 NASB). When God's fire consumes—whether consuming the altar sacrifice or the wicked offender—it is a judgment of sin. God consumes evil.

One time, during the ministry of Christ on earth, Jesus and his disciples were traveling to Jerusalem. He sent some messengers ahead into a Samaritan village to arrange lodging for the night, but the villagers refused them. The sons of Zebedee were incensed. "Lord, do You want us to command fire to come down from heaven and consume them?" they asked, apparently sure of the righteousness of their indignation, and confident of their ability to command heaven. "But [Jesus] turned and rebuked them, and said, 'You do not know what kind of spirit you are of; for the Son of Man did not come to destroy men's lives, but to save them'" (Luke 9:54–56 NASB). Jesus repeatedly makes it clear that his ministry is not one of consumption, but rather of himself "being consumed" by sinful and wicked people. The gospel, as it does for so much else, flips the consumption model on its head. In many ways, it is similar to the verse Mark 10:45, "For even the Son of Man did not come to be served, but to serve, and to give his life as a ransom for many." Or as John 12:47 says: "For I did not come to judge the world, but to save the world." Of course, Jesus is Lord and he is Judge. He will be served and he will exact a fiery judgment. We are told that the whore of Babylon will be consumed by fire (Rev 18:8) as will all enemies of God (Heb 10:27). But this is the difference between Jesus' second coming and his first. In his first advent, Jesus came not to be served, but to serve; not to judge, but to save; not to consume, but to be consumed. The Bible says that Jesus also came from the presence of God. He could have come as another occurrence of consuming fire. He did not.

While it is said that Jesus was "consumed" by zeal for his Father's house as he drove out the marketers in the Court of the Gentiles (John 2:17), mostly he was consumed by all of us who have eaten his flesh and drunk of his blood. "I am the living bread that came down from heaven," he declared to the crowds. "Whoever eats this bread will live forever. This bread is my flesh, which I will give for the life of the world" (John 6:51). "Whoever eats my flesh and drinks my blood has eternal life, and I will raise them up at the last day. For my flesh is real food and my blood is real drink. Whoever eats my flesh and drinks my blood remains in me, and I in them" (John 6:54–56). An environmental missionary may preach to a world rampant with consumerism and say, "It is better to give than to receive." This is a good rule of life, but it can also become so much yap-yap-yapping. Most importantly, it is *not* the gospel. The gospel is the invitation to come and feast upon the person of Jesus. Consume him who has given himself up for our consumption.

Jesus the consumed is distinct from the gods of this world, particularly from the consumer gods of Hinduism. Vishnu also has incarnations (*avatars*), ten of them, and each one of them comes in order to "destroy sinners and to establish righteousness." The elephant-headed god Ganesh, son of Shiva, is a consumer. A well-known legend tells of Shiva sending Ganesh to humble Kubera, the richest man on earth, who had thrown a lavish party in order to show off his great wealth. Ganesh arrives at the party and refuses to meet the other guests. "I am very hungry," he says. Ganesh eats all the sweet *laddus* and *rasmalai*, and starts in on the *idli*, *dosa*, and *samosas*. None is left for the other guests, and neither is the rice, *channa*, and *roti*. When Kubera can no longer provide food from the table and kitchen, Ganesh goes out to the orchards and fields and consumes all the crops. "I am hungry," he tells Kubera. "Give me some food or I will eat you." On September 21, 1995, when Robynn and I were in language study up in Mussoorie, India, we witnessed a crazy national moment known as the Ganesh Milk Miracle. Emanating from Mumbai, but in temples all across North India, *murthis* (idols) of Ganesh were drinking milk. If you held a spoon of milk up to the statue, it would seep off and disappear. Scientists wrote in the magazine *India Today* trying to explain natural phenomena like "surface tension" and "capillary action," but the people were believers: Ganesh was consuming milk. Prices of milk skyrocketed beyond the ability of the poor to buy it. Liters of milk ran from the floors of the temples out into the streets and into the sewers. Of all the commentary on this day, I still remember best that of an Indian Christian leader: "Wouldn't it have meant more to our country if Ganesh had *given* us milk, rather than consumed it?" (In the next chapter I will tell the story of a six-year-old boy, dying of a blood disease, in a family of Bengalis who venerated Kali. "Kali takes blood," I told them, "but Jesus gives blood.")

The gospel that an environmental missionary brings to a consumerist is the plea: feed on Jesus. We feed on so much else to fill up the empty places of our soul. We are like Ganesh. Our hunger will consume the entire world and each other, and in fact is doing so. "Whoever loves money never has enough; whoever loves wealth is never satisfied with their income. This too is meaningless. As goods increase, so do those who consume them. And what benefit are they to the owners except to feast their eyes on them?" (Eccl 5:10,11). Only the Bread of Life satisfies.

But then the gospel bids us further to come and follow him, to in fact be consumed as he was consumed. Henri Nouwen wrote his book *Life of the Beloved* around the four participles of the Eucharist: taken, blessed, broken, given. "These words also summarize my life as a Christian because, as a Christian, I am called to become bread for the world: bread that is taken, blessed, broken, and given."[26] At one point, he talks of physical pleasures, such as sharing a meal together:

> Don't you think that our desire to eat together is an expression of our even deeper desire to be food for one another? Don't we sometimes say: "That was a very nurturing conversation. That was a refreshing time"? I think that our deepest human desire is to give ourselves to each other as a source of physical, emotional and spiritual growth . . . As the Beloved ones, our greatest fulfillment lies in becoming bread for the world. That is the most intimate expression of our deepest desire to give ourselves to each other.[27]

Being consumed for the sake of each other plays itself out in the most practical of ways. Purposeful living in Christ means that on numerous occasions for numerous decisions we get to reenact a Christlike moment where we stop and ask the Holy Spirit, "Is this a situation where I'm called to consume or to 'be consumed'?" This could well be the most important question in all of creation care, and the fact that it is in the form of the lost art of inquiry makes it the subject of our next chapter: how environmental missionaries pray.

In the end, of course, there is no gospel that is unique to the preaching of an environmental missionary. Heaven forbid. The gospel of forgiveness, new life, rest, and Christ crucified is the age-old new story for a new man. The world's current ecological crisis might best be described as a new velvet background spread out behind the presentation of the gospel's diamond-like brilliance.

NOTES

1. Theodor Seuss Geisel, *The Lorax* (New York: Random House, 1971).
2. Ibid.
3. Walker Percy, *The Second Coming* (New York: Washington Square, 1980), 16.
4. Geisel, *Lorax*.
5. Sallie McFague, *A New Climate for Theology* (Minneapolis: Fortress, 2008), 44.
6. Scott Russell Sanders, *A Conservationist Manifesto* (Bloomington: Indiana University Press, 2009), 36.
7. Ibid.
8. Cal Beisner, quoted in Leo Hickman, "The US Evangelicals Who Believe Environmentalism Is a 'Native Evil,'" *Environment Blog, The Guardian*, May 5, 2011, http://www.guardian.co.uk/environment/blog/2011/may/05/ evangelical-christian-environmentalism-green-dragon (accessed October 6, 2011).
9. Ibid.
10. Jan Markell, "Mixing Paganism with the Passion," *Cup of Joe* (blog), April 28, 2011, http://cupofjoe.goodfight.org/?p=1578 (accessed July 16, 2013).
11. Ibid.

12. A. Deria, et al., "The World's Last Endemic Case of Smallpox: Surveillance and Containment Measures," *Bulletin of the World Health Organization* 85, no. 2 (1980): 279-83.

13. Third Lausanne Congress, *Cape Town Commitment*, II.B.6.

14. Sanders, Conservationist Manifesto, 53.

15. Ibid., 53–54.

16. Beisner, quoted in Hickman, "The US Evangelicals."

17. E. J. Hundert, "The Making of Homo Faber: John Locke between Ideology and History," *Journal of the History of Ideas* 33 (1972): 22.

18. Alfredo Ferrarin, "Homo Faber, Homo Sapiens, or Homo Politicus? Protagoras and the Myth of Prometheus," *The Review of Metaphysics* 54 (2000): 289–90.

19. Calvin B. DeWitt, "Seeking to Image the Order and Beauty of God's 'House,'" in *Down-to-earth Christianity: Creation-care in Ministry*, eds. W. Dayton Roberts and Paul E. Pretiz (Wynnewood, PA: AERDO, 2000), 21.

20. George Raine, "Annual Ad Spending Exceeds $141 Billion / Internet Advertising Shows Largest Percentage Gain," SFGate, *San Francisco Chronicle*, March 10, 2005, http://articles.sfgate.com/2005-03-10/business/17362937_1_tns-media-intelligence-billion-spending (accessed October 6, 2011).

21. Third Lausanne Congress, *Cape Town Commitment*, II.B.3.C.

22. *The Free Dictionary*, s.v. "Consumerism," http://www.thefreedictionary.com/consumerism (accessed October 6, 2011).

23. Victor LeBow, "Price Competition in 1955," *Journal of Retailing* 31, no. 1 (Spring 1955): 7.

24. Third Lausanne Congress, *Cape Town Commitment*, II.E.1.

25. Sanders, Conservationist Manifesto, 35.

26. Henri Nouwen, *Life of the Beloved* (New York: Crossroad, 1992), 42.

27. Ibid., 89.

11

PRAYER: MINING FOR WORSHIP AND WISDOM

Jesus told us, "If you have faith as small as a mustard seed, you can say to this mountain, 'Move from here to there,' and it will move" (Matt 17:20). Robert "Sage" Russo does just the opposite; he prays that the mountain won't move an inch. A Mennonite seminary student, Sage hikes through Appalachia. Often along the trail he will bow his head. Sometimes he'll drop to his knees. He's asking God to put an end to the practice of mountaintop removal (MTR) mining.

I first met Sage in the pages of *Backpacker* magazine, which profiled him in an article entitled "Hike. Pray. Protest." "There's a bend in a trail in a forest in West Virginia where a hiker can gaze out over Eden," the reporter says in the article.[1] "Eden" is her terminology, as is the word "Armageddon," as she continues:

> A hiker can gaze out over Eden—miles of lush, green mountains thrumming with black bears and bobcats, lungless salamanders and limb-regenerating newts. There's another view, just beyond the bend, that opens up on Armageddon: mountains stripped of their summits, resembling great piles of ash; huge lakes of toxic sludge; and mile upon mile of poisoned orange-and-green rivers.[2]

Sage prays for the 470 mountains in Appalachia leveled to become like Megiddo, which is itself, ironically, a plain. MTR mining is the practice of extracting coal by scraping over the layer of trees, soil, and rock ("overburden")

that covers the seam. The overburden is often deposited in a creek valley, further adding to the leveling.

> Where Brushy Fork used to burble, [Sage] looks at local rivers filled with 7 billion gallons of arsenic- and cadmium-infused coal slurry. In the hollows fanning out from the mountains, men and women breathe coal dust and drink diseased water. Teeth rot and gallbladders malfunction. Babies develop tumors, and girls who haven't yet ovulated suffer ovarian cancer.[3]

It's enough to drive anyone who professes Christ to his or her knees. "As we hiked along an old logging road on Coal River Mountain," the reporter writes, "my companion prayed often and quietly, dropping his head and sometimes falling to his knees. He thanked God for the 'beauty of his handiwork in all creation' and for help in stopping the destruction of MTR."[4] The first time I met Sage in person, our group added an impromptu prayer meeting to our visit. Sage and his colleague at Christians for the Mountains, Allen Johnson, had brought us to Kayford Mountain in West Virginia, the home and gravesite of the great MTR activist Larry Gibson. Overlooking an MTR moonscape, we stood at a spot on the mountain where three crosses had been planted. The last project that Allen had done with his friend Gibson was to clear out the brush leading up to these crosses. We stood in a group and prayed.

The article about Sage Russo in *Backpacker* confirmed for me many things I had come to believe about the prayer life of an environmental missionary. The first section of this chapter will briefly list those lessons. The second section of this chapter will presuppose that an environmental missionary's ministry is like the integration of the work of an Ezra and a Nehemiah, "a Bible in one hand; a shovel in the other," and so we'll look at what prayer meant in their work of postexilic restoration. In the third section, I will narrate the story of the prayers that surrounded the environmental poisioning of my landlord's son in India. And then finally, we'll return to the topic of mining—this time in Mongolia—as I explain the

Prayer

one passage in Scripture that has most recently informed my prayer life as an environmental missionary: Job 28.

Lessons from Watching Sage in the Mountains

Sage stopped "and thanked God for the 'beauty of his handiwork in all creation' and for help in stopping the destruction of MTR." Above all else, I'm convinced that environmental missions praying—if we can use that terminology—creates one of the best opportunities to recapture the role of worship in our intercessory prayers as missionaries. The Psalms of Israel and the hymnody of the church readily prove this point. Stuart K. Hine, British missionary, "when through the woods and forest glades" of the Carpathian mountains he wanders, can't help but be led to the chorus: "Then sings my soul / My Saviour God to Thee / How great Thou art!" I confess that, as a missionary, I have often made petition and intercession the totality of my prayer life. I've often led team prayer meetings where we immediately jumped into "Lord, please give me this," or "Lord, please do this." But to immerse ourselves in creation, and to yield to the praise of God that it elicits, is to remind ourselves of the lavish generosity of his character. "Here is the ocean, vast and wide, teeming with life of every kind, both large and small. See the ships sailing along, and Leviathan, which you made to play in the sea" (Ps 104:25,26 NLT). Far from the mountains of Appalachia, my perspective on prayer underwent a change on the first occasion that I ever saw dolphins out in the open ocean. Why do dolphins jump and leap out of the water? As mammals, are they grabbing a breath of air? As carnivores, are they chasing smaller fish? If so, they are seeking something they need. Or, are they just frolicking, leaping into the air just for the sheer joy of it? In the illustration of prayer that formed in my mind, the dolphin, like my soul's communion, swims continually in the bounty of God, is immersed in the ocean of his mercy and grace. God's generous love is the substance that surrounds us; it is our constant reality. Occasionally in our prayers we leap up toward God with a request: "Lord, please do," or "Lord, please give." But our leap of petition immediately falls back into the ocean of God's greatness. It's a law, like gravity for a dolphin:

ENVIRONMENTAL MISSIONS

what goes up as a need comes down as praise and thanksgiving. This image has become a discipline. I try to begin every prayer request or petition with a declaration of worship and then end it with a statement of thanksgiving. Instead of tracking "answers to my prayer," I try to identify evidences of God's subsequent goodness. This is the trajectory of the prayers of the lepers healed in Luke 17, at least of the one out of the ten who first recognizes Jesus' mastery and then comes back to say, "Thank you."

A second lesson from Sage—but also from J. O. Fraser praying as he trekked from village to village in the Burmese mountains, or from the missionary mystic Frank Laubach daily climbing up the hill behind his home in the Philippines—is the delightful prospect that environmental missions lends itself easily to prayer walking. Where we lived in India, the city's population of 1–2 million seemed to crowd upon us. We were in the Gangetic Plain, not a mountain to be seen except the heap of rubbish piled up on the side of the street. But then we moved to the ashram, on the banks of the Ganges River. We were still in the city, but when I climbed up on the flat roof of our house, I had a vista of broad river, blue sky, green fields across the river to the east. I had the night sky above me. I didn't begrudge the nighttime power cuts when the light pollution disappeared and God's starry host was on display. The scenery opened up my prayer life, something that had felt stifled in the previous years. Jesus, we are told, often "went up on a mountainside to pray" (Mark 6:46). Admittedly Jesus taught, "But when you pray, go into your room, close the door and pray to your Father, who is unseen" (Matt 6:6), but his point was not the closet so much as the closeting.

Prayer walking, as a constituted strategy of intercession, is more often the case of identifying a locale of intended ministry and walking through it with the words of prayer just audible under your breath. It's easy to draw an allusion to the Israelites marching around Jericho in expectation of the walls crashing down. Prayer walkers invoke Moses' charge: "The land on which your feet have walked will be your inheritance and that of your children forever" (Josh 14:9). The walls of Jericho represent whatever spiritual opposition to our ministry that we want the Lord to overcome.

Prayer

The foot-trodden inheritance represents whatever spiritual blessing we want to see our people group receive in Jesus' name. Consequently our prayer walking won't solely be out in the beauties of nature, but also through scenes of great environmental devastation. Sage rounds the bend to witness the moonscape (mountaintop removed) where Cherry Pond Mountain once stood. The first thing that Mitch Hescox, the director of the Evangelical Environmental Network, did upon hearing of the BP oil spill was to organize a multiweek prayer walk along the Gulf Coast. Even from the roof of our ashram in India, it was one simple glance down to the *ghats* where I could see that the Ganges was unduly drying up, kids were openly defecating into what supplied their drinking water, and the Kewat fishermen's livelihood was disrupted by a dam built downstream. (On the confines of my rooftop, I guess what I engaged in should more accurately be called prayer pacing.)

A third lesson involves the degree of faith that MTR activists like Sage must bring to their prayers. No group has more money and power in the state capital Charleston, or in the nation's capital, or in the acquiesced hopelessness of West Virginia's chronically unemployed, than does Big Coal. What hope does Sage have in stopping MTR? How could he ever hope to have the influence that the coal companies do? For that matter, there is another set of questions with which an environmental missionary will be inevitably confronted, a set of questions seemingly more benign but equally as paralyzing. What can the church do for creation care that the Sierra Club or the World Wildlife Fund can't do better? Do evangelicals possess any value other than as a potential voting bloc? The Apostle Peter had the good sense to tell the beggar in Acts 3:6: "Silver or gold I do not have, but what I do have I give you. In the name of Jesus Christ of Nazareth, walk." We have the immeasurable power of the name of Jesus. We bring it to bear in urgent and prophetic prayer. The *Cape Town Commitment* writes it up in the form of a doctrinal statement, and states it in the tone of a victory already purchased for us and operative from the Cross:

> We trust in Christ . . .

In his death on the cross, Jesus took our sin upon himself in our place, bearing its full cost, penalty and shame, defeated death and the powers of evil, and accomplished the reconciliation and redemption of all creation.

In his bodily resurrection, Jesus was vindicated and exalted by God, completed and demonstrated the full victory of the cross, and became the forerunner of redeemed humanity and restored creation.

Since his ascension, Jesus is reigning as Lord over all history and creation.[5]

Finally in this section, Sage's prayers in the context of MTR remind me of one of the best extended illustrations I have ever heard on the relationship between prayer and ministry. (Ironically for Sage, it's an illustration from mining.) Steve Wibberly, a veteran worker with Christar, was likely the first to introduce me to this quotation from S. D. Gordon: "Prayer is striking the winning blow at the concealed enemy. Service is gathering up the results of that blow among the [people] we see and touch."[6] Here's how Steve develops this principle:

It is as though God says to us, "Dig a tunnel through this mountain and carry the gospel to the other side." We immediately get out picks and shovels and start digging through the dirt. Then we come up against the solid rock of the mountain and can do little.

At this point God presents us with a pneumatic drilling machine and says, "Use this!" Such a machine makes a lot of noise and dust, but in the end all there is to show for it is a small hole in the rock. However, when we pack dynamite into the hole and set it off, the result is a very big hole with lots of small rock pieces we are able to carry off. Continual repetition of drilling and dynamiting will in the end result in us making it through the mountain.

Prayer

Our prayers are like that drill; they penetrate resistant situations, but not much of a result can be seen until God drops in the dynamite of the Holy Spirit. Then things suddenly start to shake and move, blowing the situation wide open. Then we have lots of ministry to do among the people whom the Spirit has touched.[7]

The Prayers of Ezra and Nehemiah

Prayer is a grace. Prayer is a privilege. But it doesn't take too long in one's ministry to recognize that prayer is a discipline. When we look at our schedule for the day, with each need pressing if not meaningful, it takes discipline to stop and say, "Wait, first we pray." But it is more than just time constraints that makes prayer a discipline. Prayer is rooted in faith, and faith is a discipline. The only way to see the unseen is to willfully choose to see it. We "must believe that [God] exists and that he rewards those who earnestly seek him" (Heb 11:6). We must believe that while apart from him we can do nothing, nothing is impossible for him (John 15:5; Matt 19:26). We must believe that any opposition to our good works is more than just natural (Eph 6:12).

It strikes me that environmental missionaries are going to require more than their share of discipline in prayer. We will be prone to action, ready to deploy our professional skills, ready to avail ourselves to the pickaxes and shovels of Steve Wibberly's illustration above. Dig a hole to plant a tree. Clear a wetland of an invasive species. Install a methane stove. Capitalize a new recycling business. Remediate a toxic waste site. Fill sandbags in a flood zone. Lobby government for a marine protection unit. Plant a community garden. Environmental activism is well known; environmental passivism isn't even a category. At the most, it sounds like surrender. And surrender it is: surrender to God and his chosen way of doing things, surrender to the reality of our own ineffectuality. "If you can't pray for something, you can't minister in it." That's what I tell any college student who approaches me with an interest in environmental missions. "Learn how to pray for it."

J. O. Fraser is the famous missionary among the Lisu people of Myanmar and southwest China. His ministry, not unlike Sage's, consisted of trekking from one isolated mountain village to another. At one point in his ministry, as chronicled in his biography, *Mountain Rain*, Fraser is puzzled why the church in one particular remote village is so vibrant, while the church in the village he has chosen as his home base of operations struggles. He is rarely able to visit the remote village because his preaching schedule in his home village is so full. Fraser suddenly realizes that precisely because he is unable to visit the other village as often as he would like, he actually prays for it *more* than he does for his home church. He realizes that his prayer ministry for the Lisu bears more fruit than his preaching ministry, or rather, as he concedes, his preaching ministry bears no fruit apart from prayer. "We often speak of intercessory work as being of vital importance," Fraser writes in a letter back to England. "I want to prove that I believe this is actual fact by giving my first and best energies to it as God may lead. I feel like a business man who perceives that a certain line of goods pays better than any other in his store, and who purposes making it his chief investment."[8] But Fraser is an evangelist. There is work to be done in addition to the work of prayer. Fraser attends to his own prioritization of prayer, but he also actively recruits others to pray, so that he might be freed up to preach. Almost the totality of the writing that we have of J. O. Fraser is in the form of prayer letters sent back to the church in Great Britain. "It is indeed necessary for me to go around among our Lisu, preaching, teaching, exhorting, rebuking, but the amount of progress made thereby depends almost entirely on the state of the Spiritual Tide in the village—a condition which you can control upon your knees as well as I."[9]

Like J. O. Fraser, Steve Wibberly is an active evangelist, just like any given environmental missionary might consider himself or herself a forester, a biologist, or an agriculturalist. What does prayer have to do with installing a solar panel? The two great historical books of the postexilic period in the Old Testament are Ezra and Nehemiah. Ezra was a Levitical priest. "He was a teacher well versed in the Law of Moses, which the Lord, the God of Israel, had given" (Ezra 7:6). Scripture says that "the gracious hand of his God was on him. For Ezra had devoted himself to the study and observance of the Law of the Lord, and to teaching its decrees and laws in Israel" (Ezra 7:9,10). Upon arriving back in Jerusalem—a dangerous journey bathed in prayer, by the way (Ezra 8:21–23)—Ezra learned of the lawlessness of the returned exiles as evidenced in their intermarriage with the Canaanites. There is no evidence that this teacher of the Law even opened his mouth in rebuke or exhortation. First he sat stunned and appalled and then he prayed, albeit publicly. The majority of Ezra 9 is the record of his confession and lament to God. In chapter 10, "while Ezra was [still] praying and confessing," the people of Israel gathered around him with repentant hearts (v. 1). One person—Shecaniah son of Jehiel—seems to have actually interrupted Ezra, telling him to stop praying and start preaching. "Get up," he told Ezra, "for it is your duty to tell us how to proceed in setting things straight. We are behind you, so be strong and take action" (Ezra 10:4 NLT).

Nehemiah, by contrast, was not a priest. He was a cupbearer to the king (Neh 1:11). Did this make him a courtier or a politician? He at least was a lobbyist; he had something he wanted to ask of the ruler. Nehemiah was later known as a builder of walls. He organized the returned exiles to reconstruct the ruined walls, restoring not only security to Jerusalem but a sense of national identity. He was a visionary. He was a practical man. He was a builder and an organizer. He has become the darling of any Christian CEO who wants to write a book about faith in the marketplace—Nehemiah, the patron saint of any leader who can't imagine himself or herself being an Ezra. While prayer seems so obviously a necessity for a ministry like Ezra's, it may be surprising to see the significant role of prayer in a book like Nehemiah. In fact, Nehemiah's story begins in prayer. When he heard news of the broken walls of Jerusalem, Nehemiah records, "I sat down and wept. For some days I mourned and fasted and prayed before the God of heaven" (Neh 1:4). For being such a practical man, Nehemiah doesn't immediately rush to petition and intercession. He lingers in worship and confession. In the end, he asks God, "Give your servant success today by granting him favor in the presence of this man," the king (Neh 1:11). I can imagine that this request, this verse, will be offered up to God repeatedly in the history of environmental missions; so many of our projects will require a degree of government approval. Nehemiah resorts often to prayer. He prays an imprecation over his detractors, Sanballat the Horonite and Tobiah the Ammonite (Neh 4:4,5; 6:14). (I've always considered the imprecatory psalms to be the height of maturity in prayer. I've never trusted myself to know the mind of God in such matters.) He refuses the financial allowance due him and instead entrusts himself to God for provision (Neh 5:16–19). "So the wall was completed on the twenty-fifth of Elul, in fifty-two days. When all our enemies heard about this," Nehemiah records, "all the surrounding nations were afraid and lost their self-confidence, because they realized that this work had been done with the help of our God" (Neh 6:15,16). So the wall was completed. Environmental missionaries might write in future prayer letters: so the prairie was restored . . . so the wells were dug . . . so the experimental fields were harvested . . . so the houses were weatherized . . . so the legislation was passed . . . and all onlookers—believers and unbelievers—"realized that this work had been done with the help of our God."

If the whole point of environmental missions is the integration of church planting and creation care, then let's look to Ezra and Nehemiah *as a pair* for our model. The environmental missionary is a teacher of Christ's righteousness *and* a builder of walls. Where the spirits of their ministries converge is in prayer. We can also look at Ezra and Nehemiah as a team, much in the same way an environmental missions team could consist of seminary *and* professional grads, both contributing their invaluable giftings to a common goal. In fact, in the book of Nehemiah, once the wall is built and the people are registered, Nehemiah disappears for a while as a first-person narrator. Ezra takes center stage as the one who publicly recites the Law and leads the people in repentance. When the "I" pronoun of Nehemiah returns, it signals his participation, not in building another wall, but this time in leading in praise and worship: "I had the leaders of Judah go up on top of the wall. I also assigned two large choirs to give thanks" (Neh 12:31).

Prayer

The book of Nehemiah ends as it began, in prayer. Nehemiah asks God to remember with favor all his hard work and labor (Neh 13:31).

Shivraj and "Suffer the Little Children"

I don't know how our city in India and the Ganges that flows through it stack up statistically in terms of environmentally related deaths. If you spread my heartache out over fourteen years, it might not generate the starkness of a cancer cluster that gets discovered near a chemical plant, but nonetheless I have a portion of my heart that feels like the Middle Ages. I remember corpses. The one child whose death I remember the most, and whose dying we most intimately accompanied, was our landlord's six-year-old son, Shivraj. He contracted aplastic anemia, a disease whereby the bone marrow is deficient in making new blood cells. Attribution studies are not common in India, so the cause of Shivraj's illness was never precisely identified, but aplastic anemia is often the result of exposure to benzene, an ingredient in the gasoline so wantonly spilt about the property, both there and at our landlord's farm in Madhya Pradesh. So the reader will have to decide whether this qualifies as an "environmental missions" story; certainly we didn't think in those terms back then. In the end, this might be just a general lesson in prayer, except for a central point: namely, that which "belongs" to God—i.e., the earth and *all* it contains—is as much a basis for prayer as it is for creation care.

We all noticed that something was wrong when Shivraj developed little blue spots all over his skin, like stains from a ballpoint pen. Then he began to bleed through his gums. Robynn and I, as well as our whole team and church plant, ministered as we could. We prayed and recruited prayer, just as J. O. Fraser did in years past. We gave blood. Since I was a blood-type match, I donated often. After our first transfer, the family's joke was that Shivraj would come home speaking fluent English since his blood was now American. We gave money to help with medical expenses. We gave advice. We gave encouragement. We ministered in all the ways our love for Shivraj could conceive. Eventually Shivraj was taken to Mumbai for special treatment. When no compatible bone marrow donors were found among his family members, Shivraj was sent home with the prospect of emergency blood transfusions as the only hope to prolong the inevitable.

One Wednesday morning, Robynn and I woke up with a conviction that Shivraj and his family needed to be prepared for death. We made an appointment to talk that afternoon to his mother and father and his aunt and uncle. We spent the entire morning in prayer seeking a boldness and clarity commensurate to the situation. Our landlord's family had Bengali roots and were thus worshipers of the goddess Kali. At the far end of their property they maintained a temple to her. Kali, one of the consumer gods of Hinduism discussed in the last chapter, is generally considered the most bloodthirsty of all the pantheon. Blood drips from her long tongue. She wears a necklace of skulls about her neck. The infamous *thuggi* cult emerged around her worship. Every year, this family offered a goat to Kali on the night of Diwali. In other words, it was a blood sacrifice, and Shivraj's uncle claimed his family had been offering the sacrifice without fail for eight hundred years. Of the many things we told this family that day in our urgent presentation of the gospel was a sense that this year "Kali intends to take the blood of your son, Shivraj." "Kali takes blood," we said, "but Jesus gives blood." Jesus gave his own blood at the Cross, for the forgiveness of our sins and for a newness of life in him. We told them: "As Shivraj's mother and father, and his aunt and uncle, you have spiritual authority over Shivraj. You need to give him to Jesus. Jesus might heal him, or he may choose not to. If not, there is nonetheless life available for Shivraj in the presence of Jesus. Jesus is trustworthy and he loves children." That night our entire church plant met with the family, prayed at their invitation over Shivraj, and shared a gracious meal together with them.

Two weeks to the day, Shivraj would be dead. I helped carry his body down to the river. In these intervening weeks, we had indeed seen Shivraj's grandmother reading to him stories of Jesus from the Hindi-language children's Bible we had given him. Shivraj's mother, clutched as she was to Robynn's chest as her son was carried away, told my wife through her sobbing tears, "I gave Shivraj to Jesus. Just like you told me. I gave him." The strangest event of that heartbreaking period was an evening in the final week of Shivraj's life. I had gone up on the roof to pray before bedtime, another episode of prayer pacing. From our roof I could peer down into the courtyard of our landlord's house, even see the light behind the door of the room where Shivraj was lying. I tried to pray for him, my regular set of prayers for healing, deliverance, and salvation. But . . . I felt blocked in my spirit. Try as I could, I could no longer intercede for that little boy. Instead, from some deep place in my heart, I felt overwhelmed with a tearful joy. I began to laugh out loud. I felt like I was being told that there was nothing left to pray for: Shivraj was in the hands of Jesus. Now that didn't mean that Shivraj would live or die, nor even that he would be in heaven or not. It meant only that Shivraj was in the hands of Jesus, and that Jesus was trustworthy. I found my comfort in the fact that, as I word it now, Jesus came not to consume but to be consumed.

Months later, also up on the roof below a starry night, with the polluted Ganges River flowing below me, I would ask myself the question: Will I see Shivraj again when I too go to the presence of Jesus? Will he be resurrected into the same glory that I imagine for the Ganges River of the new heavens and new earth? I take comfort in the passage where Jesus turned away no mother who brought her children to him (Matt 19:13–15; Mark 10:13–16; Luke 18:15–17). Certainly others, touched by Shivraj's story, have rushed to my rescue with well-meaning assurances. But in the end, I too am left with what I told Shivraj's parents: "Maybe Jesus will save him; maybe he won't. But Jesus is trustworthy. He is gracious, compassionate, slow to anger, and abundant in lovingkindness." And what belongs to him, belongs truly to him.

Ownership is a troublesome issue in creation care. Beginning 130 years ago, speculators from the American northeast traveled through Appalachia with "broad form leases" in hand, and bought the mineral rights in perpetuity from unsuspecting landowners, often for dollars on the acre. Years later when the "surface owners" complained about mountaintop removal mining (as compared to the traditional practice of sinking a shaft), the Supreme Court of Kentucky, for one, ruled repeatedly that surface mining need not have been anticipated in the leases. Consequently coal companies own the rights to claim easement and to dig up whatever of the surface they need in order to get to the coal seams below. Certainly *personal property rights* are often invoked whenever some new environmental regulation is proposed: "It's *my* forest (or farmland, or territorial waters, etc.) and I can do with it whatever I want." In a classic tale of the preservation of the remaining tallgrass prairie here in Kansas, when Secretary of the Interior Stewart Udall stepped out of his helicopter in 1961 near Twin Mound, he was met by a rancher with a shotgun. (Ironically the rancher was only leasing the grazing rights on land owned by another.) MTR activist Larry Gibson passed away with only fifty acres of Kayford Mountain still in his ownership. A family-owned cemetery remains, but it is surrounded by 7,500 acres of MTR devastation. The Gibsons don't own the easement, and must get a permit in order to visit the cemetery. When Allen Johnson and Sage Russo gathered our group around the three concrete crosses up on Kayford Mountain, the topic of ownership was part of our prayers: "Lord, this mountain, indeed all of Appalachia, all of the world, belongs to you. And so, your kingdom come, your will be done, on [this piece of] earth as it is in heaven."

Evangelism, of the variety we did with Shivraj's family, is often conceived of as bringing Jesus (or the light, or the gospel, etc.) to people. In some ways, we entrust people with the gospel. And then they do with it whatever they please. Some receive it with joy. People, however, are not trustworthy, and so some reject the gospel, or despise, mock, or abuse it. Prayer feels like it flows in the opposite direction: we entrust people (or species or ecosystems) to Jesus. We give them to him, he to whom they have belonged all the time. And he is trustworthy. He will do rightly with that which is entrusted to him.

Mongolia and Job 28

All prayer, particularly that in a new category within missions, is well advised to begin with the disciples' request of Jesus: "Lord, teach us to pray, just as John taught his disciples" (Luke 11:1). It is one of the privileges of being apprenticed to a spiritual master: Jesus will teach his disciples every bit as much as John taught his. My admonition to young potential environmental missionaries has been: "Learn how to pray for it. If you can't pray for something, you can't minister in it." I give that admonition in full expectation that Jesus will take up his responsibility as Master and teach us. Eden Vigil publishes a free e-letter entitled "The Environmental Missions Prayer Digest." Every month we pray for a handful of requests from around the world, but admittedly one of our motivations is to train ourselves how to pray in a new category. In one issue of EMPD, we took up the topic of mining—not in West Virginia this time, but in Mongolia; not of coal, but of gold—and we found Job 28 to be helpful in informing our supplication.

The largest mining exploration project in the world is currently being conducted in southern Mongolia. The Oyu Tolgoi mine hopes to work a copper and gold ore deposit that is larger than the state of Florida. As one reporter describes the prospects:

> Over the forecast sixty-five-year lifespan of the mine, its rev-
> enues are expected to become a third of Mongolia's gross do-
> mestic product. It's a big deal, and the discovery of it and a
> wealth of untapped deposits of coal, gold, silver, tin, uranium,
> and "rare earth minerals" used in most of today's advanced
> electronics has mining-industry shills proclaiming Mongo-
> lia the next "Saudi Arabia of insert-name-of-precious-metal-
> here."[10]

The financial benefit to Mongolia of course will depend on how wisely the government can avoid what development experts call "Dutch disease," a phenomenon whereby discovery of a wealth of natural resources can actually lead to a host of unintended economic woes, particularly for the poor and other nonowners of those resources. Witness the Netherlands' overvalued guilder and depressed export market following the discovery of natural gas in the North Sea in the 1960s (hence the name, Dutch disease). The Netherlands had a developed economy and stable political structures. Nigeria had neither when Shell Oil began pumping from the Niger River delta. As for Mongolia, 27 percent of her urbanized population is below the poverty level and 50 percent of her rural population. Mongolia has not had to wait to feel some of the environmental distress of mining. Mining for gold is water intensive and results in a toxic waste that cannot be returned to the watershed. The Onk River once supplied water to sixty thousand people and 1 million head of livestock. Ten years ago, due to the gold mine's consumption, it ran dry. Tens of thousands of people were forced to relocate. Those who remained dug wells to reach the water, but the water was so contaminated that many children suffered liver damage.[11]

If any environmental issue has an air of inevitability about it, it is that new mines will almost always be sunk wherever mineral wealth is discovered—this, despite whatever opposition might mount against them. (This is one of the reasons why I purposefully chose mining as the backdrop for this entire chapter on prayer.) Onodelgerekh Ganzorig of the Mongol Environmental Conservation says, "We fought for eight to ten years to stop mining companies, and it doesn't happen. Why? Because it happens with or without you. Because it's what the other half of the people want. It's an economic development concept."[12] And then there is the uncertainty that the person who prays brings to his or her prayers. "One problem with the doctrine of dominion, however," writes Cal Beisner,

> is that it simply does not give direct, pat answers to lots of the specific questions that arise in environmental discussions. Should we drill for oil? Here? How? Should we mine coal? There? By boring (which is much more dangerous to the miners), or strip-mining (which can leave ugly scars on the land, although the scars can be restored to beauty)? Should we log old-growth forests? Where? How much, if any should we preserve? Inferring specific answers to these and many other specific environmental questions from specific passages of Scripture, or even from general principles of Scripture, is not only not easy, it is impossible.[13]

Job 28 suggests a solution for our dilemmas. It begins:

Prayer

> There is a mine for silver
>> and a place where gold is refined.
> Iron is taken from the earth,
>> and copper is smelted from ore.
> Mortals put an end to the darkness;
>> they search out the farthest recesses
>> for ore in the blackest darkness.
> Far from human dwellings they cut a shaft,
>> in places untouched by human feet;
>>> far from other people they dangle and sway.
> (Job 28:1–4)

Job's monologue starts out as a tribute to human ingenuity. What is astonishing is that the book of Job is written in pre-Abrahamic times. From early times, we humans have known how to mine the earth and how to smelt what we extracted.

> No bird of prey knows that hidden path,
>> no falcon's eye has seen it.
> Proud beasts do not set foot on it,
>> and no lion prowls there.
> People assault the flinty rock with their hands
>> and lay bare the roots of the mountains.
> They tunnel through the rock;
>> their eyes see all its treasures.
> They search the sources of the rivers
>> and bring hidden things to light.
> (Job 28:7–11)

If a twenty-first century Job wrote a sequel, he might very well gaze up in the opposite direction, to the moon, another place where proud beasts don't tread nor lions prowl. But we humans have been there! Part of the inexorability of most environmental issues seems bound up in the advance of human ingenuity. If we can figure out how to do something—human cloning, for instance—we'll do it. For however much grief that results from hydrological fracturing (hydro fracking) to extract natural gas, you can't help but be astonished at the technology behind it and the scale at which oil and gas companies can operate. Hubris wouldn't be hubris if it wasn't grand.

Job 28 also indicates that silver, gold, iron ore, lapis lazuli—the riches underground—seem to be as much a part of God's great bounty in creation as the God-given ingenuity that humans use to extract them. Mining has every much a claim as agriculture to the stewardship mandate of Genesis. I look at the wedding ring on my left hand and see an intrinsic beauty that is apart from the dear marriage that it symbolizes. I am grateful to the South Africans (probably) who mined the gold and to the New Delhi goldsmiths who fashioned it. God sanctions mining. Would we really give up the benefits of the Industrial Revolution for the sake of having kept the coal in the ground? "Oil is the devil's excrement." This famous quotation is from former Venezuelan Oil Minister and OPEC cofounder Juan Pablo Perez Alfonzo. "Ten years from now, 20 years from now," he predicted in the 1970s, "you will see, oil will bring us ruin."[14] Was he right, or wrong, or simply irrelevant?

It isn't until the little twist between verses 11 and 12 of chapter 28 that Job lands on the main point of his monologue. Humans "search the sources of the rivers and bring hidden things to light. But where can wisdom be found? Where does understanding dwell?" Chapter 28, in the end, is not about human ingenuity at all. It is about two things: how divine wisdom is more precious than anything we might dig out of the ground, and how difficult it is to find wisdom.

> It cannot be bought with the finest gold,
>> nor can its price be weighed out in silver.
> It cannot be bought with the gold of Ophir,
>> with precious onyx or lapis lazuli.
> Neither gold nor crystal can compare with it,
>> nor can it be had for jewels of gold.
> Coral and jasper are not worthy of mention;
>> the price of wisdom is beyond rubies.

Prayer

The topaz of Cush cannot compare with it;
  it cannot be bought with pure gold.
(Job 28:15–19)

The wisdom literature of Scripture, of which Job is a part and Proverbs is the embodiment, precipitates a crisis of faith. Do we truly believe that wisdom is more precious than anything that can appear on a mining company's fourth-quarter earnings statement? Would we trade anything that we might find in the ground—i.e., "leave it there"—if wisdom could be bought as a result?

Humanity, for whatever our history with ingenuity, hasn't had a great track record with wisdom. We might laud David Ballard's underwater discovery of the Titanic. We may thrill at David Cameron's CGI re-creation of it on film. But the "world's largest metaphor" remains on the bottom of the ocean with 1,500 souls lost at sea. "Where then does wisdom come from? Where does understanding dwell? It is hidden from the eyes of every living thing, concealed even from the birds in the sky. Destruction and Death say, 'Only a rumor of it has reached our ears'" (Job 28:20–22). But we are not left alone to fulfill the stewardship mandate of Genesis. As we till and keep, as we subdue and rule, we can turn to God for wisdom. We can ask him.

God understands the way to it
  and he alone knows where it dwells,
for he views the ends of the earth
  and sees everything under the heavens.
When he established the force of the wind
  and measured out the waters,
when he made a decree for the rain
  and a path for the thunderstorm,
then he looked at wisdom and appraised it;
  he confirmed it and tested it.
And he said to the human race,
  "The fear of the Lord—that is wisdom,
    and to shun evil is understanding."
(Job 28:23–28)

❧ ENVIRONMENTAL MISSIONS ❧

Often when Scripture talks about God's establishment and exercise of wisdom, the text closely associates it with creation and images from nature. "By wisdom the Lord laid the earth's foundations, by understanding he set the heavens in place; by his knowledge the watery depths were divided, and the clouds let drop the dew" (Prov 3:19,20). Wisdom as a personification declares:

> I was there when he set the heavens in place,
> when he marked out the horizon
> on the face of the deep,
> when he established the clouds above
> and fixed securely the fountains of the deep,
> when he gave the sea its boundary
> so the waters would not overstep his command,
> and when he marked out the foundations of the earth.
> Then I was constantly at his side.
> I was filled with delight day after day,
> rejoicing always in his presence,
> rejoicing in his whole world
> and delighting in mankind.
> (Prov 8:27–31)

Wisdom is built into the warp and woof of the creation and is the basis of any stewardship we share with Christ over it. It's the most natural thing in the world that we should pray for wisdom in issues of creation care.

Brian Awehali is the reporter who traveled to Mongolia to report on its mining operations. He was the one who recorded Ganzorig's despair: "We fought for eight to ten years to stop mining companies, and it doesn't happen. Why? Because it happens with or without you." Awehali sympathizes and concludes, "The practical question, then, becomes how to have mining operations without losing other important environmental or cultural resources." This strikes me as an unverbalized prayer for wisdom. When it comes to mining, wisdom might shut down some operations altogether. But wisdom might also suggest that other operations proceed, albeit with them being wisely redesigned for less human, environmental, and cultural damage. We used Awehali's article to pray for Mongolia. "Even in a country with advanced environmental laws and strict enforcement," he writes, "the very best case scenario for a mine involves an accident-free exploration and extraction phase followed by an aggressive long-term, well-funded reclamation plan that creates some approximation of the natural order that went before."[15] And so in the Environmental Missions Prayer Digest, we prayed, "Gracious Lord, grant all parties wisdom that it may be so!" On the flip side, Awehali writes,

> There is no single worst-case environmental scenario for a mine. It could be staggering levels of water consumption, poisoned watersheds, or toxic silt-choked rivers that asphyxiate fish. It could be gaping open-pit mines and a surrounding dead zone created by any number of toxins leaching into the ground, or areas known in the mining industry as glory holes, where "block-caving" operations, which involve blasting deposits into tunnels dug below, create large areas of permanently unstable earth on the surface.[16]

And so we prayed, "Oh Lord, heaven forbid! The fear of the Lord, and the shunning of evil, would dictate otherwise."

When Beisner asks, "Should we drill for oil? Here? How? Should we mine coal? There?" these need not be rhetorical questions. In Christ Jesus, we have been given the privilege of approaching the owner of all things and offering up to him what theologians have called the Prayer of Inquiry. He gives wisdom generously and without reproach to all who ask of him (Jas 1:5).

NOTES

1. Tracy Ross, "Hike. Pray. Protest.," *Backpacker* (March 2011): 82.
2. Ibid.
3. Ibid.
4. Ibid., 89.

5. Third Lausanne Congress, *Cape Town Commitment*, I.4.A.

6. S. D. Gordon, *Quiet Talks on Prayer* (New York: Revell, 1904), 19.

7. S. M. Wibberley, *Knowing Jesus Is Enough for Joy, Period* (Maitland, FL: Xulon, 2010), 270.

8. James O. Fraser, quoted in Eileen Crossman, *Mountain Rain* (Wheaton: Harold Shaw, 1982), 170.

9. Fraser, quoted in Crossman, *Mountain Rain*, 148.

10. Brian Awehali, "Under the Eternal Sky," *Earth Island Journal* (Winter 2011): 26.

11. National Geographic TV, "The True Cost of Gold," Wild Chronicles, YouTube video, 6:54, July 22, 2009, http://www.youtube.com/watch?v=lgAKeTGHx5g (accessed May 23, 2012).

12. Awehali, "Eternal Sky," 29.

13. Beisner, *Wilderness*, 17.

14. Juan Pablo Perez Alfonzo, quoted in Nick Cohen, "The Curse of Black Gold," *New Statesman*, June 2, 2003, http://www.newstatesman.com/node/145564 (accessed May 23, 2012).

15. Awehali, "Eternal Sky," 29.

16. Ibid.

12

TOPICS IN ENVIRONMENTAL MISSIONS

R alph Winter, founder of the US Center for World Mission, was a big fan of new sodalities—smaller-defined initiatives that, like the monastic orders of the Middle Ages, advanced the kingdom in ways sometimes decisively, sometimes incrementally, but always forward. Winter's first major teaching on sodalities was presented in Seoul, Korea, in August 1973. In July 2008, in one of the last addresses before his death, Winter appeared again in Seoul and told the Korean World Missions Conference, "The biggest trend in world mission is the polarization occurring among mission agencies that either focus exclusively on personal salvation or, in contrast, physical needs when they should be doing both."[1] Or the "polarization of some doing good things and some saying good things when the two need to be put together." Sodalities are good, but integrated sodalities are better.

When I first encountered the Evangelical Climate Initiative, a call to action in response to climate change, I looked through the extensive list of signatories for any of "my people": cross-cultural church planting missions executives. I couldn't find any. There were nationally known pastors (Hybels, Warren), university presidents (Mouw, Liftin), and many from the relief-and-development community. As it turns out, many of the "missional" signatories were recruited when Jim Ball, the draftsman of ECI, made a presentation at a member's meeting of the Association of Evangelical Relief and Development Organizations, now known as Accord Network. Church planting signatories would have more likely been found in a ministry association like Missio Nexus, of which, for example, Christar is a member. When I finally met Jim Ball, I asked him, "Why didn't you seek signatories in the missions arm of the church?" Jim replied, "I didn't think they would be interested."

Back then, Jim's assessment was probably correct, but that's changing, and environmental missionaries are definitely interested in the issues raised by the Evangelical Climate Initiative. But does this mean that those environmental missionaries who, like me, were born and bred in traditional church planting agencies need to switch their membership from Missio Nexus to Accord if they want to find a home? The answer is certainly no, but environmental missionaries are nonetheless on the vanguard of Winter's appeal to be workers who say good things and who do good things. We focus neither "exclusively on personal salvation [nor], in contrast, physical needs when [we] should be doing both." Like my original illustration back in the preface, we have one foot in environmental issues (as if on the eastern bank of the Ganges River) and one foot in traditional church planting issues (as if on the western bank of my religious Indian city). We have one foot in the discussions occurring in Accord, and one foot in the discussions occurring in Missio Nexus. Visualizing this, however, reveals the tension: it's quite a stretch to straddle the Ganges River. Probably for the time being, environmental missions does not yet have a settled home anywhere despite, in actual fact, the welcome of both Accord and Missio Nexus. Again, speaking from personal experience, when I have been with Accord members, I spend a great deal of time talking about gospel preaching and church planting among least-reached people groups. When I'm with Missio Nexus members, I spend a great deal of time talking about the moral mandates and strategic opportunities of creation care. To both audiences, I probably sound less integrated than I wish to be.

In this final chapter of this book, I want to briefly touch upon some specific issues that have traditionally been the concern of Accord: poverty alleviation, refugeeism, natural disasters, population growth, and political activism. Even now, by their own admission, Accord members are just beginning to learn how these are also creation care issues. We hope additionally that they begin to see how an environmental missions approach can also speak profitably into these concerns. For those who, Missio Nexus–like, come into environmental missions through church planting, they will very quickly encounter these five topics in their ministry, and so this chapter hopes to provide some helpful suggestions in how to best forge partnerships, how to best promote integration.

Poverty Alleviation

There is an intriguing quotation that is making the rounds. Nazmul Chowdury, manager of Practical Action's Disappearing Lands project in Bangladesh, has said, "Forget about making poverty history. Climate change will make poverty permanent." His words make reference to two contemporary campaigns—poverty alleviation and climate mitigation—and to one presupposition about poverty that even Jesus himself seems to challenge. "Make Poverty History" is the star-studded campaign based on Jeffrey Sachs' book *The End of Poverty: Economic Possibilities for Our Time*.[2] Sachs suggests that "clinical and extreme" poverty—the less than a dollar a day earnings, which keep whole countries on the bottom rung of development—can be eliminated by the year 2025. Chowdury's quotation is right in drawing our attention to climate change's impact on the poor. "It is the poorest of the poor in the world, and this includes poor people even in prosperous societies, who are going to be the worst hit," confirmed IPCC chair Rajendra Pachauri at the release of the Fourth Summary Statement on Climate Change in 2007.[3] As an example, one Yale University study estimates that African farmers on rain-fed land will lose $28 per hectare per year for each 1°C rise in average global temperatures.[4] We are already at almost a 1°C rise, with the international climate negotiations (Copenhagen, Cancun) hoping for only a 2°C rise at best. This represents a hole dug in Africa's dustiest fields that make African farmers even further out of reach of Sachs' bottom rung of economic development.

As for the permanency of poverty, it is Jesus himself who told us, "The poor you will always have with you" (Matt 26:11; Mark 14:7). He was responding to Judas, who was objecting to the pint of pure nard that Mary had, in his opinion, "wasted" on the anointing of Jesus' feet. But Jesus, in wanting to exert the supremacy of devotion, was not being disparaging of the poor. As Jesus replied to Judas, he was apparently quoting from Deuteronomy 15:11: "There will always be poor people in the land. Therefore I command you to be openhanded toward your fellow Israelites who are poor and needy in your land." There will always be poor people in the land—even when that land is beset by drought, flooding, sea-level rise, disease vectors, or any other of the projections of global climate change. Our mandate is to be openhanded to them. In the various words of the book of Proverbs alone, we are commanded: "Don't oppress, mock, exploit, shut your ears to their cries, take interest or profit at their expense; but instead, be kind, be generous, give, open your arms to, share your food, judge fairly, defend their rights, and care about justice."

Scott Sabin's environmental missions organization Plant With Purpose grew out of a commitment to poverty alleviation: plant a tree as a way to feed a community. (See appendix 3 for a full discussion.) The link between creation care and the poor will also eventually bring one around to a discussion of "environmental justice," that often our environmental distress is built on the backs of the poor for the enrichment of the wealthy. As mentioned in a previous chapter on environmental sin, we North American evangelicals seem to want to keep such discussions at arm's length, but justice is a thoroughly biblical subject and, for that matter, a core attribute of God. We are under his command: "The righteous care about justice for the poor, but the wicked have no such concern" (Prov 29:7). In the case of creation care, environmental missionaries will very quickly encounter two specific forms of injustice towards the poor: NIMBY and commoditization of God's good gifts.

The deceptively cute acronym of NIMBY stands for "Not in my backyard!" One must have a voice to voice such a sentiment, so in this case it's the wealthier portions of town who are telling city zoning officials, "Don't you dare threaten my wealth, well-being, or property values by placing factories, power plants, or garbage dumps near my neighborhood." Majora Carter, director of Sustainable South Bronx, is one of the more well known urban environmentalists. She in fact calls herself a social justice environmentalist. In a recent podcast, she was introduced with this background about her neighborhood:

> The South Bronx, where she grew up, is one of New York City's poorest neighborhoods and historically perhaps its most environmentally toxic. It has a higher concentration of industrial facilities than other sections of the city. Power plants, waste transfer stations, and high diesel truck traffic contribute to increased pollution and poor community health. An estimated 17 percent of Bronx school-age children have asthma, three times the national average.[5]

And one's backyard can also be defined as one's own country. For example, most developed countries export a great deal of their "e-waste" (i.e., obsolete computers and other electronics). The US has very stringent laws for the disposal of e-waste, particularly because our electronic junk contains elements of lead, cadmium, and mercury. Often it's cheaper for companies to ship the junk to a country like Ghana than to dispose of the waste properly within the US. In Ghanaian sites, like the big Agbogbloshie market, children like twelve-year-old Yusef Nashedu will scavenge the junk, looking for copper, in turn exposing themselves to the dangerous heavy metals.[6] Such exports are not illegal. A nation's e-waste must occupy space. That space is either hazardous or costly to supply. And so, while no one would come out and say it: better Ghana's backyard than ours, better Yusef than one of our own kids.

An environmental missionary's response to NIMBY will likely involve some of the political activism described in the final section of this chapter. Hands-on action, though, starts with the declaration of any incarnational ministry: "Your backyard is now my backyard too, and all of it is God the Creator's backyard anyway." If a sending country exports its waste, then a sending church is determined to export the knowledge of safe and sustainable waste management and mitigation, which should have gone with it.

Commoditization is often another form of environmental injustice. Natural resources can be turned into commodities, and thus one legal defi-

nition of commodity is: "an article of trade or commerce, especially an agricultural or mining product, that can be processed and resold."[7] Commoditization is a normal and necessary practice in economics. But what happens
when goods and services that are normally provided free, just by virtue of
God's good creation, end up being commoditized? Thomas Taha Rassam
Culhane is the director of Solar Cities, an NGO that, among its other projects, installs solar water heaters in the slums of Cairo, Egypt. His clients
are Coptic Christians and traditional Muslims. From the rooftops, Culhane
gazes out over the great Nile River basin and thinks about economics:

> In . . . pre-industrial times, the poor could depend on the
> sun shining at certain times, the rain falling at certain times,
> the river flowing, rising, depositing fertilizer . . . This subsidy
> from nature meant that even if you were financially poor, you
> could lead a fairly rich life in terms of comfort. The predict-
> ability is now gone. The poor can't depend on their environ-
> ment for any kind of subsidy, and so it now is, can you earn
> enough money to buy the resources that were mined out of
> the environment by the rich and then put in warehouses now
> sold at commodity prices? Having no subsidy left, the poor
> are completely dependent on fluctuations in market prices.[8]

Life, liberty, and the pursuit of happiness were all listed by America's
founding fathers as inalienable rights and the endowments of our Creator. Is clean water an inalienable right? Is clean air an endowment? As in
NIMBY, the easiest way to understand the injustice of commodization is
to pick an example close to one's own backyard, but our example—bottled
drinking water—also has a surprising cross-cultural component among
the poor. Most tap water in the US is clean, safe, and free (though in essence commodified by our payment of the municipal water treatment tax.)
Water is fully commodified when it is packaged in little plastic bottles and
sold to consumers. Clean water used to be free to anyone willing to carry
a bucket to the nearest stream and fetch it. Even the poorest families in
the village owned a bucket or, lacking one, could dunk their heads in and

drink freely. Often the advertising industry aids and abets commodification. A 1997 study in *American Demographics* showed that "black, Asian, and Hispanic households are more likely than whites to use bottled water, even though blacks and Hispanics as a group have lower-than-average household incomes."[9] A more recent study (2007) updated the results for Latinos. Hispanic women are the one group in the US most likely to purchase bottled water.

Of the study population [all Latinos], 41.2% never gave their children tap water and 30.1% never drank it themselves. Immigrant Latinos were even less likely to consume tap water or to give it to their children than non-Latinos. The primary factor influencing this behavior in immigrant Latinos seems to be a fear that tap water is a potential cause of illness.[10]

Previously free clean water can be commoditized. So can previously free clean air if, like the mothers of New Delhi or the South Bronx, one must also purchase inhalers and nebulizers for her asthmatic children. Even sunlight can be commoditized. How do you charge a cotton farmer in Andhra Pradesh, India, for sunlight? Sell it to him as oil. (Fossil fuel is prehistoric plant life that has converted the sun's energy through time and geologic pressure from carbohydrates to hydrocarbons.) Fertilizers, pesticides, and herbicides are all petroleum based. Tractors and combines need a full tank of gas. As a final example, one of the most threatening forms of commoditization is the laws that prevent the millenia-old practice of "seed saving." Traditionally farmers have been allowed to set aside a portion of their harvest to use as seed for next year's planting; not so today with hybrid seed that has been patented by a multinational agribusiness. Farmers in India sign contracts in which they promise to purchase new seed each year.

Environmental missionaries are protective of both God's abundant bounty and of his love for the poor. In appendix 3 you can read how missionary Jean Grade once explained to a Ugandan village how the ready availability of local herbal remedies—free for the plucking—is a sign of the generosity of a God who didn't hesitate to send his Son too for our salvation. Working with Latino mothers, environmental missionaries can educate and reassure: "The reason other mothers are buying bottled water is for

convenience or consumerism. Tap water is safe for your children, saves you money, and is better for God's creation." Dirty water can be cleaned up. Polluted air can be rendered breathable again. Heritage seeds, owned by no one other than the farmer willing to do the labor of seed saving, can be made more widely available. God's lavish banqueting table can once again be declared open.

Refugees

Sociologist Norman Myers writes:

> There is a new phenomenon in the global arena: environmental refugees. These are people who can no longer gain a secure livelihood in their homelands because of drought, soil erosion, desertification, deforestation and other environmental problems, together with associated problems of population pressures and profound poverty. In their desperation, these people feel they have no alternative but to seek sanctuary elsewhere, however hazardous the attempt. Not all of them have fled their countries, many being internally displaced. But all have abandoned their homelands on a semi-permanent if not permanent basis, with little hope of a foreseeable return.[11]

By way of example, the Marsh Arabs are Shi'ite Muslims who, like their Sumerian ancestors, have made their living on the Mesopotamian marshlands of southeastern Iraq. After the first Gulf War in 1990–91, and after the failed Shi'a rebellion, Saddam Hussein targeted the Marsh Arabs. Villages were attacked and burned, often with missile fire. Drinking water was reportedly poisoned, but most devastating of all, rivers were dammed and the wetlands were drained. Hussein's Ba'athists—whether military or civilian—were targeting the land as much as the people. The marshlands for centuries had been a hiding spot for rebellious factions, much like how South Carolinian swamplands served American patriots, or the Dakota Badlands served Wild West outlaws. The central Qurnah marsh once covered nearly 300,000 square miles; it is now all but dry.[12]

With the marshlands gone, the social and economic livelihood of the Marsh Arabs has fallen apart. Essentially now
a refugee population, this unique human community and a
5,000 year-old way of life has also been flushed away by the
drainage scheme. Given that the flight of the Marsh Arabs
was triggered by massive environmental deterioration, there
is a strong case for them to be considered as "environmental refugees." These were defined in a UNEP commissioned
study "as those who had to leave their habitat, temporarily or
permanently, because of a potential environmental hazard or
disruption in their life- supporting ecosystems."[13]

The United Nationals Environmental Programme (UNEP) report
quoted above demonstrates a dilemma. "Environmental refugee" is not an
officially recognized designation. As far back as 1988, Jodi Jacobson published Worldwatch Paper 86: *Environmental Refugees: A Yardstick of Habitability.* Her opening paragraph describes how the citizens of Chernobyl,
ten thousand in number, have been forced to relocate due to the world's
worst nuclear disaster. Then she writes:

These people are refugees, though not by any standard definition. According to widely accepted doctrine, refugees are people who decide to seek asylum out of fear of political, racial, or
religious persecution, or who leave their homes because of war
or civil strife. This conventional notion, however, leaves out a
new and growing class—environmental refugees.[14]

Jacobson estimates the number of environmental refugees in 1988 to
be "at least 10 million," and then claims that this "rivals that of officially
recognized refugees and is sure to overtake this latter group in the decades to come."[15] In fact, in 2008 World Vision Canada announced that
environmental refugees now outnumber those displaced for any other reason—political, military, economic, etc.[16] The UN High Commissioner for
Refugees (UNHCR) admits, "There is a protection gap in the international system that needs to be addressed." Whereas previously the UN-

HCR had "refused to embrace the new terminology of 'climate refugees' or 'environmental refugees' fearing that this would complicate and confuse the organization's efforts to protect the victims of persecution and armed conflict," now they are willing to consider new protocols.[17] There's a lot at stake for environmental refugees to be included in these official definitions. Recognized refugees have a right to demand asylum in other countries. In addition, those who force refugees off their land can be held liable for repatriation or relocation.

While the international community attempts to settle these disputes, we can ask what exactly is the nature of ministry that environmental missionaries might have among environmental refugees? Adaptation work for an environmental missionary can mean helping people develop new ways of living on devastated land so that they don't have to move off of it, or assisting in restoring the land so that refugees can move *back* to it. One ethnographer interviewed Marsh Arab expatriates who had ended up in San Diego. Ninety percent of them said they would return to Iraq if the marshes were restored.[18] There have been some encouraging signs:

> With the demise of Saddam Hussein and the Baathist regime in 2003, and with good water years from 2003 to 2005, water returned to about 60 percent of the former marshland area (Richardson et al. 2005). Some areas rejuvenated beautifully, with lush growth of reeds and rebounding fish populations. The Ma'dan people who lived as environmental refugees throughout the 1990s were returning to the marshes with their water buffalo. However, despite the rehydration of such a large area of the marshes, much of the marsh ecosystem is in poor condition. According to a paper in *Science* (Richardson et al. 2005), less than 10 percent of the original marshes in Iraq remain fully functioning wetlands (also Reiss et al. 2003; Stevens 2006).[19]

But additional "good water years" are not going to be sufficient to restore the Mesopotamian marshlands. Reduced water flow has meant increased salinity. The region also suffers from what taxes the rest of the country: "(1) water resource pollution (including groundwater); (2) ecosystem and biodiversity degradation; (3) waste and sanitation disposal; (4) oil and other cement, fertilizer, and pesticide industry pollutants; and (5) the direct impacts of military conflicts."[20] In other words, there's plenty of good work to occupy an environmental missionary.

However, the whole point of the story of the Marsh Arabs, and central to the heart of environmental missions, is that the human story is as compelling as that of the ecosystem. Adaptation means the reintroduction of the Marsh Arab to his former homeland, an important process that Michelle Stevens calls *eco-cultural restoration*. She writes:

> Because the marsh ecosystem is adapted to human management, any effort to restore the ecosystem must also be an effort to reestablish Marsh Arab culture and make use of their traditional management practices. Thus maintaining the integrity, identity, and culture of the Marsh Arab society must be preeminent in restoration planning, and this must include encouraging the sustainable livelihoods of Marsh Arabs who have returned to the area. "The future of the 5,000-year-old Marsh Arab culture and the economic stability of a large portion of southern Iraq are dependent on the success of this restoration effort" (Richardson et al. 2005), however, the converse is equally true, the success of the restoration effort depends on the actions of the Marsh Arab culture and the economic stability of a large portion of southern Iraq.[21]

Unfortunately, while ecologists talk about restoring the Marsh Arabs *to* the marshes, they don't talk about the restoration *of* the Marsh Arabs themselves. Stevens hopes to *maintain* "the integrity, identity, and culture of the Marsh Arab society," without thought to the fact that their integrity has already been shattered, their identity drained off, their culture silted over. The good water years of 2003–5 were followed by drought in 2007 and 2008. Water flow to the marshlands, necessary to their restoration,

was cut off this time, not by Saddam Hussein, but by water rights disputes with others in the Tigris-Euphrates watershed. The Marsh Arabs have broken relationships with others. They have a broken relationship with self. The last survivors of the Sumerian civilization, their population is diminished to the point of extinction. Where will they find hope? And that question is pertinent because love compels us to say it: the Marsh Arabs remain Shi'ite Muslims in a universe where Christ's ascendancy to the throne is more important than Ali's to the caliphate. The Marsh Arabs, like all of us, have a broken relationship to God that can only be restored in Christ Jesus.

Another avenue for refugee ministry by environmental missionaries is to give attention to that piece of property that, while labeled a refugee camp, is nonetheless still part of God's creation. Refugee camps brutalize the local landscape and often result in replicating the devastation of what the refugees left behind. For example, while food and water can be shipped into a camp, sanitation waste is rarely shipped out. In 1999 the government of Guinea, West Africa, invited UNEP to research the impact of the 800,000 refugees who had fled to Guinea from the unrest in Liberia and Sierra Leone. The complexity of their findings is illustrated in this paragraph from the report:

> A predominant problem throughout refugee-hosting areas is the *shortening of the fallow periods*. The traditional rotational bush fallow system requires long fallow periods to restore soil fertility. Increasing demand for arable land means that it is no longer possible to maintain the required long fallow periods and that agriculture is also expanding to upland areas. There is an urgent need to develop and adopt agricultural and agroforestry models that are able to increase yields and cope with shorter fallow periods on one hand, and prevent soil depletion, erosion, and encourage the retention of existing forest on the other.[22]

But I want to reserve my last comments about environmental refugees for church planting. We church planters, by and large, like to work with stable populations. Survey is the first stage of church planting, and so we pore over the demographic data, including drawing the geographic boundaries of our particular people group. A "local, indigenous church" is, by definition, local. The very etymology of the word "indigenous" means "of a place," and would seem to preclude the *dis*placed, the refugee. Modern church planters may no longer start with a vision for a piece of property on which the church might eventually build a building that they themselves own. Nonetheless house churches do presume a house, not a white tent with the light blue UNHCR logo painted on the side. Or house churches presume a stable host household—some already established member of the neighborhood, preferably employed, preferably respected by the community. In other words, refugees are rarely on the radar screen of traditional church planters.

Estimates, depending on who issues them, are that by 2050, environmental refugees will number 150 million, 250 million, even 1 billion.[23] Is it possible that, by 2050, upwards of 1 billion of the world's unreached will be effectively off the radar screen of the church planting mission of the church? Fortunately for the Marsh Arabs, *Operation World* is determined to get the church praying for them: "Restoration of the marshes is now occurring, but the younger generation remain rooted in the cities, not in their traditional marsh homelands. There are no known Christians and no sustained outreach specifically to them."[24]

Environmental missionaries can form new, robust partnerships with refugee workers whereby church planting is reconceptualized for refugee populations. If we want to be ready by 2050, we'd best get busy problem solving now. In chapter 4, the profile of a country that may need to flee *in toto*, I invoked Paul's sermon to the Athenians at the Aeropagus in Acts 17. Paul makes a statement about God's sovereignty over the movement of people groups: "From one man he made all the nations, that they should inhabit the whole earth; and he marked out their appointed times in history and the boundaries of their lands" (v. 26). But then Paul identifies the unfailing purpose behind the sovereignty of our Lord:

God did this so that they would seek him and perhaps reach out for him and find him, though he is not far from any one of us. "For in him we live and move and have our being." As some of your own poets have said, "We are his offspring." (Acts 17:27,28)

This is the great hope of the refugee. We are all his offspring. He knows where we are, even when we don't.

Disasters, Natural and Man-made

Natural disasters that are related to extreme weather events (hurricanes, floods, drought, tornadoes, etc.) have received an unfortunate new name in this era of global climate change. They are called the "New Normal." But what about *man-made* disasters, those most likely to be called environmental disasters, those akin to, say, the Bhopal gas leak of 1984, where a Union Carbide pesticide plant leaked a cloud of methyl isocyanate, killing at least 3,787 people? At Urbana 09, I used a slide in my presentation commemorating the first anniversary of the Kingston coal ash spill in the Emory River of Tennessee. But before the Environmental Missions Consultation was convened the next summer, twenty-nine men would be dead at the Upper Big Branch coal mine in West Virginia and eleven dead on the Deepwater Horizon oil rig in the Gulf Coast. In terms of the worst oil spills in human history, the BP Gulf Oil spill, with an estimated 206 million gallons released, was second only to Saddam Hussein's sabotage of oil terminals and tankers in the first Gulf War in 1991. And today the world is still following news from the Fukushima Daiichi nuclear plants, the victim of the Japanese tsunami.

Accidents happen. The Bhopal gas leak is twenty-eight years old; the Exxon Valdez spill is over twenty years old. What basis, one might ask, do we have for saying that man-made environmental disasters (as compared to "acts of God") are part of the New Normal? The Gulf and Fukushima disasters are two examples. In September 2009, seven months before the accident, the Deepwater Horizon set a world's record, drilling the deepest-ever oil well to a vertical depth of 35,050 ft. Where it had drilled at the time of the explosion, the seafloor was almost a mile beneath the rig. This capability is truly a marvel of human technology. But it is also a marvel (i.e., horror, terror) of human need. We wouldn't be operating at such great depths, under such risky conditions, if all the easy and safer oil fields had not already been tapped. As geologist Chris Rowan writes,

> The offshore drilling industry is currently undergoing a transition. Most easy targets have already been developed, and yet global demand for oil is not abating. In an attempt to quench this thirst, attention is moving into more technically challenging areas, with more complex geology and often in the deeper waters of the continental slope. The increasing complexity of the equipment required to drill in such areas increases the number of things that can go wrong, and the location of the drilling makes dealing with catastrophic failures much more difficult.[25]

The Fukushima nuclear power plants are a similar example of the New Normal in that its technology, by all appearance and history, is the height of human ingenuity. Nonetheless, in the end, the reactors proved inadequate for new realities of rock and water. The leak of radiation from the reactors, the unfortunate result of an earthquake—"an act of God"—may be different than the leak of Deepwater Horizon's oil—"an act of man" as the present investigations of BP, Haliburton, and Transocean are trying to ascertain. This nuclear disaster may even prove different than Chernobyl or Three Mile Island. But my point in this example is that if natural disasters become the New Normal, then so is our best technology's inability to withstand those disasters.

Environmental missionaries bring an integrated perspective to a disaster situation, which can multiply the restorative effects of the church's best relief efforts. I'll mention just two considerations. First, disaster management leadership in the New Normal is already shifting more energies away from relief activities to rehabilitation and development instead, activities in which environmental missionaries can be fully invested partners. Steve

ENVIRONMENTAL MISSIONS

Corbett and Brian Fikkert, authors of the influential book *When Helping Hurts*, write: "Relief can be defined as the urgent and temporary provision of emergency aid to reduce immediate suffering from a natural or man-made crisis."[26] Relief features a strong *provider*, who gives assistance to a *receiver*, who due to the immediacy of the crisis is often incapable of helping himself or herself. Rehabilitation "seeks to restore people and their communities to the positive elements of their precrisis conditions," and development is "a process of ongoing change that moves all the people involved—both the 'helpers' and the 'helped'—closer to being in right relationship with God, self, others, and the rest of creation."[27] Notice how the authors mention what we've been calling the labor of the environmental missionary: restoring broken relationships with God, self, others, and creation.[a] Corbett and Fikkert argue that the relief phase of any crisis is a

---

[a] When Corbett and Fikkert turn the corner in their book and begin to present positive ways to restructure our ministries, they begin by introducing us to some development "best practices": Asset Based Community Development (ABCD), Participatory Learning and Action (PLA), and Appreciative Inquiry (AI). Maybe it's just the use of acronyms, but while asset mapping, participation, and appreciation all point to relationship cultivation, the techniques seem to quickly lose themselves again in the development world. How do these techniques apply (as an important example) to restoring one's relationship with God? At the beginning of the book, Corbett and Fikkert give readers an "opening exercise." Our pretend church is to send a team to assist with the restarting of small businesses in Indonesia wiped out by the December 2004 tsunami. How will we go about it? (For some of our colleagues, of course, this is no pretend example.) After reading through the book, readers are brought back around to the "Extended Exercise: Indonesia Reconsidered." We are asked twenty-three questions that specifically apply the teaching of the book to our reconsideration of ministry in Indonesia. For example, one question was "Did you bring in outside resources when local resources were insufficient to solve pressing needs?" However, among the twenty-three questions, not a single one asked: "How did you incorporate the preaching of the gospel into your trip?" The closest questions seem to be: "How might this framework [of relational understanding of poverty] alter the approach you took?" and "Did you address the

lot shorter than most of us would think, and that the sooner we can begin working *with* victims and not *for* them, the better. "One of the biggest mistakes that North Americans make—by far—" the authors warn us, "is in applying relief in situations in which rehabilitation or development is the appropriate intervention."[28]

Secondly, the New Normal represents greater strategic opportunities for church planting among the least reached. I spoke extensively in chapter 1 about how the Pakistani earthquake of 2005 seemed to present some strategic opportunities, of historic proportions, for church planting. The official death toll of the Pakistani earthquake of 2005 stands at 74,698. Is it ghoulish to talk about it or any other disaster as an opportunity to promote a church planting agenda? Is a church planter's "disaster survey trip" any different in essence than disaster tourism? These are tough questions. But, if we can find a space in between disasters during the New Normal, if we can ask these questions not from Battagram, Pakistan, but from our mission agency boardrooms, then maybe we can revisit some more fundamental questions about the Great Commission. If relief efforts, relief organizations, or relief longings do not make room for evangelism, discipleship, and church planting, then I think Corbett and Fikkert can make a case that they have fallen prey to *When Helping Hurts*' most devastating equation:

> Material Definition of Poverty + God-complexes of Materially Non-Poor + Feelings of Inferiority of Materially Poor = Harm to Both Materially Poor and Non-Poor[29]

(See also the previous footnote.) People are poor and their lives are disasters because the four relational walls of God, self, others, and crea-

---

brokenness in both individuals and systems?" Those questions might be close enough—the authors truly are committed to preaching a restored relationship with God through Jesus Christ—but the lack of explicit reference to how evangelism, discipleship, and church planting might be advanced in Indonesia following the tsunami is further proof of just how new a category environmental missions might be.

tion have been shaken by sin and have crashed down around them. Where those walls have crashed down on their created bodies, short-term medical relief teams need to be sent to help bind up their wounds. But evangelists and disciple makers, even from among those doctors and nurses, need to tend to the other broken relationships. Whenever I've talked about breaking down the walls between church planters and relief workers, between Accord and Missio Nexus organizations, I have been cautioned. Many relief organizations have spent a great deal of energy over the years to build up trust with reluctant governments. They have tried to distance themselves from any hint of proselytizing for fear that when a crisis hits, they will be denied access to the place of need where they know the Lord wants them. This is a tricky problem. But I would argue that the Great Commission, incapable of being suspended by even the most strident demands of a recalcitrant government, suggests that this is a problem that we should try to solve.

One idea that Eden Vigil is batting around is to send environmental missionaries to disaster relief efforts as "relief chaplains." It's a way to understand what I and my friends (church planters, each of us) brought, or could have brought, to the table in Pakistan in 2005. A relief chaplain is probably more of a church planter than a relief worker. He tries to help the doctors and other relief professionals as best as possible, but doesn't begrudge that he lacks the skills and credentials of his colleagues. A relief chaplain in the midst of the heavy physical demands of a field hospital seeks opportunities for spiritual ministry. Charles, Tom, and I prayed regularly with patients in Urdu and in the name of *Hazarat Isa Masih*, our Lord Jesus Christ. Charles shared the gospel with the soldiers in Battagram with whom he broke the Eid fast every evening. It would be the relief chaplains who would receive the offer to "re-build the entire medical infrastructure in this district." They would identify the church planting networks, resources, and opportunities that emerge from the disaster, and write it up as a strategic plan afterwards. If they can't sell that plan to current SIM or Christar teams (the particular agencies with which we worked in Pakistan), then maybe another agency would be interested in a new turnkey project. In other words, relief chaplains would "market" these plans to the sending church. If relief teams are truly committed to moving quickly past relief to rehabilitation and development strategies, and if rehabilitation and development is really just the holistic restoration of the four broken relationships, and if restoration of right relationship is the essence of church planting, then church planters in the form of environmental missionaries are the natural successors in this Great Commission moment.

Population Growth

Environmental missionaries find themselves at the very center of population worries—those worries being, on one hand, that impossible human numbers will swamp a finite ecosphere, and on the other hand, that draconian measures will be used to deal with it.

Environmental missionaries often work among "the highly populated" as a people group. The population of our city in India was between 1 million and 2 million; we always said, "Nobody stands still long enough to get accurately counted." But even at 2 million, ours was a small city by Indian standards. Mumbai now exceeds 18 million. (I once took a train out of Mumbai's CST train station. The train picked up and maintained high speed quickly, but looking out the window forty minutes later, we had still not left the urban sprawl. It was mind blowing.)

The country of Yemen is experiencing a severe water crisis. They have exploited their aquifer above hope of recharge. In the twenty years leading up to this crisis, the population of Yemen had doubled. At the time, they had one of the highest rates of population increase in the world, at 3.5 percent.[30] Even in bringing those trends up to date, Yemen's population has increased by 35 percent since 1994, and is additionally taxed by the arrival of 300,000 Somali refugees by 2007. Missionaries live and love at this local level. I've met Christian workers who love the Yemeni and wouldn't want there to be any fewer of these dear people. But these are the same workers who join their Yemeni neighbors in pumping water up to their roof tanks only once a month, if they are lucky. Local scarcity can also be the result of distribution inequities. In 2007 and 2008, "food

riots" were recorded in numerous African, Asian, Caribbean, and Latin American countries. (Yemen was among that number.) Rioters protested shortages of basic staples, drastically higher food prices, and higher prices because of those shortages.

Christian ecologist Rusty Pritchard admits that many evangelicals are concerned that

> worries about overpopulation and admiration of population control strategies are regularly found in environmentalism . . . Enviros certainly aren't universally agreed on those points, but they have been entirely too tolerant in the past of a mind-set that views people as a blight on the planet. Many are beginning to repudiate that position, and at least one major environmental organization has actually quietly closed down its population program. Christians should rejoice that prolife values are beginning to be more clearly reflected in environmental circles, and we should continue to press the point.[31]

Regardless of how near or far secular environmentalism might be from pro-life values, environmental missionaries must be given the freedom to grapple with—or at least grieve over—how high populations can add to the suffering caused by resource scarcity in a particular locale.

There are, in fact, two ways in which environmental missionaries can contribute to population control efforts without violating their pro-life convictions. One way is to understand population as "populations." Wes Jackson, paraphrasing economist Herman Daly, asks the question, "What do mice and elephants and humans and Holstein cows and deer and toasters and Deepfreezes and houses and garages and so on have in common?" He answers: "Well, one is they are all members of populations. In other words, there is a population of houses and a population of pop-up toasters and a population of Deepfreezes, and so on, just as there are populations of people and deer and whatever . . . They all occupy space."[32] It's possible that the true population problem isn't with human beings but with the stuff that we humans like to accumulate, consume, and discard. One could say to the Yemeni, "If you want to give water to your people, then decrease the "population" of the water-intensive crop, *qat*" (a mild narcotic). One could say to the Chinese, "If you want the best chance to feed your people, then reverse the population trend for pigs." Consumption of pork has tripled in China since 1980. If it ever reaches the same luxury level of consumption as in Hong Kong, pork production will require an additional tonnage of corn for use as hog feed equal to half the annual crop (in a good year) of the United States, the world's largest corn grower.[33] These, of course, are intrusive conversations, but not outside the *Cape Town Commitment*'s call for us to urgently and prophetically confront the idolatry of consumerism. The average American house size—now at 2,349 square feet—has more than doubled since the 1950s, even though the average number of people living in each has diminished.[34] Back in the 1950s and '60s, a single bathroom was considered adequate, and two or three brothers or sisters could share a bedroom. So the population of 2x4s and drywall sheets has increased. This population has its own set of resource demands, consuming its added share of fossil fuels in order to be heated and cooled. Could we self-impose population controls on the population of houses? Perhaps nothing better highlights the population problem of stuff than the fact that four Kenyan children use the same amount of resources as about one-eighth of one American kid.[35] If we multiply out the ratio—that is, one American child uses the same resources as 32 Kenyan kids—we can ask the question: Where's the population problem? Is it with an African woman who irresponsibly produces 32 children? (Is such a thing even possible?) Or is it with the American mother who surrounds her one toddler with a population of the latest and greatest plastic doo-dads?

Herman Daly often uses the analogy of the *Plimsoll line* when talking about how ecologically oriented economics differs from neoclassical economics:

> In 1875, Samuel Plimsoll supported Britain's Merchant Shipping Act, requiring that a load-limit line be painted on the hull of every cargo ship using British ports. If the waterline exceeded the Plimsoll line, the ship was overloaded and pro-

hibited from entering or exiting the port. Because of England's seafaring dominance, the practice was adopted worldwide. Yet shipowners who profited from overloading their ships fiercely resisted the measure. They could buy insurance at rates that made it profitable to occasionally risk losing an overloaded ship. The Plimsoll line has saved the lives of many sailors.[36]

If we want to fill earth's boat with people and more people, that may be fine, but we have to then be willing to govern the rest of the cargo, lest it violate the Plimsoll line. If we don't, in the end we risk the very lives of the people we claim to love. So how does an environmental missionary engage in this form of "population control"? By propogating the most ubiquitous of all creation care messages: "reduce, reuse, and recycle." When environmental missionaries go the extra mile to design and make mechanisms for reducing, reusing, and recycling more easily available, then they have certainly done more than yap-yap-yapping about overpopulation.

Another means for environmental missionaries to enter population advocacy is with the realization that family planning is only one of four possible means that have been proven to stabilize local populations. The four factors are:

- The widespread education of girls.

- The social and political empowerment of women to participate in the decisions of their families, communities, and nations. (This includes, but isn't limited to, the right to vote.)

- High child-survival rates, leading parents to feel confident that most or all of their children will survive into adulthood. (This includes access to quality medical care, as well as safety and security concerns.)

- The ability of women to determine the number and spacing of their children.[37]

Working for the fourth factor might scare some evangelical missionaries off, but there's enough to do in the love of Christ for the empowerment of women and the care of their daughters and sons to satisfy a lifetime of ministry.

Political Activism

Environmentalism, like any other human endeavor, has its own folklore, and few parables are as famous as the tale that ecologist Garret Hardin told in *Science* magazine in 1968. He coined the term "The Tragedy of the Commons."[38] Hardin explains how each herdsman in a group that shares an open pasture will rationalize that the benefit of adding one more animal to his herd will outweigh the cost of overgrazing, since he alone gets the whole benefit of one more animal while the cost of overgrazing is shared by everyone. "At this point," Hardin writes, "the inherent logic of the commons remorselessly generates tragedy." Since each herdsman makes the same calculation of maximum utility, it isn't long before the field is grazed bare and all the animals—added or otherwise—die off.

The point of Hardin's parable is not the tragic inexorability of exploitation; instead it's the obvious need for the commons to be managed by the *commonwealth*. In other words, "in order to form a more perfect union, establish justice, insure domestic tranquility, provide for the common defence, promote the general welfare, and secure the blessings of liberty to [themselves and their] posterity," the herdsmen must come together to form "government" and submit to its policies. The herdsmen must see themselves as a *polis*. For the sake of their herds, wise herdsmen (stewards) must devote a portion of their time to *politics*.

The first time I ever presented my slide presentation about a missionary perspective on climate change, I did so to a small group at our church. Afterwards, a member of the audience went up to our pastor and asked, "Why is Lowell getting involved in politics?" I felt I had gone out of my way not to "be political," but the assumption was that the topic of climate change automatically means politics. The second assumption was that missionaries shouldn't involve themselves with politics. Now, five years after that first presentation, I have to admit that his first assumption may have

been correct: not that environmental topics *automatically* mean politics, but they likely will end up there at some point.

The relief-and-development community also has a folklore, and one of its most famous tales is "The River." As it goes, one day a man from a certain town went walking down by the river that flowed alongside the village. He spotted a distressed child, half-drowned, floating in the current, barely holding on to breath. The man dashed out into the river, rescued the child, and brought him to shore. He revived him and then brought him to the town's only doctor. News of the rescue spread through the town, but the exclaim was even greater the next day when this man spotted—and rescued—not just one but two other children from the river. Drowning children soon became a regular occurrence, and the kind-hearted townspeople responded. They formed teams and specialties. They performed training drills. They built a new hospital. After a few months, they thought, "Surely we could do more and do it better," so they called a town meeting. Committees of townspeople presented elaborate proposals to improve their practices. In the end, though, the meeting was disrupted by one small voice that asked, "Shouldn't we send someone upstream and stop whoever is throwing all these babies into the river?" Environmental topics will likely end up at politics, but only if some brave voice pipes up and asks what's going on upstream. Otherwise we violate Thoreau's famous insight: "For every thousand hacking at the leaves of evil, there is one striking at the root." Often the upstream root causes are discovered to be some systemic breakdown in the governance of the commonwealth. While the immediate problem on the commons is overgrazing, the root cause of the tragedy is poor organization of the *body politic*.

I would change my friend's first assumption to sound something like: if we are going to pursue solutions for environmental problems with both integrity in our compassion and efficacy in our solutions, we will likely at some point have to become politically engaged. But if his first assumption is correct, what about his second: that missionaries should nonetheless not get involved in politics? My only answer to that question is to pose a different one, not to the general audience of North American Evangelicalism, but to the individual environmental missionary with his or her specific environmental issue: where do you sense the integrity of your compassion and the efficacy of your solution is leading you? In other words, how is God calling? Christendom has a long history of embracing a William Wilberforce, a Lyman Beecher, a Martin Luther King, or a Nelson Mandela, but only after years of first rejecting them. Or if not forcibly rejecting them, then at least advising them to the "gradualism" that Wilberforce lamented in a Lord Dundas, or MLK in the pastors mentioned in his *Letter from a Birmingham Jail.*

I once heard of a Catholic missionary in Latin America who said, "When I feed the poor, they call me a saint. When I ask why they are poor, they call me a Communist." At the very least, environmental missionaries should be prepared to be called names. It's been some time since North American missionaries have been called "the scum of the earth, the garbage of the world" (1 Cor 4:13)—these names hurled at the apostles ("sent ones") as much by the sending church as by the pagans. If anything, we missionaries have been on a post–World War II, Jim Elliot pedestal. We have also been conditioned by the support structures of a "faith missions" model. Admittedly it's hard to sit down and write a prayer letter without feeling like it needs to be a glossy public relations flyer. We don't want to step on toes, alienate, or offend any of our supporters. My friend at my first presentation of a church planting missions perspective on global climate change was simply raising an eyebrow and raising a question. I've subsequently been lumped with "Communists, socialists, Al Gore-dupes, Eco-Nazis," and something called "libtards." Robynn and I have lost financial supporters. Most of this loss has been gracious, but it still hurts when those who previously "believed in you" no longer do.

In the end, environmental missionaries can take inspiration from E. Stanley Jones, who, for all the ways that he is currently honored as a towering figure in the history of twentieth-century missions, was a controversial figure to some in his time. He was a loyal friend to the Mahatma Gandhi and a vocal supporter of the nationalist movement in India. In 1944, trying to return to India, Jones, an American Methodist, was denied a visa by the British colonial government because of his support for nationalism. "It was a privilege to be kept out of India on that issue," he later wrote. "I believed fundamentally in the method and motive of the struggle for political independence."[39] In his classic *Christ of the Indian Road*, Jones shares his personal philosophy of living within history. "Some time ago I got hold of a phrase that has been of incalculable value to me: 'Evangelize the inevitable.' Certain things are inevitable; no use to grumble against them—get into them and evangelize them."[40] As an example, he felt that much grief could have been spared if the church in England had sought to evangelize the labor movement there rather than help repress it. He saw Gandhi's nationalist movement in India as equally inevitable.

> You could not scatter as much education and Christian teaching through India without there being an uprising of soul demanding self-expression and self-control. It is as inevitable as the dawn. We could have felt that we had failed if this had not come. When I saw the inevitableness of it I felt there was only one thing to be done—get into the movement and evangelize it. Stand down in those national currents and put Christ there.

> That does not mean that we should get into the politics of the country and become politicians, but it does mean that the Indian Nationalist senses at once that we are in spiritual sympathy with the finest and best in his movement. That is all he asks for, but he does ask for that.[41]

I have visited E. Stanley Jones' beloved Sat Tal ashram in the Kumaoni region of the Himalayan mountains. I have even prayed at his graveside that the Lord might grant me a double portion of this man's spirit. On his grave marker is an inscription from 1 Corinthians 3:22,23: "Everything belongs to you, yet you belong to Christ, and Christ belongs to God." You can turn from the white marble of his gravestone and contemplate the thinning forests of the Himalayas and the melting glaciers on the mountaintops. You can look down to the plains near Lucknow where Jones got his start and contemplate cycles of drought and flood. I can easily imagine that Jones, who courted controversy one last time in his life when he advocated a freeze on nuclear weapons, would consider the environmental movement to be one of history's inevitabilities. It was not that Jones' politics were liberal, but that his gospel was generous. His advice to us: evangelize it! "Stand down in those national currents and put Christ there."

NOTES

1. Michelle Vu, "Prominent Missiologist Identifies Biggest Trend in Global Mission," *Christian Post,* July 30, 2008, http://www.christianpost.com/news/ prominent-missiologist-identifies-biggest-trend-in-global-mission-33570/ (accessed July 16, 2013).
2. Jeffrey Sachs, *The End of Poverty: Economic Possibilities for Our Time* (New York: Penguin, 2005).
3. Rajendra Pachauri, quoted in Bruce E. Johansen, "Poverty and Global Warming," in *The Encyclopedia of Global Warming Science and Technology,* vol. 1 (Santa Barbara, CA: Greenwood, 2009), 488.
4. "Adapt or Die," *The Economist,* September 11, 2008, http://www.economist. com/node/12208005 (accessed October 5, 2011).
5. Majora Carter, "Discovering Where We Live: Reimagining Environmentalism," interview by Krista Tippett, *Speaking of Faith,* January 11, 2007, http:// www.onbeing.org/program/discovering-where-we-live-reimagining-environmentalism/transcript/4514 (accessed July 16, 2013).
6. Ron Claiborne, "U.S. Electronic Waste Gets Sent to Africa," *ABC Good Morning America,* August 2, 2009, http://abcnews.go.com/GMA/Weekend/ story?id=8215714&page=1 (accessed October 6, 2011).
7. "Commodity Law and Legal Definition," US Legal, http://definitions.uslegal.com/c/commodity (accessed October 5, 2011).
8. Thomas Taha Rassam Culhane, quoted in Liane Hansen, "Slow but Sure Environmental Progress in Cairo," *Weekend Edition Sunday,* National Public Radio, May 4, 2008, http://www.npr.org/templates/story/story. php?storyId=90109734 (accessed October 6, 2011).
9. Marcia Mogelonsky, "Water off the Shelf," *American Demographics* (April 1997): 26.

10. Wendy L. Hobson et al., "Bottled, Filtered, and Tap Water Use in Latino and Non-Latino Children," *Archives of Pediatrics and Adolescent Medicine* 161, no. 5 (May 2007): 459.

11. Norman Myers, "Environmental Refugees: A Growing Phenomenon of the 21st Century," *Philosophical Transactions of the Royal Society of London: Biological Sciences* 357, (2002): 609.

12. Nolan Fell, "Outcasts from Eden," *New Scientist,* 151 no. 2045 (August 31, 1996): 25.

13. Hassan Partow, *The Mesopotamian Marshlands: Demise of an Ecosystem; Early Warning and Assessment Technical Report,* rev. 1 (Nairobi: United Nations Environment Programme /DEWA/GRID, 2001).

14. Jodi L. Jacobson, *Environmental Refugees: A Yardstick of Habitability,* Worldwatch Paper 86 (Washington, DC: Worldwatch Institute, 1988), 5.

15. Ibid., 6.

16. Justin Douglass, "The Environmental Refugee Phenomenon," *Childview* (World Vision Canada), Summer 2008, 16–21.

17. Alister Doyle, "World Needs Refugee Re-think for Climate Victims: U.N.," *Reuters,* June 6, 2011, http://www.reuters.com/article/2011/06/06/us-climate-refugees-idUSTRE7553UG20110606 (accessed October 6, 2011).

18. Michelle Stevens and Hamid K. Ahmed, "Eco-cultural Restoration of the Mesopotamian Marshes, Southern Iraq," in *Human Dimensions of Ecological Restoration,* eds. Dave Egan, Evan E. Hjerpe, and Jesse Abrams (Washington, DC: Island Press, 2011), 289.

19. Ibid., 291.

20. Ibid.

21. Ibid., 293.

22. United Nations Environment Programme, *Environmental Impact of Refugees in Guinea* (March 2000), http://www.grid.unep.ch/guinea/reports/reportfinal3b.pdf (accessed October 6, 2011).

23. John Houghton, "Sir John's Word to Pastors" (speech, Center for Applied Christian Ethics, Wheaton College, January 25, 2007), http://www.wheaton.edu/CACE/CACE-Audio-and-Video (accessed October 6, 2011); Myers, "Environmental Refugees," 16.1; Christian Aid, *Human Tide: The Real Migration Crisis* (London: Christian Aid, 2007), 27.

24. Jason Mandryk, *Operation World,* 7th ed. (Colorado Springs: Biblica, 2010), 473.

25. Chris Rowan, "Drilling for Oil Is More Risky than It Used to Be," *ScienceBlogs*, May 4, 2010, http://scienceblogs.com/highlyallochthonous/2010/05/drilling_for_oil_is_more_risky.php (accessed February 27, 2012; page discontinued).
26. Steve Corbett and Brian Fikkert, *When Helping Hurts* (Chicago: Moody Publishers, 2009), 104.
27. Ibid.
28. Ibid., 105.
29. Ibid., 67.
30. Christopher Ward, "Yemen's Water Crisis" (lecture, British-Yemeni Society, September 2000), http://www.al-bab.com/bys/articles/ward01.htm (accessed October 5, 2011).
31. Rusty Pritchard, "Global Warming Skeptic at Religious Right Conference Apologies for Slanderous Charges," SustainLane, September 23, 2009, http://www.sustainlane.com/reviews/global-warming-skeptic-at-religious-right-conference-apologizes-for-slanderous-charges/MD2LZ844ONT78J73MZZFO-HI47AQI (accessed October 6, 2011; site discontinued).
32. Wes Jackson, "Q&A: Wes Jackson," interview by Jesse Finfrock, Mother Jones, October 29, 2008, http://motherjones.com/environment/2008/10/qa-wes-jackson (accessed October 6, 2011).
33. Agrimoney.com, "Chinese Hunger for Pork Could Be Corn Growers' Best Friend," March 6, 2013, http://www.agrimoney.com/feature/chinese-hunger-for-pork-could-be-corn-growers-best-friend--200.html (accessed May 21, 2013).
34. Margot Adler, "Behind the Ever-expanding American Dream House," *All Things Considered*, National Public Radio, July 4, 2006, http://www.npr.org/templates/story/story.php?storyId=5525283 (accessed October 6, 2011).
35. Sharon Astyk and Aaron Newton, *A Nation of Farmers: Defeating the Food Crisis on American Soil* (Gabriola, Canada: New Society, 2009), 243.
36. Herman E. Daly and Joshua Farley, *Ecological Economics* (Washington, DC: Island Press, 2004), 5.
37. Al Gore, *Our Choice* (Emmaus, PA: Rodale, 2009), 229.
38. Garret Hardin, "The Tragedy of the Commons," *Science* 162, no. 3859 (1968): 1243–48.
39. E. Stanley Jones, *Gandhi: An Interpretation* (New York: Abingdon-Cokesbury, 1948), 6.
40. Jones, *Indian Road*, 82.
41. Ibid., 83.

EPILOGUE

Putting Wheels on the Vehicle

Bill McKibben, who occasionally describes himself as "just a Methodist Sunday school teacher from Vermont," is credited with writing the first popular treatment of climate change. (*The End of Nature* was published in 1997.) McKibben's latest book is entitled *Eaarth*. Why the aberrant spelling? McKibben explains. He first tells the story of astronaut Bill Ander's famous photo entitled "Earthrise." The photo was taken from the Apollo 8 spacecraft on Christmas Eve 1968 and shows our planet illuminated by the sun, captured on film from space. At this point in the story, McKibben interrupts:

> *But we no longer live on that planet.* In the four decades since, that earth has changed in profound ways, ways that have already taken us out of the sweet spot where humans so long thrived. We're every day less the oasis and more the desert. The world hasn't ended, but the world as we know it has—even if we don't quite know it yet. We imagine we still live back on that old planet, that the disturbances we see around us are the old random and freakish kind. But they're not. It's a different place. A different planet. It needs a new name. Eaarth . . . It still looks familiar enough—we're still the third rock out from the sun, still three-quarters water. Gravity still pertains; we're still earth*like*. But it's odd enough to constantly remind

ENVIRONMENTAL MISSIONS

us how profoundly we've altered the only placed we've ever known.[1]

A new planet would seem to demand a new category of missionary who can go to the uttermost ends of it, as per Acts 1:8.

If McKibben's idea of a new planet is too far-fetched for you, I'm afraid you won't be greatly comforted by those who argue, "Same planet, new era." The geologic age that the Apollo 8 astronauts gazed down upon has been called the *Holocene*, a period scientists claim began twelve thousand years ago. *-Cene* always means new (as in "a new era") and *holo-* means "whole" or "entire." Thus *Holocene* means "whole or entirely new." And so scientists recognize that this current interglacial period of the past twelve thousand years represents something new. In 2000, Nobel Prize–winning scientist Paul Crutzen had an epiphany of geologic proportions. As he describes it, "I was at a conference where someone said something about the Holocene. I suddenly thought this was wrong. The world has changed too much. So I said: 'No, we are in the Anthropocene.' I just made up the word on the spur of the moment. Everyone was shocked. But it seems to have stuck."[2] In the word *anthropocene*, the root *-cene* still means "new," but *anthropo-* recognizes that the human species has proven itself capable of altering the landscape and the climate, and perhaps in no place more indicative than in the inversion of carbon. What was buried underground now floats in the atmosphere. Who worked this seismic inversion? *Anthropos.* The *anthropocene* is no rhetorical flourish of an amateur wordsmith. In 2000, Crutzen published the term in a newsletter of the *International Geosphere-Biosphere Programme*, and other scientists have affirmed it.[3]

Can what we call *modern missions* still be considered modern when it no longer operates in the same geologic epoch?

In the end, we don't need to state it as dramatically as McKibben and Crutzen. Missionaries throughout the ages have recognized that ages change and bring with them new realities. The sons of Issachar of 1 Chronicles 12:32 were "men who understood the times and knew what Israel should do." In creation care, the evangelical missionary movement can

Epilogue

find new means for reaching the least reached and for loving them in the fullness of Christ, their Creator, Sustainer, and Redeemer.

This entire book has emerged from the Environmental Missions Consultation of July 2010, the gathering which collaborated to write the definition of environmental missions, which is the core of this book. (You can read the story of the Consultation in appendix 2.) We began our sessions by reading a letter sent to us by Ed Brown. He set the agenda for our Consultation, and sets the agenda for this epilogue:

> Finally, we are very much aware from conversations with people who have been in this field longer than either of us that this wheel has been invented dozen of times already. I have seen documents and books from the 1970's to 2000 that all try to call the evangelical church to an energetic mission of caring for God's creation. Some of you at this consultation are veterans of these earlier efforts. Perhaps the problem is that all those wheels were invented but left on the shop floor. We'd like to attach them to the very healthy vehicle that is the mainstream evangelical missions movement by trying to devise ways and means to integrate creation care concerns and environmental projects into mission organization goals and programs.

I still believe now, as Ed did then, that the mainstream evangelical missions movement is not in need of a major overhaul. Neither the Consultation nor this book intends to propose the formation of something outside existing structures, though new environmental mission sodalities will likely emerge. Nonetheless, for all the appreciated health of the vehicle, the missing wheels do signify. Traditional agencies like Christar, but also the others represented at the Consultation, will gain no traction toward addressing the environmental needs of their people groups, nor seizing the opportunities for new expressions of church planting, without a degree of retrofitting. And so, as Ed charged us, there must be some people, however loyal to their agencies, who do the work of attaching the wheels to the vehicles.

What I leave you with in this epilogue is a "to do" list. Now that I've finished writing and revising this book, I am very much left with the question, what's next for Eden Vigil? How best to employ our time in cultivating the category of environmental missions and facilitating the work of environmental missionaries? I suspect it will be something like the list I've written up. And of course, the list is offered to you as well, my best suggestions for how to put the wheels on the vehicle—for the planting of churches and trees, for the saving of soils and souls, for the glory of God alone.

❑ Learn to pray for environmental missions and creation care. If you can't pray for something, you can't minister in it. Eden Vigil will continue publishing *The Environmental Missions Prayer Digest*, available at http://www.edenvigil.org.

❑ Encourage traditional church planting mission agencies to adopt creation care as a value. Encourage and assist traditional church planting mission agencies in identifying which of their already-existent projects are legitimately "environmental missions" projects. Encourage and assist these agencies to think through all of their other projects so as to be mindful of the environmental needs of their people groups, while transforming some of these projects into full-fledged environmental ones. (Putting the category heading of "Creation Care" into any future SWOT (Strengths, Weaknesses, Opportunities, and Threats) analysis is a practical first step.) Add creation care to the discipleship priorities in our local, indigenous church plants. As an important mark of valuing creation care, help each mission agency to evaluate its own operations to determine how sustainable they are, how greatly they contribute to the care of God's creation. (Are our facilities as energy efficient as they can be? Do we add recycling services into our conferences? And—this one is going to be tough!—are we limiting unnecessary air travel? Etc.) Our message to mission agencies and their offices: Go Green!

Epilogue

❏ Help facilitate new, strategically placed environmental missions projects by mobilizing personnel, resources, and creation care expertise. In other words, pursue "project brokerage" as an important component in the missions sending process. Create a database of all known environmental missions projects among mission agencies, so that mobilized environmental missionaries can quickly be linked up with suitable projects. In other words, be a headhunter for environmental missions. Construct a database that either shadows or supplements the Joshua Project by supplying a helpful environmental profile of every least-reached people group in the world. Create new mission agencies that specialize in sending environmental missionaries. Consider using Christian Veterinary Mission as a suitable model. (See appendix 3.)

❏ Be a part of the church that blesses our young students who go into environmental studies and other related programs. Actively mobilize among these students as well as among environmental professionals. Build a vision for them of how God can use their background, skills, and gifts for bringing the whole gospel to the least reached. Multiply the number of environmental studies programs at Christian colleges, and promote a missional focus among them. Provide or facilitate training among environmental missionaries. Environmental professionals will need training in Bible, theology, and cross-cultural ministry skills. Bible and seminary grads will need training in environmental development skills.

❏ Build and maintain a network of creation care expertise. Help on-field environmental missionaries gain instant access to supportive agencies such as ECHO or to Christian professors at universities. These experts can answer questions and help problem-solve. An actual on-field visit by them can confer great legitimacy to an environmental missions project.

❏ Encourage greater cross-pollination between Accord (relief and development organizations) and Missio Nexus (church planting

associations). Rethink our approach to natural disasters so as to take a bigger "four broken relationships" approach to them. Start a "relief chaplaincy," which sends ministers and church planting strategists to work alongside relief teams. Ask the large relief agencies to create, maintain, and deliver field hospitals, which qualified mission agencies could staff at disaster sites. Research the unique needs of those who are "environmental refugees." Adopt them as a needy and least-reached people group.

❑ Promote the *Cape Town Commitment* and the Lausanne creation care "Call to Action," and draw the attention of the church to its language on environmental missions. (Of course, please read it first yourself!) Purposefully seek out the non-Western (and/or non-North American) church for what they can teach us about creation care. What has God been doing among them that he would like to do among us? Receive instruction with humility. Bless and encourage the "young leaders," not only of the Lausanne Movement, but in our own churches and agencies. If they do indeed have an intuitive respect for creation care, fan that flame.

❑ Read (or research and write) on a theology of creation care and environmental missions. Research more fully the historical antecedents of environmental missions, with a particular eye for better informing our current practices. Add creation care and environmental essays to chapter 12 (Christian Community Development) in the *Perspectives* course.

❑ Introduce yourself to, align yourself with, and consider supporting evangelical creation care ministries like Care of Creation, A Rocha, Evangelical Environmental Network, Flourish, Blessed Earth, Restoring Eden, Renewal, and the other organizations mentioned in the pages of this book.

❑ Feel free to correspond with me with questions, comments, ideas, and proposals at lowell@edenvigil.org.

Epilogue

NOTES

1. Bill McKibben, *Eaarth: Making a Life on a Tough New Planet* (New York: Times, 2010), 2–3.

2. Paul Crutzen, quoted in Fred Pearce, *With Speed and Violence: Why Scientists Fear Tipping Points in Climate Change* (Boston: Beacon, 2007), 21.

3. Jan Zalasiewicz et al., "Are We Now Living in the Anthropocene?," *GSA Today* 18 (2007): 4–8.

APPENDIX 1

The Lausanne Global Consultation on Creation Care and the Gospel: Call to Action[1]

St. Ann, Jamaica, November 2012

The *Lausanne Global Consultation on Creation Care and the Gospel* met from 29 Oct 2 to Nov 2012 in St. Ann, Jamaica to build on the creation care components of the *Cape Town Commitment*. We were a gathering of theologians, church leaders, scientists and creation care practitioners, fifty-seven men and women from twenty-six countries from the Caribbean, Africa, Asia, Latin America, Oceania, North America and Europe. We met under the auspices of the Lausanne Movement in collaboration with the World Evangelical Alliance, hosted by a country and region of outstanding natural beauty, where we enjoyed, celebrated and reflected on the wonder of God's good creation. Many biblical passages, including reflections on Genesis 1–3, Psalm 8 and Romans 8, informed our prayers, discussions and deliberations on the themes of *God's World, God's Word and God's Work*. Our consultation immediately followed Hurricane Sandy's devastation of the Caribbean and coincided with that storm's arrival in North America; the destruction and loss of life was a startling reminder as to the urgency, timeliness and importance of this Consultation.

Two major convictions

Our discussion, study and prayer together led us to two primary conclusions:

Creation Care is indeed a *"gospel issue within the lordship of Christ"* (*CTC* I.7.A). Informed and inspired by our study of the Scripture—the original intent, plan, and command to care for creation, the resurrection narratives and the profound truth that in Christ all things have been reconciled to God—we reaffirm that creation care is an issue that must be included in our response to the gospel, proclaiming and acting upon the good news of what God has done and will complete for the salvation of the world. This is not only biblically justified, but an integral part of our mission and an expression of our worship to God for his wonderful plan of redemption through Jesus Christ. Therefore, our ministry of reconciliation is a matter of great joy and hope and we would care for creation even if it were not in crisis.

We are faced with a crisis that is pressing, urgent, and that must be resolved in our generation. Many of the world's poorest people, ecosystems, and species of flora and fauna are being devastated by violence against the environment in multiple ways, of which global climate change, deforestation, biodiversity loss, water stress, and pollution are but a part. We can no longer afford complacency and endless debate. Love for God, our neighbors and the wider creation, as well as our passion for justice, compel us to "urgent and prophetic ecological responsibility" (*CTC* I.7.A).

Our call to action

Based on these two convictions, we therefore call the whole church, in dependence on the Holy Spirit, to respond radically and faithfully to care for God's creation, demonstrating our belief and hope in the transforming power of Christ. We call on the Lausanne Movement, evangelical leaders, national evangelical organizations, and all local churches to respond urgently at the personal, community, national and international levels.

Specifically, we call for:

1. **A new commitment to a simple lifestyle.** Recognizing that much of our crisis is due to billions of lives lived carelessly, we reaffirm the Lausanne commitment to simple lifestyle (*Lausanne Occasional Paper* #20), and call on the global evangelical community to take steps, personally and collectively, to live within the proper boundaries of God's good gift in creation,

to engage further in its restoration and conservation, and to equitably share its bounty with each other.

2. **New and robust theological work.** In particular, we need guidance in four areas:

- An integrated theology of creation care that can engage seminaries, Bible colleges and others to equip pastors to disciple their congregations.

- A theology that examines humanity's identity as both embedded in creation and yet possessing a special role toward creation.

- A theology that challenges current prevailing economic ideologies in relation to our biblical stewardship of creation.

- A theology of hope in Christ and his Second Coming that properly informs and inspires creation care.

3. **Leadership from the church in the Global South.** As the Global South represents those most affected in the current ecological crisis, it possesses a particular need to speak up, engage issues of creation care, and act upon them. We the members of the Consultation further request that the church of the Global South exercise leadership among us, helping to set the agenda for the advance of the gospel and the care of creation.

4. **Mobilization of the whole church and engagement of all of society.** Mobilization must occur at the congregational level and include those who are often overlooked, utilizing the gifts of women, children, youth, and indigenous people as well as professionals and other resource people who possess experience and expertise. Engagement must be equally widespread, including formal, urgent and creative conversations with responsible leaders in government, business, civil society, and academia.

5. **Environmental missions among unreached people groups.** We participate in Lausanne's historic call to world evangelization, and believe that environmental issues represent one of the greatest opportunities to demonstrate the love of Christ and plant churches among unreached and

unengaged people groups in our generation (*CTC* II.D.1.B). We encourage the church to promote "environmental missions" as a new category within mission work (akin in function to medical missions).

6. **Radical action to confront climate change.** Affirming the *Cape Town Commitment*'s declaration of the "serious and urgent challenge of climate change" which will "disproportionately affect those in poorer countries," (*CTC* II.B.6), we call for action in radically reducing greenhouse gas emissions and building resilient communities. We understand these actions to be an application of the command to deny ourselves, take up the cross and follow Christ.

7. **Sustainable principles in food production.** In gratitude to God who provides sustenance, and flowing from our conviction to become excellent stewards of creation, we urge the application of environmentally and generationally sustainable principles in agriculture (field crops and livestock, fisheries and all other forms of food production), with particular attention to the use of methodologies such as conservation agriculture.

8. **An economy that works in harmony with God's creation.** We call for an approach to economic well being and development, energy production, natural resource management (including mining and forestry), water management and use, transportation, health care, rural and urban design and living, and personal and corporate consumption patterns that maintain the ecological integrity of creation.

9. **Local expressions of creation care,** which preserve and enhance biodiversity. We commend such projects, along with any action that might be characterized as the "small step" or the "symbolic act," to the worldwide church as ways to powerfully witness to Christ's Lordship over all creation.

10. **Prophetic advocacy and healing reconciliation.** We call for individual Christians and the church as a whole to prophetically "speak the truth to power" through advocacy and legal action so that public policies and private practice may change to better promote the care of creation and better support devastated communities and habitats. Additionally, we call the church to "speak the peace of Christ" into communities torn apart by

environmental disputes, mobilizing those who are skilled at conflict resolution, and maintaining our own convictions with humility.

Our call to prayer

Each of our calls to action rest on an even more urgent call to prayer, intentional and fervent, soberly aware that this is a spiritual struggle. Many of us must begin our praying with lamentation and repentance for our failure to care for creation, and for our failure to lead in transformation at a personal and corporate level. And then, having tasted of the grace and mercies of God in Christ Jesus and through the Holy Spirit, and with hope in the fullness of our redemption, we pray with confidence that the triune God can and will heal our land and all who dwell in it, for the glory of his matchless name.

We, the participants of the 2012 Jamaica Creation Care Consultation, invite Christians and Christian organizations everywhere to signify your agreement with and commitment to this Call to Action by *signing this document as an individual or on behalf of your organization, institution or other church body.*

NOTES

1. Lausanne Global Consultation on Creation Care and the Gospel, "Call to Action" (St. Ann, Jamaica: Lausanne Movement, 2012), http://www.lausanne.org/en/documents/all/2012-creation-care/1881-call-to-action.html (accessed July 17, 2013).

APPENDIX 2

Origin of the Terms: A Brief Survey

Francis Schaeffer published his book *Pollution and the Death of Man* in 1970, the year the first Earth Day was observed, and three years after Lynn White Jr.'s article "Historical Roots of Our Ecologic Crisis" famously laid blame at the feet of the church.[1] Schaeffer didn't use the words "creation care" to describe our ministry. Rather, as befitting a worldview where Christianity engages all the disciplines of the world in the spirit of Christ, Schaeffer speaks freely about "the modern field of ecology" and the "problem of ecology." He defines "ecology" as "'the study of the balance of living things in nature.' But as the word is currently used, it means also the problem of the destruction man has brought upon nature."[2] A recent republishing of the book (2011) includes a concluding chapter from Schaeffer's protégé Udo Middelmann, who now reserves the term "ecology" for study and uses the terms "environment," "environmental," "environmentalism" for the problem of destruction.

Dean Ohlman, recently retired from RBC Ministries and very much a father figure in the creation care movement, notes how in the later twentieth century the word "stewardship" began to be applied more broadly in the evangelical church beyond the annual "stewardship sermon" where, usually at the deacon board's urging, the pastor appealed to the congregation for more generous giving. Stewardship could apply to giving one's time and talents as well, and came to mean the wise and intentional management of what in fact God has given us, not what we have presupposed to own outright.

Ohlman claims the first use of the word "earthkeeping" was a play on the popularity of *Good Housekeeping* magazine. Of course the Greek root *oikos* in *oikologia* (ecology) means "household." In 1980 Calvin College gathered a group of scholars, including Cal DeWitt, and published *Earthkeeping: Christian Stewardship of Natural Resources.* When the book was substantially revised and reissued a decade later, the title had changed to *Earthkeeping in the Nineties,* but the subtitle had the more significant shift: *Stewardship of Creation.* General editor Loren Wilkinson explains:

> In this edition by using [the word "creation"] more consistently to describe this vast, dynamic, beautiful, but suffering planet, we hope to contribute to a recovery and deepening of the full biblical doctrine of creation: that heaven and earth are the Lord's, the product of the Creator's ongoing love—a love which calls us, through creation and through Christ, back to our original task in creation, which is to be gardeners of the earth, stewards of what God has entrusted to us.[3]

Wilkinson's comments appear to signal a shift. Around the same time, the Christian Environmental Council, of which Dean Ohlman was a member, helped launch the Evangelical Environmental Network (EEN), and Ohlman could say, "By the mid-Nineties, mostly because of frequent use, the term 'creation care' became the most common reference to our responsibility to take better care of what the Creator has given us."[4] EEN uses "Creation Care" as the title of their magazine and as the domain name for their website. The Lausanne Movement has also adopted the terminology.

Assuming that creation care is missional in itself, how should the church describe creation care that is additionally evangelistic or cross-cultural? As described earlier in this book, Ghillean Prance read a paper at the Au Sable Institute entitled "Missionary Earthkeeping." Prance and Au Sable founder Cal DeWitt subsequently conducted an entire forum under that title and then edited and published a book in 1992, a collection of the forum's essays. (The term was recently resurrected for use at a seminar that

Au Sable conducted at Calvin College in January 2013.) "What is 'missionary earthkeeping'?" the two editors of the book ask in the preface:

> It is mission work that honestly acts upon a full understanding of Creation, of its degradation, and of biblical principles for its proper care and keeping. It is enterprise whose goal is the wholeness, integrity, and renewal of people and Creation and their relationships with each other and the Creator; it is reconciliation of *all things* (1 Cor 15:20–22; Col 1:15–20; Rom 5).[5]

With such a wonderful explanation, and with such notable antecedents, I want to explain briefly why Eden Vigil and my book promote the terminology of environmental missions instead of missionary earthkeeping. The other great published work that uses Prance's nomenclature is *Down-to-earth Christianity: Creation-care in Ministry*, published in 2000 by the EEN for AERDO.[6] In *Down-to-earth*, the editors refer us particularly to their final chapter, which "tries to fit things together and is particularly valuable to 'ordinary everyday cross-cultural missionaries.'" They write, "We hope it will help all of us to learn to 'tread softly' on the planet God has given us to use, enjoy and care for, and to approach our respective ministries with an enlightened, scriptural attitude towards God and the Creation."[7] Years after editing *Missionary Earthkeeping*, Prance commented in an interview,

> I have seen excellent missionaries who have understood the needs and ways of local people. I have also seen mistakes. Back in the 1970s, I ran workshops and in 1993 I published a book called *Missionary Earthkeeping* to encourage people to learn the whole of what the Bible teaches about caring for God's creation—care for the environment and care for individual tribes. Nowadays the approach is better but that's a message the West still needs to hear.[8]

So I infer from these quotations that missionary earthkeeping was a vision for "ordinary, everyday cross-cultural missionaries" to reform their practices for greater creation care, a cry still vividly relevant for today. Business as usual on the missionary compound had not yet been mobilized for creation care, and in fact often harmed indigenous people and local ecospheres. In addition, DeWitt et al., owing in large part to the influence of Peter Harris, had a genuine vision for extending creation care beyond the borders of the UK, US, and Canada. Any mandate of the Creator is, by necessity, global.

I have only seen one person referred to in print as a "missionary earthkeeper." It was William Carey himself, and Cal DeWitt was the one to give him that appellation. DeWitt wrote, "William Carey, widely acknowledged as a principal founder of modern missions, was a missionary earthkeeper engaged in responsive and responsible stewardship."[9] Dennis Testerman, the author of the lead essay for the book *Missionary Earthkeeping*, came close to being known by that label. He was once introduced in print as

a commissioned agricultural missionary to Nigeria and Pakistan. Since 1990 his principal workplace has been Cabarrus Soil and Water Conservation District in Concord, North Carolina, where he continues in a bivocational ministry of missionary earthkeeping as a conservationist and public servant.

Missionary earthkeeping is identified as a ministry, but Testerman himself is considered an "agricultural missionary" and a "conservationist and public servant."

Our agenda in the early twenty-first century is to launch a new category within cross-cultural church planting missions, an agenda that isn't necessarily evident in the term "missionary earthkeeping." We are in no way contradicting DeWitt and Prance when we want to ensure that environmental missions is more than just creation care applied cross-culturally. Grammatically, the main activity in the term "missionary earthkeeping" is the "keeping of the earth." It will be easier to invest the (nonnegotiable) value of earthkeeping in a term like "environmental missions," than to infuse church planting into earthkeeping, however "missionary" that earthkeeping might be. Having said all this, I think "missionary earthkeeper" is

Appendix 2

a more evocative term. (It makes me feel like a superhero. The environmentalist Robert F. Kennedy Jr. gets to be a "riverkeeper" after all.) Nonetheless I've always gotten in trouble when I've strayed too far from the term "missionary." Accepting the baggage of the term while trying to transcend that baggage often leads me into a humility to which God applies grace. The church understands and can accommodate new categories within missions. It has a harder time with new terminology. If the great need of the ecological crisis is a rapid mobilization of workers, we are well advised to refit existing infrastructure—missionaries in missions sent through mission agencies—rather than try to introduce new conceptual entities.

Neither do I wish to stray too far from the perspective expressed by Francis Schaeffer and Udo Middelmann. If missions is, by nature, outreach, then we should stick as close as possible to the terminology that our audience is using: "environmental" and "ecological." Interestingly, the secular world has adopted the terminology of "environmental *stewardship*." Peter Illyn of Restoring Eden recently told me that many people believe Cal DeWitt should be credited "almost single-handedly" for introducing the use of the concept of stewardship so broadly among secular environmental and governmental groups. Such can be the influence of the church in society, as per Schaeffer's vision.

This whole discussion is helpful in bringing us to the essence of the definition of environment missions: it must be an integration of what we've known of gospel preaching, disciple making, and church planting missions; and what we've learned from Prance, DeWitt, and Harris of our stewardship in God's creation. The earliest reference to "environmental missions" I've ever tracked down is from Peter Harris in his essay "Creation Care and Mission," adapted from his contribution to *Down-to-earth Christianity*, and thus dated 2000. He sets the context for environmental missions by writing:

> Furthermore we understand that everything about all people is in some measure created—body, soul, spirit, person. The old and agonised discussions about the priority of evangelism over social work, and maybe the newer ones about the impor-

tance of creation care, set against evangelism, can only survive if we regard people, quite unbiblically, as souls on legs, or some other disembodied entity. God's care is manifest to all his creation, and not merely a part of it. His care is for the created person, in need of redemption in all its fullness, and not merely for some non-material entity deemed to be eternal. Moreover, the understanding that all people, in every place and in every condition, share an equal status as created beings gives us a renewed motivation for crossing cultural barriers, and reaching out everywhere with the good news.[10]

Then Harris uses the term:

> So—if we see the growth in the number of environmental missions we should rejoice, but then beware of thinking we can leave any of this to the professionals. For as we have seen, whatever our work or our life, it is inevitably something that we will all do, and the choice we face is merely whether we will do it well or badly, whether we will do justice to the gospel, or will distort it.[11]

In July 2010 Ed Brown and Eden Vigil collaborated to host the first-ever Environmental Missions Consultation. Twenty-five missions and creation care leaders convened in Manhattan, Kansas, for four days of discussions. Agencies represented included Christar, Christian Veterinary Mission, Frontiers, SIM, Wycliffe/SIL, and TEAM. People group experience included work among Hindus, Muslims, and African and Asian tribals. For creation care, the academic disciplines represented included forestry, landscape architecture, veterinary medicine, and marine biology. We were a small group, all of us middle-level managers, and we made no claim to be a grand adjudicatory body of the church. For example, our national representation was all Western: British, Canadian, American, and New Zealander. Of all the outcomes that we had hoped for from the Consultation, a workable definition of environmental missions was foremost. We didn't want to close the final session without one. I knew that so many of

our discussions would be open ended and that often we would feel like we were merely scratching the surface of a topic, but for a sense of accomplishment, nothing would serve us better than a good, agreed-upon definition. On the morning of the last day of the Consultation, I wrote a definition up on the board: *An environmental missionary is a missionary who also does environmental thingies.*

Environmental *thingies* are important: watershed management, marine protection units, sustainable subsistence farming, renewable energies. In addition to an analogy, Ed's statement about environmental missions (see chapter 2) offered an example: "In Kenya, this means reforestation." Having these examples is, I am trying to say, important. They give us a preliminary sense, as does the analogy of medical missions, of what environmental missions might look like. The definition on the board about *thingies* was meant to raise an early morning smile. It was meant to alert everyone to that day's definition-writing agenda. It was also meant to hint at some of the dangers of not possessing a definition.

In the end, one of our consultants, Dr. Katie Weakland, a professor of biology and forestry at Bethel College in Mishawaka, Indiana, offered us the best first draft from which to construct a final version. Katie had come to the Consultation with definitions of environmental missions already abuzz in her head. She regularly leads a group of her students to Hakalau Forest National Wildlife Refuge in Hawaii to participate in a rainforest reforestation project. On one May trip, they had planted 2,800 koa trees and helped to propagate endangered plants. After her last trip, Katie began to feel a vision starting to coalesce. In writing up her thoughts, she wrote:

> Here is my vision. It really fits all of my experiences and interests . . . This is it: run an 8-week summer mission program for students (or others) in environmental and ecological stewardship, to give students exposure to international conservation and missions and to serve developing countries who struggle with finances for conservation issues (kind of like "Doctors without Borders," but really "Ecologists without Borders").

I am calling it "EcoMission" right now, for lack of a better title at this time.[12]

Dr. Katie Weakland, holding up a scrap of paper from the back of the room, is the last bit of background imagery behind the definition that is offered in this book, a definition that is more than just the product of my, the author of this book's, conceptualization. This definition, as unpacked in chapter 2, has the weight of progression, reflection, comparison, and collaboration.

To conclude this appendix, I want acknowledge two earlier calls for environmental missions, namely, those of Luther Copeland and Dana Robert. As early as 1985, Copeland, missions leader in the Southern Baptist Convention, wrote:

> No doubt many missionaries, like [William] Carey, especially agriculturists, have been actively engaged in protecting the environment. Most, however, like other Westerners, have been indifferent to environmental issues. Earthkeeping now should be seen as an essential part of the Christian mission. There is a call for Christians who will give themselves specifically to this vocation and for some to fulfill this calling as cross-cultural missionaries. The larger summons is for all of us to support this aspect of the Christian mission and to contribute to it according to our abilities.[13]

Dana Robert, professor of world Christianity and history of mission at Boston University, mentioned environmental mission in her keynote address at Edinburgh 2010. In an earlier speech, however, she made a comment about categorical inevitability:

> Both the history of missions, and contemporary concern for the environment show that a beneficial relationship with nature is intrinsic to mission "best practices"—whether framed as human survival or for the sake of God's creation itself. The days are gone when an abundance of forest and wildlife can be seen as the "howling wilderness" waiting to be subdued

Appendix 2

for Christian civilization. In a context of overpopulation and environments on the edge of extinction, the paradigms of stewardship need to replace those of dominion. The question before us is how—not when, or even whether—evangelical missions will enter the realm of earth care, for "eco" projects are springing up in missions like mushrooms after the rain. It is time that a mission forum or formal clearinghouse be established to study, to collect examples of best practices, and to give solid practical and theological advice to missionaries who find themselves of choice or by necessity entering the realm of earth care.[14]

NOTES

1. Lynn Townsend White Jr., "The Historical Roots of Our Ecologic Crisis," *Science* 155, no. 3767 (March 10, 1967): 1203–7.
2. Schaeffer, *Pollution*, 9.
3. Loren Wilkinson, preface to *Earthkeeping in the '90s*, ed. Loren Wilkinson (Grand Rapids: Eerdmans, 1991), x.
4. Dean Ohlman, "What Is Creation Care?," Wonder of Creation, June 26, 2011, http://wonderofcreation.org/2011/06/26/what-is-creation-care (accessed May 18, 2013).
5. Calvin B. DeWitt and Ghillean T. Prance, "Preface," *Missionary Earthkeeping*, eds. Calvin B. DeWitt and Ghillean T. Prance (Macon: Mercer University Press, 1992), ix.
6. W. Dayton Roberts and Paul E. Pretiz, eds., *Down-to-earth Christianity: Creation-Care in Ministry* (Wynnewood, PA: EEN, 2000).
7. Roberts and Pretiz, *Down-to-earth Christianity*, 4.
8. Ghillean Prance, "Faith v Science?," interview by Nigel Bovey, *Rejesus* (blog), http://www.rejesus.co.uk/site/module/faith_v_science/P7 (accessed October 5, 2011).
9. Calvin B. DeWitt, "Contemporary Missiology and the Biosphere," in *Antioch Agenda: Essays on the Restorative Church in Honor of Orlando E. Costas*, eds. Daniel Jeyaraj, Robert W. Pazmino, and Rodney L. Petersen (New Delhi: ISPCK, 2007), 322.

10. Peter Harris, "Creation Care and Mission," A Rocha, http://www.arocha.org/int-en/3286-DSY.html (accessed October 5, 2011).

11. Ibid.

12. Katie Weakland, email message to author, June 29, 2010.

13. Luther Copeland, *World Mission, World Survival* (Nashville: Broadman, 1985), 123.

14. Dana L. Robert, "Historical Trends in Missions and Earth Care," *International Bulletin of Missionary Research* 35, no. 3 (July 2011): 128.

APPENDIX 3

Lessons from Four Environmental Mission Leaders

I t's been my privilege to meet each of the four leaders who are profiled in this appendix. My first encounter with each of them, though, was through writings by or about them. (In Dr. Val Shean's case, it was a DVD documentary.) In each case, their involvement in environmental missions is introduced in the form of a memoir. In other words, we are invited to hear their stories and learn from them. And that's how I've chosen to write up this appendix: as a chance for environmental missionaries to learn from four remarkable teachers.

Peter Harris, A Rocha:
Conservation and a Philosophy of Ministry[a]

The 2010 Prairie Festival at the Land Institute was an august gathering—this, despite meeting in a barn on a small research station just a few miles south of Salina, Kansas. Of course the Land Institute itself brings its own *gravitas*; it is the home of MacArthur Genius winners and National Geographic fellows, plant geneticists assiduously attending to the development of "perennials grown in polycultures," food crops which can grow back and be harvested each year without violence to the soil. The conference was also weighty because of the list of speakers. No less a personage than Wendell

---

[a] A full account of Peter Harris' environmental missions and the organization A Rocha can be found in Harris' two books: *Under the Bright Wings* (Vancouver, Canada: Regent College Publishing, 1993) and *Kingfisher's Fire* (Oxford: Monarch, 2008).

Berry, Kentucky farmer and essayist, gave Saturday morning's keynote address. He was followed by ecological economist Josh Farley, toxicologist Sandra Steingraber, conservationist Scott Russell Sanders, seed saver Kent Whealey, and finally Land Institute founder himself, Wes Jackson, named in 2005 by Smithsonian Magazine as one of "35 who made a difference." Sanders began his talk,

> So considering what I would say here today and imagining the audience I would be saying it to, I wanted to avoid repeating the bad news about the planet that you already know. I wanted to offer an uplifting speech and even if possible an amusing speech, but I couldn't get the bad news out of my head.[1]

He was speaking to a similarly dispirited audience. For all the joy of camping in a hayfield, drinking coffee in the orchard, and sitting in a barn on a pleasant autumn day listening to some of the most articulate ecologists on the planet, September 2010 was a gloomy month for environmentalists. The year began with the failure of climate change talks in Copenhagen. No one knew what was worse: the Gulf Oil spill or how quickly it faded from American consciousness. Any sort of energy bill in the Senate fizzled out that summer without a floor debate, ignored by a much-hoped-for president who no longer seemed interested. It's not surprising that after each speaker at the Prairie Festival finished reading from his or her notes, as questions were sought from the audience, people would invariably ask, "Where's the hope?" Where do you see hope? It rarely sounded like a question. It was a plea. Give us hope!

Each speaker tried his or her hardest. Unabated mountaintop removal mining in Kentucky still makes Wendell Berry angry. Now, at eighty-two years of age, it also seems to make him weary. But Berry probably rivals Pope John Paul II in being our era's most prolific writer on hope. "Hope is a duty," he has admonished. That four-word statement has been adopted by many as a byword. The Land Institute itself is predicated on hope. Jackson knew from the beginning that the nature of cross-breeding wheat and perennial prairie grass varieties would require at least fifty years of patient har-

Appendix 3

vest, sorting, and replanting. So each speaker tried valiantly. Some spoke of the hope gained by witnessing emerging local environmental efforts. Others spoke of hope in the younger generation's intuitive grasp of creation care. Still others helpfully answered, "You are not responsible to save the planet; just do right."

Centuries earlier, the Apostle Paul told us where to find hope: "Indeed, we felt we had received the sentence of death. But this happened that we might not rely on ourselves but on God, who raises the dead. He has delivered us from such a deadly peril, and he will deliver us again. On him we have set our hope that he will continue to deliver us" (2 Cor 1:9,10). Our hope is in Christ. And our hope encompasses creation.

> For the creation waits in eager expectation for the children of God to be revealed. For the creation was subjected to frustration, not by its own choice, but by the will of the one who subjected it, in hope that the creation itself will be liberated from its bondage to decay and brought into the freedom and glory of the children of God.
>
> We know that the whole creation has been groaning as in the pains of childbirth right up to the present time. Not only so, but we ourselves, who have the firstfruits of the Spirit, groan inwardly as we wait eagerly for our adoption to sonship, the redemption of our bodies. For in this hope we were saved. But hope that is seen is no hope at all. Who hopes for what they already have? But if we hope for what we do not yet have, we wait for it patiently. (Rom 8:19–25)

What do Christians bring to creation care that other environmental leaders cannot bring? We bring the hope that is found in Christ Jesus, the Creator, Sustainer, and Redeemer of all creation. If so, then an Anglican pastor and lifelong birdwatcher like Peter Harris must have an inside track on understanding hope. To wake up on a freezing cold morning, pull on one's Wellington boots and woolen jumper, and trudge, binoculars in hand, out into the marshlands in search of one flitting glimpse of a tiny winged creature, must represent a spiritual discipline particularly suited to hope. Peter Harris founded the Christian conservation trust A Rocha in 1983. Every environmental missionary should have an early encounter with Peter Harris. (Greg Parsons of the US Center for World Mission calls him "the Ralph Winter of the environment.")[2] Hope sustains any environmental career, and Harris knows where to find it.

Whenever I introduce someone new to A Rocha, our conversation follows a predictable pattern. First, I give the name. Then we have to clarify the pronunciation: *uh-RAW-sha*. Then I have to explain: "It's Portuguese; it means 'the rock.'" As quickly as possible I follow up with their positioning statement, *A Rocha: Christians in Conservation*. Finally, I get a chance to explain, though I doubt if I do it as succinctly as their current published statement: A Rocha is "an international family of conservation organizations working to show God's love for all creation through community-based efforts." Most people assume correctly that "the Rock" is a reference to Jesus, and not to Alcatraz. Actually, the first reference in the organization to A Rocha is of *Quinta da Rocha*, a peninsula in Portugal between two rivers of an estuary, near where Harris would launch his first field study center. "We decided to adopted the name A Rocha, the Rock, for the project," Harris claims, "because it seemed to do justice to all that we were planning—the beginning of field studies, geology, and the only sure foundation for the whole of life, the Rock who is Christ."[3]

Back in the early 1980s, Peter Harris was serving as the curate in an Anglican parish in Merseyside, UK. He was content to be in the ministry, but found his soul flitting whenever he saw a bird take wing. Once, he organized a group of students who were doing environmentally related courses and took them on a bird watching expedition to southern Sweden. "For many students," he commented, "the only Christian teaching that they heard on Creation had to do with the contentious issue of its origins. There was little interest in the environment or concern about the present disasters overtaking the world that Christians believed God had made."[4] Among those on the expedition was a zoologist, Les Batty, who served for Harris the role of a friend who helps define and bless. Batty was a big

fan of Francis Schaeffer's L'Abri, a retreat center in Switzerland, and proposed a nature field study center characterized by Christian scholarship and Christian hospitality. Batty reawakened a longstanding tension for Harris. "Some years before, we had decided not to look for work in nature conservation, but to give our full energies to what we then understood as 'full-time Christian work.'" Peter and Miranda Harris applied to the Bible Churchman's Missionary Society to serve as Anglican missionaries in Tanzania, possibly to pastor a church and to help with theological education. Nonetheless they began to pray some sheepish private prayers and drop some quiet hints. Perhaps the Lord would sovereignly direct them back to conservation, or—greatest of hopes!—they might be able to do both: ministry and creation care. At one point Harris asked Batty whether he still intended to open a field study center in Northumberland. When Batty said yes, Harris replied, "Pity about that. Not that it isn't a wonderful area, but it's just that there are a lot of field centres in the UK already, and not many in the south of Europe. Ditto committed Christians. Ever thought of Portugal?"[5]

There it is! The first statement from which a whole philosophy of ministry would eventually emerge. Peter Harris refuses to separate conservation from the missionary movement. "Since student days," he writes, "when I had seen something of the struggles of tiny churches in Asia, I had had an unsophisticated conviction that it was better to spend your life where Christian resources were limited."[6]

The Lord of the harvest did intervene in the decision of an African bishop who didn't think his diocese could offer placement as previously planned to the Harrises. They were free to explore other options, and quite quickly proposed a survey trip to Igreja Lusitana, the Anglican communion in Portugal. They found the Portuguese church welcoming. Interestingly, all of their clergy, including the bishop, had other full-time jobs and so could understand a priest who wanted to be bivocational as a conservationist. Secondly,

> they were not holding to a definitely traditional evangelical
> line that might have made them cautious about a Christian

centre given over to environmental issues, although they were looking for help from BCMS which was clearly evangelical. Maybe like us they were pleasantly surprised by the changes that were taking place in evangelical thinking.[7]

The Algrave region of Portugal's coastline is home to a large volume of migratory bird traffic. "Strategically paced in the southwesternmost corner of continental Europe, the area was ideal for studies of migration. The mix of Atlantic and Mediterranean habitat types gave it a particular character, and there was work to do on nearly every aspect of its natural history." The result of their survey trip, and the blessing of BCMS and Igreja Lusitana, was the formation of a field study center on the Alvor estuary, which finally settled near the village of Cruzinha, all supported by a charitable trust in the UK given the name A Rocha. Harris admits, "We were greatly helped also by the august group who agreed to join our Council, because at first we faced questions about the seriousness of any 'mission work' that was concerned with the environment and the protection of wildlife." Theologian John Stott, whose passion for ornithology Harris claims is "almost legendary," was one of these early supporters.[8]

In 1983 the Harris family and their team moved to Portugal, engaging what all missionaries have experienced as priority number one upon arrival: language study. But it wasn't long before they were happily out in the marshland doing bird surveys, tagging migratory species, collecting data. And it wasn't long before conservation students, whether from Portugal or abroad, found their way to Cruzinha, not only for field study but for Bible study. The field study center remains A Rocha's primary model of ministry, even after twenty years of expansion to nineteen other countries. In creation care ministry, their purpose is to apply knowledge to local conservation issues. Early on in Portugal, A Rocha visited a nearby marsh that "was alive with migrant waders": collared pratincoles, whimbrels, purple herons, little bitterns, black terns, and little gulls. On a return visit, they were surprised to discover red and white surveyor markers. The marsh was eventually drained in order to build a golf course to support the burgeoning tourist industry. The development had apparently been permitted

because the government biologist who filed the report claimed, "The area was occasionally used by gulls and nothing else."[9] Often the effect of an A Rocha field study center, particularly in the early years, was to encourage young conservation movements in their host countries. The A Rocha field study center near Bannerghatta National Park in South India studies elephants and Indian star tortoises, as well as monitoring birds, plants, and butterflies. One film they've produced is entitled *Elephants and Farmers: Can They Co-exist?*

"All conservation is local." This is a statement traceable to columnist Thomas Friedman, but has been used more widely.[10] It was an early discovery of A Rocha as well. During a heated debate over a proposal for a nature reserve in Alvor, Harris felt not only his weakness but that of the government in Lisbon. He concluded,

> The only ones left with any credibility in the argument were those for whom Albor was their *terra*, their own place. The right to contribute was earned by having lived there, and not by being important elsewhere. Jesus chose to be unimportant in Jerusalem or Rome in order to be in Galilee with the unimportant, and that is how mission will always be best conducted. It has also been of some consolation at times when we have felt most useless. "Well at least we are here," we have thought, "and if we weren't, there would be no one else for a few miles in each direction able to explain about Jesus, if anyone should ever want to know."

> This was the part of our work which was more easily understood by many of those who were supporting A Rocha. As we slowly worked towards fluency, our aim was to gain an understanding of the local and national church and the different organizations that work within it in order to see what our contribution could be. This was not, however, the "Christian side" to our work. It was simply an important band in the spectrum of work to which we were called.[11]

❧ ENVIRONMENTAL MISSIONS ❧

The evangelism and discipleship component in A Rocha, as expressed through the field study centers, might best be understood as the successful replication of L'Abri's model of ministry. If you build it, they will come . . . and they'll stay for a while, and they'll watch you at work and worship, and they'll ask the questions they never felt safe asking elsewhere. *They* refers to anyone who knocked at the front door—so long as they had a genuine environmental interest and weren't simply tourists. Many visitors were Portuguese; others were British and other nationalities. Many were unbelievers who had never heard the gospel. Others were believers who had never heard that their conservation interest could be an integral component of their love for Christ. The field study center in Cruzinha considered themselves part of the Christian outreach of Igreja Lusitana.

> The needs of the Christian world seemed as overwhelming as those of the conservation groups. We could only hope to help and support a few people even when we were well established, so it seemed sensible to concentrate our limited efforts in three areas: first, in student work, with Christians encouraging them to relate their beliefs to the rapidly changing society around them, but also with others to present a clear statement of the meaning of Christian belief; secondly, in building interdenominational bridges so that we could help out wherever we were asked; and thirdly, in establishing a local church among our friends and neighbours. Over the years we have probably done only the first, which was the easiest, halfway reasonably, but our intentions have remained the same as those we established at the beginning in Vila Verde.[12]

Harris keeps returning to the church planting potential of environmental missions. Commenting in 1993 on the twelve ladies, one elderly man, and various Portuguese children who made up the congregation of their monthly Sunday service, Harris wrote,

> In our defence I have to say that for most Portuguese towns that is a reasonable sized Protestant church, and in Yemeni

terms it would be a revival. Either way that's where we are. We have often thought that we have not so much planted a church as dug a hole where in time one might be planted.[13]

I would love to commission a graduate student to write his or her dissertation on A Rocha's model of ministry. John Stott could get the researcher started: "As for methods of evangelism, an activity which Peter Harris clearly and rightly distinguishes from both propaganda and proselytism, he lays his emphasis on the importance of the Christian community."[14] An equally worthy field of study would be Harris' whole philosophy of ministry. (Dave Bookless is also a prolific writer for A Rocha.) Perhaps because Harris has so often felt the need to justify his conservation work, even in the early years to his own soul, no environmental missionary seems to have such a fully embodied philosophy of ministry as Peter Harris. Harris speaks of the word "missionary" as "that unfortunate but apparently indispensable term," and wants to promote the broader implications of *mission* (as compared to traditional *missions* with an *-s* at the end), working not only in the church, but also in the world. "Mission is not defined," he writes, "by any particular activity (although some, such as witnessing to Jesus, will be common to them all), but by the clear intention to live out what the Kingdom of God means."[15] While mission will not necessarily require the crossing of cultural boundaries, Harris believes the call of the least reached will likely necessitate it. A Rocha's expansion to such countries as Lebanon, India, or Uganda is evidence of the Spirit's guidance. In fact, Harris believes there are three reasons why conservation is so conducive to missions work: (1) it's international; (2) by its nature, it's religious; (3) with field study centers, you can constantly be with people.[16] According to Greg Parsons, "On almost every project they have done, they [A Rocha] see people come to the Lord: either those they are helping or others with concern about the environment who are shocked to find believers involved."[17] That's the power of hope.

❧ ENVIRONMENTAL MISSIONS ❧

Scott Sabin, Plant With Purpose:
Reforestation and a Model of Ministry[b]

Scott Sabin is the executive director of Plant With Purpose, a Christian NGO that seeks to alleviate rural poverty primarily through the planting of trees. Many of its field operations still use the old organizational name Floresta. Among the wonderful things about Plant With Purpose is its website (http://www.plantwithpurpose.org), a pleasant place to visit where they get their message across in the simplest of terms. For example, their fundraising campaign is called "Trees Please," and on the day that I'm writing this, you could see on the website that their staff has planted 5,801,172 trees since 1984, primarily in Burundi, Tanzania, Thailand, Haiti, Dominican Republic, and Mexico. That's some serious acreage.

It's ironic that Sabin, one of the highest profile environmental missionaries, didn't start out particularly creation care–minded, and even now experiences moments of skepticism about environmental action. "I was a sailor," he told me. He graduated from college and was commissioned into the Navy on the same day, spending seven years in service, three of them at sea. He was a gunnery and ordinance officer on a frigate and later, when he switched to shore duty, he helped train in carrier battle group tactics. "I look back," he says, "and can see that it's surprisingly related to what I do now. I had a sense of mission, a sense of duty. It was the Cold War, and I asked myself, 'What is the central conflict?' 'What is the best way of *saving the world?*'"

Sabin went on to study for a master's degree in international politics. To help fulfill a foreign language requirement, he traveled to Guatemala. "In many ways my journey toward becoming an environmentalist began when I spent a summer in a Spanish immersion program in Guatemala," he admits, but it was still a journey, and one that had only just begun, and one that would first go through the topic of poverty alleviation before

---

[b] A full account of Scott Sabin's environmental missions and the organization Plant with a Purpose can be found in Sabin's book *Tending to Eden: Environmental Stewardship for God's People* (Valley Forge, PA: Judson, 2010).

ending up at environmental missions. One weekend, in the middle of his studies, Sabin visited a dump in Guatemala City. He watched the ragpickers and their children ply what he had a hard time calling "their trade." He found himself reflecting on a slightly revised question, "What is the *real* conflict in this world?" He writes, "When Jesus described the place of damnation, he called it *Gehenna*—the name of the garbage dump outside of Jerusalem. The image of hell as a refuse pile took on new meaning for me. This place was as close to hell on earth as I could imagine."[18]

What I love about Scott Sabin's personal story is the difficulty he has in acknowledging all the influences—that is, keeping track of every last one of them—that brought him face-to-face with creation care and missions. It sounds so typical of all of us, and of how God chooses to guide, Damascus Road experiences being so few and far between. God taps us on our shoulder and we turn, degree by degree of angle, until we are finally pointed in the direction he intends. In his book *Tending to Eden*, Sabin fills four pages with one thought-provoking incident after another, one seemingly no more influential than the other: the garbage dump, a ragpicker's school, Pastor Salomón Hernández, a bus trip to a mountain village, a Wycliffe widow, Canadian latrine builders, a missionary under death threats, (and then upon returning to the States) Mother Teresa, a chance sermon by Tony Campolo, the riots in L.A., a pastor's unfortunate building program, reading in Luke and Isaiah. "What happened," Sabin summarizes, "is that I had my eyes opened to living out faith on the edge. I had heard people talk about the 'adventure of the Christian walk,' but I had never experienced it." Growing up in Southern California, he felt that "comfortable Christians had reduced faith to praying for a parking space." At the *Gehenna* on the edge of Guatemala City, Sabin concluded, "God was there." It was a chance to be part of the light shining in the darkness.

"Looking for a way to spend myself for the hungry," Sabin says, "I began volunteering for Plant With Purpose, simply because it was the Christian antipoverty organization closest to my home. Mine was a humble beginning: stuffing response cards into envelopes and calling donors." We other humble beginners in environmental missions need to hear such stories. Sabin was still not an environmentalist. He was a sailor with a heart for the poor. His father wasn't particularly encouraging, telling him at one point, "Planting trees for Jesus? That's as marginal as you can get."[19] Sabin in fact was looking for an organization that was more traditionally humanitarian. "When did you make the switch?" I asked him. "It was gradual," he said. "A major catalyst was my first trip to Haiti, when I saw mile after mile of barren hillside." He remembers meeting Christian ecologist Cal DeWitt for the first time and hearing him speak. And he remembers witnessing the repeated success of Plant With Purpose's ministry model. "The poor farmers, their only assets are the soil and the rain that collects on it. We were seeing actual transformations." Even now, Sabin admits to lapsing into some environmental skepticism, but then he hears himself giving a presentation, and he finds himself reconvinced. "At first, my environmentalism was utilitarian," meaning he valued creation's restoration as a means to alleviate poverty. But then, under endless influences, Sabin began to see the truth of God's pronouncement over creation: "It is good."

If Peter Harris and A Rocha can introduce us to a philosophy of ministry, Plant With Purpose can introduce us to an equally solid model of ministry. The model is more than just reforestation, which is simply a form. Of course, reforestation as a form strongly recommends itself. Eden Reforestation Projects is a related ministry. ERP founder Steve Fitch has acquired similar evidence of reforestation's power to bless:

> In September 2004, I was requested by President Haile Marium of the Southern Peoples Region of Ethiopia to take over an abandoned seedling nursery that was associated with a desperately needed reforestation project. The President reported that villages near Hawassa had experienced loss of life from flooding, serous erosion, soil degradation, and declining water tables. All of these symptoms were connected to destruction of the region's forest. The diagnosis was tragic; if things didn't improve, the villagers would become eco-refugees. So, the challenge was accepted and Eden Reforestation Projects (ERP) was born, and in the last six years over 22 million new

trees have been planted in Ethiopia, Madagascar, and Haiti. Today, the flooding around the reforestation sites in Ethiopia has stopped. The soil quality has been enhanced, the farming has greatly improved, the water tables are rising, and the animal life is returning to a restored eco-system. All of this dramatic ecological healing is the result of employing over 3,000 Ethiopian "eco-workers" who desperately needed a job.[20]

I would characterize the ministry model of reforesters like Plant With Purpose and ERP as "simple solutions directed to root causes." Thoreau supplies the quotation that, despite the irony, may stand as their banner: "For every thousand hacking at the leaves of evil, there is one striking at the root." The founder of Plant With Purpose is not the envelope-stuffing, socially awakened Scott Sabin, but rather a San Diego businessman named Tom Woodard. In 1979 Woodard went to the Dominican Republic as a part of a relief team following the devastation of Hurricane David. He found himself frustrated with the limited goals and long-term ineffectiveness of food distribution. He sought to understand the roots of Dominican poverty. Succinctly stated, "The people were without food because deforestation made the land too poor to farm." Deforestation contributes to degradation, first of farmland, then of communities, in numerous ways. Healthy forests prevent erosion, retain water in the soil, stabilize rainfall patterns, filter out impurities from drinking water, and filter out pollution in the air. Forests also prevent a whole second tier of misfortunes:

> Deforestation hurts us all, but especially the poor who cannot afford to have water piped into the home or to buy bottled water to drink. Instead, family members, mainly the women, walk hours to fetch water and the firewood necessary to boil it to make it safe to drink. As firewood becomes scarcer, costing more time and money, people are less likely to boil their water or adequately cook their food, compounding health risks and contributing to the downward cycle of desperation. Families

who have no safety net are forced to take greater risks with their health and the well being of their families.[21]

If the problem is "not enough trees," then the solution is seemingly simple: "trees please." What could be simpler than to dig a hole and plant a seedling? Of course, forestry has its complexity, and the issue of invasive species should be well heeded. Many missionaries have been hoodwinked by the fast-growing eucalyptus tree, but this Australian export is notoriously thirsty. An African woman once told Ed Brown, "If your neighbor has a eucalyptus tree, forget it. Your own farm will be dry." But for whatever complication forestry might send our way, nothing compares to an encounter with the cycle of poverty among the rural poor, and poverty's accompanying mentality. How do you treat poverty in a country like Haiti without creating "a nation of beggars," as has often been the accusation? Sabin's book *Tending to Eden* is not a tree-planting manual. It reads like a companion piece to Corbett and Fikkert's book *When Helping Hurts*, or the more sweeping and secular *Dead Aid: Why Aid Is Not Working and How There Is a Better Way for Africa* (by Dambisa Moyo).[22] One of Sabin's more memorable stories is of the Haitian woman who listened in at the meeting where Plant With Purpose proposed tree planting in their village. She confronted them. Numerous aid agencies had been through the region, bringing food and clothes, but leaving and never returning. How would Plant With Purpose be different? Sabin told her, "Well, first of all, we are not going to give you anything." As she soaked that in, he said, "Second, we are not going to leave until you ask us to." Sabin reflects, "Once we understand God's heart for justice and the vicious cycle of deforestation and poverty that traps the poor, how do we respond? The desire to help is admirable in a world where far too many pass by on the other side of the road. But determining how to respond can be complicated."[23]

Sabin, like many devoted development specialists, expresses frustration at poverty's complexity, but it seems to me that the genius of Plant With Purpose's ministry model is to let the complexity reside in the search for root causes, while applying a noncomplex solution to each level of causation that they discover. For example, we could conclude that *a* root cause—without

assuming that it is *the* root cause—of hunger among Haitian farmers is that they don't grow enough food. A simple solution is to simply pass out food to the hungry farmers, something that Plant With Purpose is quite happy to participate in when rescue efforts like the 2010 earthquake dictate it. But bravely facing the complexity encourages Plant With Purpose to look for one more root cause, the next one. Why can't Haitian farmers grow enough food? Because the soil is poor? Why is the soil poor? Because of erosion? Why the erosion? No tree roots to hold the soil in place. At this level of exploration, the simple solution is to plant trees, and so Plant With Purpose has done so—hundreds of thousands of them since 1984. But you can't stop there. Deforestation is a problem, but what's the root cause of the deforestation in this particular locale? Cattle grazing? Commercial logging? Agricultural clearing? Firewood and charcoal production? There are root causes behind each of these root causes. What is the new simple solution to implement at the next layer of complexity?

As a result of this ministry model, it would be inaccurate to say that Plant With Purpose plants trees. They don't plant trees; the farmers they work with do. In his "One Year Later" report, Sabin announced from Haiti:

> Since the earthquake, we have raised over $1 million for im-
> mediate relief efforts, which were used to distribute over 107
> tons of seed to rural communities and to employ 4,300 people
> through our "Cash for Work" program. In the last year, the
> farmers we work with planted 540,000 trees and constructed
> nearly 600 miles of soil conservation barriers. As a result of
> these efforts, thousands of families were able to feed their
> households, as well as the Internally Displaced People (IDP)
> who came to live with them after fleeing Port au Prince. They
> also experienced improved health and increased incomes.[24]

A "Cash for Work" program is a simple solution for one of the root causes of deforestation—the farmers think they can get more income only by clearing more cropland, even the marginally fertile hillsides. Haitians

apparently have a saying: "Either this tree must die, or I must die in its place."

I would restate the ministry model this way: build simplicity into solutions, channel all complexity into the next layer of root cause. When you discover that next root cause, build simplicity into *its* solution, and channel the complexity into another systematic, discerning search for the *next* layer of root cause. All along we pray for the success of our solutions, and wisdom for our searching. Too often we get it the other way around. We apply simplicity to the root causes because we assume we see the whole picture. Then we build increasing complexity into our solutions, particularly when the inadequacies of those solutions begin to be revealed, as they must. Applying simple solutions to the deepest level of underlying cause that one discovers means that a missionary need not be paralyzed. There's always something we can do to roll up our sleeves and be helpful. But being on a relentless search for the next layer means you have a greater chance at effective ministry. Hacking at the leaves takes just as much energy as chopping at the roots, with very little revitalizing sense that we are actually making a difference. Leaves grow back. How much of missionary burnout is the result of efforts that are actually simple enough as a solution, but inadequate for the next layer of complexity? Environmental missions is well positioned to be a relentless searcher of root causes. Such tenacity is grounded in modern environmentalism's founding mythology, in particular Rachel Carson's discovery of the effects of DDT as the cause of the loss of songbirds, a silent spring. Ecologists are detectives.

A final word from Scott Sabin:

> It is easy to romanticize the poor, their communities, and their traditional beliefs. It is just as easy to demonize a whole culture, people, and way of life. We must avoid either extreme.

> Rather, we must be confident in the truth and goodness of the gospel we've been given to proclaim while being respectful of both the people and the work God is doing in their midst. As we humbly share the hope Christ has given us, we become

more aware of our own cultural and spiritual blind spots. We must remember that we are not the saviors, Jesus is. And spiritual development is a process of mutual discovery and growth in the body of Christ.[25]

Craig Sorley, Care of Creation Kenya: Sustainable Agriculture and a Model of Discipleship[c]

Craig Sorley's story was encapsulated in the paragraphs of *Time* magazine, when he was named one of their "Environmental Heroes of 2008."

Craig Sorley's conversion to environmentalism came after doctors removed a tumor from his brain. It was 1989 and Sorley was a student at a Christian college in St. Paul, Minn. As he recuperated, Sorley says he "sensed a very clear call" to find out what Christians were doing to solve the world's environmental problems. "It was one of the most defining moments in my life in terms of my walk with Christ."

Sorley's revelation was an unusual one. Environmentalists and Evangelicals come from very different traditions: many greens are dismissive of conservative Christians' creationist beliefs, which are starkly at odds with scientific views on evolution. Sorley believes he can bridge this divide, bringing the two groups together by emphasizing the common goal of saving the planet.

Soft-spoken and reflective, Sorley is an environmentalist who cites chapter and verse to push his point. From his office outside Nairobi, Kenya, he's working to convince conservative Christians that it's their God-given duty to care for the earth.

---

[c] A full account of Craig Sorley's environmental missions and the organization Care of Creation Kenya can be found in Sorley's two books: *Christ and Creation* (Nairobi: Care of Creation, 2009) and *Farming that Brings Glory to God and Hope to the Hungry* (South Hadley, MA: Doorlight, 2011).

"God was the first gardener and the first farmer," Sorley says, and it's man's responsibility to tend God's garden.

Sorley's group, Care of Creation Kenya, organizes conferences and seminars in East Africa and the US. Participants have included Kenyan Nobel prizewinner Wangari Maathai and Anglican Archbishop Benjamin Nzimbi. But Sorley's primary occupation is to use the Bible to make an environmental case: God delighted in his creation (Genesis 1:31) and put man in his garden "to work it and take care of it" (Genesis 2:15); Jesus found more glory in the wonders of nature than in the constructions of man (Matthew 6:28,29); all things were created by Christ and for Christ (Colossians 1:16). Conservative Evangelicals are far more receptive to an environmental message, explains Sorley, when it's presented to them in "the language they appreciate most . . . the language of the Bible."

After his bout with cancer, Sorley dropped out of his Christian college (it didn't offer classes in environmental science) and enrolled at the University of Minnesota. "In the '90s, nobody in my church would ever want to talk about this issue," he says. But the tide may be turning. Last year, the National Association of Evangelicals, a grouping of 45,000 American churches, declared "creation care" one of its top priorities, and Christian colleges now offer degrees in environmental science. Still, a lot of work remains to be done before conservative Christians embrace conservation as a matter of faith. Says Sorley: "Our worldview on this topic is still more often defined by politics, by secular economic thought, by our materialistic culture, and by a knee-jerk reaction to the extreme ends of the environmental movement, than it is by Scripture." He's preaching to change that.[26]

In environmental missions, look for the convergence of three stories: (1) of the individual, (2) of the land, and (3) of the Bible, both Old and New Testaments. What the *TIME* magazine article doesn't mention of Sorley's personal story is that he grew up in Africa (Ethiopia, Uganda, and Kenya). "Growing up in Africa," he writes, "afforded me with a privilege that few boys from the West can enjoy. One of those privileges was the opportunity to witness firsthand the glory and beauty of God as seen in the unique wildlife found here." Being the son of medical missionaries also influenced him toward environmental missions, and he lists three lessons that his parents' ministry taught him: (1) that God loves the whole person; (2) that training local believers produces the best results; and (3) that, as in the AIDS crisis, commitment to Christ can transform society.

Sorley found one other thing: a friend who blessed his interests. Simon Thomsett, according to Sorley, is "East Africa's expert on birds of prey," and introduced the teenager to the sport of falconry. Thomsett took Sorley on excursions throughout Africa's wild places, and also helped him begin to develop his "story of the land." "During these months I began to learn more about the new crisis that was unfolding in this part of Africa, which took on new meaning as I was on the verge of entering the next chapter in my life." That next chapter was his cancer, experiencing in his own body what he was seeing in the land. And then experiencing that same hope of healing. He's been cancer free for over twenty years. Could the ancient land of Kenya also have its "youth renewed like the eagles"? After treatment, a return to Kenya and a reunion with Thomsett helped him interpret his story:

> Together Simon and I spent long hours reflecting on the beauty and wonder of Africa, its landscapes, its birds and wildlife, its rivers and forests, and how that beauty and diversity was so essential to the well-being of Africa's people. Unfortunately, we also grieved over the fact that this beauty was fading, and it was fading fast. What struck me most deeply one day was a question that Simon posed. "What are Christians doing about these issues? They don't seem to care at all about what is hap-

pening to the environment!" Little did Simon know how God would use that question to strengthen and confirm the calling I had sensed in the hospital. It would serve to fan the fire that had already been lit within my heart, leading to a conviction that would direct the course of my life.[27]

Sorley's subsequent training at the University of Minnesota means that when he tells the story of the land it will be done in terms of charts and tables and yields of beans per acre. In Kenya's villages, large gunnysacks are often used to measure yields. It's not a precise measurement, but it does work for comparisons, and it jogs the memories of the old farmers whom Sorley interviewed. In one community, maize yields had dropped from thirty bags/acre in the 1980s and early '90s to a current average yield of seven bags/acre. Beans had fallen from a harvest of twenty bags/acre to five. Potatoes: one hundred bags/acre to ten bags/acre. In other words, the same plot of ground is only providing 10–25 percent of the food that it used to supply. Meanwhile, the population of Kenya has increased. At one point in the 1980s, Kenya's 4 percent population growth rate was the highest in the world. Decreased yields, according to Sorley, are

> understandable given the fact that many landscapes in East Africa have been continuously cropped, year after year, without rest. Compounding the problem are the rapid rates of deforestation, the erosion that follows, the intensification of farming practices due to a rapidly growing population, the growing scarcity of productive and arable land, more frequent droughts, and the increasingly erratic nature of rainfall patterns.[28]

The story of the land cannot be captured totally in statistical analysis. Sorley collects stories from old farmers and retired missionaries. He collects mentors like Dr. Dan Fountain, Baptist community development veteran from Central Africa, who wrote *Let's Restore Our Land*, a story itself of a rural church leader.[29] Sometimes the story of the land gets told through one special walk through the woods. That was the experi-

ence of Brian Oldrieve, a pioneer in zero-tillage farming and another of Sorley's mentors. Back in the 1970s, Oldrieve was farming near Harare, Zimbabwe. Growing increasingly discouraged at lower and lower crop yields, one day Oldrieve went for a walk at the edge of a field. "I would go into the virgin bush for times of prayer," Oldrieve reflected, "and one day God began to reveal to me His ways in nature (Romans 1:19–22)."[30] As Sorley narrated the story to me, Oldrieve stopped and looked over into the forest and saw the lush fertility of even the ground cover. Then he looked over at his fields, dry and eroding. "That over there," he said to himself, referring to the forest, "is untouched by human hand. The only farmer that land has known is God himself." He then began to ask himself, if God farms, then how does he do it differently from me? In Oldrieve's own words, "There I saw that there is no mechanism in nature in which the soil is inverted and that there is a thick blanket of fallen leaves and grass which covers the surface of the soil."[31] Oldrieve had heard of the agricultural practice of zero tillage, but when he brought the idea to a local research authority he was told that "it wasn't feasible for our region." "I was in such a desperate situation," he writes, "that I thought I must try and God gave me the faith to launch out."[32] Beginning with small test plots, simply planting next year's seed straight into the wheat straw from the previous crop proved so successful that within six years, one thousand hectares of the farm were under zero tillage, and the profits were used to buy up surrounding farms. Soon 3,500 hectares were being "farmed God's way." At that point, Oldrieve understood the age-old principle that we are blessed in order to be a blessing. He could verbalize his calling even in a specific sense: "Teach Africa to make a profit." Craig Sorley and Care of Creation Kenya have adopted the curriculum "Farming God's Way" as a cornerstone of their creation care discipleship.

Other training programs at Care of Creation Kenya are entitled "Harvesting God's Water" (rainwater), and "Planting God's Trees" (native species). Mulch, borrowing an Oldrieve term, is referred to as "God's blanket." A recent article in the *Guardian* (UK) newspaper about Sorley indicates how integrated environmental issues are. Trees do more for cropland than retain rainwater. A local farmer invited Sorley out to his maize fields. Rats were infesting their small four-acre farm. Normally Sorley's old childhood friends, the raptors, would maintain the rat populations, but farmers like this one had long since cut down the indigenous trees for firewood. The remaining eucalyptus trees, an exotic species, are not suitable for nesting. Sorley commented to the farmer and to the reporter, "You mess with one part of God's creation and you'll pay for it with another."[33]

> The story of an individual. The story of the land. The third metastory, which converges with the personal and the geographic, is the story from Scripture itself, with the unique feature that the Old Testament is preached as fully as the New Testament, a practice that Sorley didn't necessarily pick up from Bible college in the States. It all begins in the beginning: the book of Genesis, including Genesis 2:8: "Now the Lord God had planted a garden in the east, in Eden; and there he put the man he had formed." Sorley comments, Genesis 2:8 holds a golden nugget of truth that can usher in one of the most necessary shifts in worldview, the very key that can open the door to transforming the minds of hopeless farmers. God was not someone who just walked across the red carpet after someone else had designed and planted the garden. He himself was the One who planted the garden . . . There is another word that we often use interchangeably for someone who plants a garden. We identify such a person as being a farmer.[34]

The effect of Genesis 2:8 is just one of the "necessary shifts in worldview" that Sorley hopes will result from the training offered by Care of Creation Kenya. The ministry itself is a branch of Care of Creation, directed by Ed Brown. Craig and his wife, Tracy, and two girls, along with the staff, recently moved operations to Moffat Bible College in Kijabe, Kenya. For all the agricultural and reforestation work they do—rightfully under the rubric of environmental missions—Care of Creation Kenya is emphatic: they are first and foremost a discipleship ministry. Applying the

❧ Appendix 3 ❧

lessons learned as the child of medical missionaries, Sorley disciples local believers. The best-informed agriculture practice and the technology to accompany it is useless without a fundamental shift in worldview, and none is more profound than the truth that all farms, all trees, all water, even the mulch on the ground, are God's. Discipleship is evident in Sorley's teaching. He is fond of presenting lists of principles. There are fourteen general principles in his book *Christ and Creation* and sixteen specific ones in *Farming that Brings Glory to God*. Disciples ruminate on such principles as #3: "Farming is a meaningful and noble way of life because God was the First Farmer." Worldview change here is crucial. "The unfortunate but honest reality," Sorley says,

> is that we generally show little respect to our farmers and little appreciation for the hard work they do. When farming is increasingly viewed as a demeaning or futile way of life, when it is characterized by discouragement and a loss of hope, we need to recognize the long-term and potentially-devastating consequences of such trends.[35]

Care of Creation Kenya, with its mobilization of the local church and its principle-ridden curriculum, presents a discipleship model for environmental missions. In some ways, there are two other audiences for discipleship. Sorley is intent on recruiting and nurturing a Kenyan staff, training up the next generation of African conservationists, just as Simon Thomsett had invested in him. I know from personal conversations with Craig Sorley that it's not been easy. Some interpersonal conflicts have been painful, and at times harmful to the progress of the work. And yet that too is the nature of discipleship. The other audience for discipleship is the national church. Care of Creation Kenya was instrumental in convening the International Conference on God and Creation at the Brackenhurst International Conference Center near Nairobi. Nobel Prize–winning tree planter, the late Wangari Maathi, spoke to the crowd about her own Christian commitment and later told organizers that she "fully agrees that a biblical viewpoint on the environment needs to be widely promoted across the country."

When the conferees met again, two hundred church leaders signed the document *A Declaration to Care for Creation*, March 11, 2006. Among the affirmations these leaders made was the paragraph: "We confess that the church has responded poorly to this issue. Our failure in promoting and exercising proper stewardship over the creation has undermined our witness for Christ, and we hereby declare that we repent of our sin and negligence in this matter."[36] The declaration ends by quoting 2 Chronicles 7:14: "If my people, who are called by my name, will humble themselves and pray and seek my face and turn from their wicked ways, then I will hear from heaven, and will forgive their sin and will heal their land."

Val Sheen, Christian Veterinary Mission: Ethnovet Medicine and Community Transformation[d]

Dr. Valery Shean is a missionary with Christian Veterinary Mission in northeast Uganda. The Karamojan people of this region are cow herders (when they can prevent rustling from nearby subtribes) and farmers (when they can get access to their fields without getting shot at as a reprisal for rustling). They are an isolated people, tucked up in to the borders with Kenya and South Sudan. Raiding between villages has been a fact of life for years, but became deadly beginning in 1979 when automatic weapons were introduced to the region. A raid would occur, perhaps to acquire dowry. A villager would be killed. A counter-raid would be organized to retaliate for the murder. Soon the retaliations would escalate until a hundred people armed with machine guns would sneak in and massacre a village in the night. The violence was so well known that the UN and USAID refused to risk sending their development workers into Karamoja.

When Val Shean was a vet student at Oregon State and Washington State, she made a handful of short-term trips to Africa. After working for one year upon graduation as a dairy vet in Oregon's famous cheese-making region, Shean moved to Uganda in 1992. The two Karamojan subtribes

---

[d] An account of Shean's ministry can be found in *Cattle, Guns and Murder . . . or Peace?*, produced by Ron Hauenstein (Spokane, WA: acts5:20video, 2009), DVD.

she worked among were the Pian and the Bokora. What these two deadly enemies had in common, other than a common ancestry, were cows. "We knew they loved their animals," Shean explains, and so this CVM missionary began to "care about what they cared about."[37] The fact that she could work in both tribes helped build trust. Shean established the CLIDE Consultancy: Community Livestock Integrated Development. Dr. Val is apparently known by two names among the Karamojan. She is *Naler*, which means "the one of the harvest" and *Namwaar*, "the lady with the horned vehicle." The former name has biblical overtones; the latter name is a reference to her Land Rover. One day she and her colleagues were driving across no man's land between the two subtribes, when suddenly shots were fired their direction. When she got to the village and discovered that the assailants had actually been friends she asked, "Why did you shoot at me?" They apologized, albeit without any evidence of horror, and explained, "We didn't recognize your vehicle. We thought you were the army." Now the CLIDE Land Rover has two large cow horns that stick up at such an angle as to be visible above the tall grass.

When Shean's former CVM colleague Jean Grade arrived in Uganda in 1998, she found a project that was already deeply interested in ethnoveterinary medicine, the use of local knowledge and resources to treat livestock. Grade gravitated to the subject with alacrity, eventually studying in Belgium for a doctorate in ethnobotany. CVM Uganda now has a catalog of over two hundred plants that can treat internal parasites, help retain placenta, or even address foot and mouth disease. Some of these treatments, according to Grade, "are not even in Western world pharmacopeias."[38] *Ebuto* is a huge underground tuber, which when cut up and mixed with water can be rubbed on an animal or a child to remove lice or ticks. *Ekapangiteng* is used for intestinal worms. It is a shrub tree with small leaves from which you strip the bark, pound it, and administer it orally. CLIDE is working with twenty of these traditional herbal veterinary medicines, patenting, producing, and marketing them as modern commercial products. Their people-related goal is to help the tribes develop a business, which can be a substitute livelihood for the deadlier one of raiding each other's cattle. Forty commercial woodlots are also cultivated to help provide the raw material for these medicines.

On one occasion, Grade was visiting a new village on the northeast border of Uganda. Seeing the group's white faces, the villagers swamped their arrival with a multitude of requests for aid. A fellow missionary called this "the biggest closed door in Africa to the gospel"; that is, a flurry of handouts precludes any serious listening to the good news of Jesus able to heal body and soul. But while this missionary was rehearsing in his mind how to negotiate the demands, Grade asked one petitioner, "What problem do you have?" The village man said he suffered from headaches. Grade reached up to a nearby shrub, snapped off a twig, and then first giving the local name for the shrub said, "Here, boil this as a tea and drink it. It should cure your headache." The villagers began to quiz her about other plants. In each case, she would first give them the local name of the plant, then say which was good for cattle or for humans, and how best to prepare it. The fellow missionary who witnessed this later remarked, "The biggest closed door to the gospel has now become the biggest open door, because I can say God loved you so much that he put all of these things right under your feet. And he loved you even more," adding, "he sent his Son to die on the cross for your sins."[39] For an environmental missionary to help open the eyes of a local population to the glories of God's provision built right into their own landscape, surely that is one of the first declarations of God's fatherly love over that people.

> Then God blessed Noah and his sons, saying to them, "Be fruitful and increase in number and fill the earth. The fear and dread of you will fall on all the beasts of the earth, and on all the birds in the sky, on every creature that moves along the ground, and on all the fish in the sea; they are given into your hands. Everything that lives and moves about will be food for you. Just as I gave you the green plants, I now give you everything." (Gen 9:1–3)

Admittedly in the covenantal blessing over Noah (as much our father as Adam is), God also spoke of murder, juxtaposing it to the command for human flourishing: "Whoever sheds human blood, by humans shall their blood be shed; for in the image of God has God made mankind. As for you, be fruitful and increase in number; multiply on the earth and increase upon it" (Gen 9:6,7). Between the villages of the Pian and the villages of the Bokora in Karamoja stands a sizeable protrusion in the grasslands called Mt. Napak. The cattle rustlers and the retaliatory mobs use raiding corridors that sweep around both sides. The result is the de facto creation of a no man's land. Herders cannot bring their cattle out there to graze for fear of the violence lurking in the tall grass. Young couples can't settle new villages and till new ground out there; they would be set upon in the night. The ground of no man's land is much more fertile than the marginal land where each subtribe has hunkered down for safety. In addition, the pastures close enough to the village for safety become quickly overgrazed. Farmers don't have the luxury to let any of their limited plots lay fallow. Sometimes underutilization of land (in this case, the grass and soil around Mt. Napak) can be as bad a case of poor stewardship as overutilization. Val Shean understood that access to no man's land would mean healthier herds for both subtribes. It would also mean the ability to grow enough extra food that they could sell some of it. The income would indicate that there are other ways to earn money than the raiding of each other's cattle.

Shean organized the Napak Peace Project. Drawing on the trust that she had engendered among the Pian and Bokora as a veterinarian, trained by Ken Sande's book *The Peacemakers*, and ready to preach the commands of Jesus to a people who professed to be Christians, Shean called for her first peace camp, November 10, 2007. Each subtribe hiked in from their direction into no man's land, where the conference would be held. Shean and her team—people who bore the title "peace builders"—waited anxiously. When they heard the approaching sound of dancing and the singing of Christian hymns, they took it as a good sign. The two groups met over the gospel of reconciliation. They repented of their sin, one toward another. They sang and danced and performed skits. Young men and young women began to eye each other across the campfires. Shean proposed the creation of a *peace village*, right there in no man's land. The Pian would send half the settlers, as would the Bokora. The young people would intermarry. Fields would be plowed and sown.

As of January 2010, there are now sixty-two peace villages in Karamoja with eleven thousand settlers. I heard Dr. Shean speak at Kansas State University. The crowd listened enraptured, as had the European Union (EU) and the UN World Food Programme (UNWFP) when they first heard of a single woman missionary succeeding where their big budgets and complex programs had failed. Walter Renberg, CVM board member, asked me on the side, "How does one get nominated for a Nobel Peace Prize?" Why not? If Craig Sorley can be an Environmental Hero of the Year, why can't Val Shean be equally recognized for her heroism?

On the third anniversary of the first peace camp, Shean reported back from Mt. Napak:

> "We had an excellent trip to the peace villages this weekend and found the peace councils and peace builders actively pursuing their mandate in their communities." Nabwal is the first established area of the peace villages. They are having difficulties with their bore holes (wells) and have to walk about 6 miles to get to a working one. A pastor has been holding services at their church whenever he can make it on his bicycle. The school building was recently completed and three volunteer teachers are teaching primary grades 1–3.[40]

The peace village named Nakayot, established one year after Nabwal on the opposite of Mt. Napak, was still having trouble with its lone bore well. A partner NGO (quite possibly the EU or UNWFP, which have rushed in to support the Napak Peace Project) has been slow in delivering five new wells. "As a result, people from about one thousand homes are walking 3-4 kilometers to get water from a pool fed by a spring up on the mountain. The water is quite dirty and unsafe." Environmental sustainability is one of the stated values of CLIDE Consultancy, but Shean also understands

sustainability as crucial to what always seems like a tenuous peace process. Pastor Samuel Nagarik is an official with the church of Uganda who works near the peace villages. He says of CLIDE, "We have planted some bore holes and then we have repaired so many broken bore holes. We have given food, we have given seedlings, we have given agricultural inputs. So many things, and now people are, they are like saying, 'Thank you, God.'" He talks of CLIDE's environmental work as providing the space where people can finally listen to both the word of God and to each other.

Early on in the development of environmental missions, I've had the intuitive conviction that CVM represents a model for how environmental mission agencies and practitioners can organize and proceed. "While the animals might be our patients, their owners are our *clients*" is the mantra taught at university Vet Med programs. Veterinary medicine is a human service attending to the livestock and the pets that are an integral part of human flourishing. When you add the words "Christian mission" to veterinary practice, then the humanitarian nature of the discipline is multiplied. CVM director Kit Flowers explains, "The goal of our work is the transformation of individuals, groups, and communities through balanced ministry to spiritual, physical, mental, social, and ecological needs." When the CVM values statement mentions a "veterinary focus," it explains: "The skills and knowledge of veterinary medicine are used to transform lives."[41] Those *lives* are invariably human ones: the cattle owner in Uganda, the goat herder in Nicaragua, the Mongolian small animal clinician in Ulan Bator. CVM has developed effective structures for mobilizing industry professionals for the sake of the cross-cultural preaching of the gospel. But their model also supplies a key conceptual bridge.

Ed Brown had said of environmental missions, "It's very similar to medical missions in its approach to the mission field. When you take out the word 'medical' and put in the word 'environmental,' that's what we are." That's helpful, but it's easy to picture a compassionate medical doctor working on a human patient, while the hospital chaplain looks over her shoulder, ready to pray with, comfort, and share the gospel with that patient. The public perception of veterinarians, however, is that they primarily work with animals, seeing to the care and healing of cows and goats, or cats and dogs. Humans are a secondary consideration. Similarly, when one considers the work of an environmentalist, human beings as the focus of ministry don't immediately come to mind. Environmentalists work on soil and water and air. They tend to rainforests and wildlife. Save the whales! Clean up the Hudson River! I have met environmentalists, wounded souls, for whom people are considered nothing more than "polluters." Responsible environmentalists, however, also speak in terms of human impacts. Dumping factories and trucking routes into the South Bronx of New York City mean that children there have asthma at three times the rate of the national average. Damming the Ganges River downstream means that the *hilsa* fish no longer migrate as far enough upstream, which makes the Kewat fishermen there susceptible to unemployment and alcoholism. Nonetheless, when the public think of environmentalists, they probably think more about air quality and fisheries than they think of schoolchildren and fishermen.

CVM missionaries work hard at being veterinarians who love people. When Proverbs declares, "The righteous care for the needs of their animals, but the kindest acts of the wicked are cruel" (12:10), it affirms that animal care and kindness are somehow "right" actions in their own right. Attending to animal welfare is a means of glorifying God. Similarly, we would argue that creation care can be intrinsically good. And yet environmental missions must aspire to more. That more is the people, as much a part of the ecosphere as any sequoia or polar bear. The vast majority of CVM's veterinary work is livestock, or "large animals." Even then, as part of their Community Animal Health Training, working with herding villages means they work more with training the human herders than treating the bovine herds. I asked Dr. Flowers if they do small animal practice. Yes, he said, referring to a project in Mongolia's capital as an example of another of their ministry tracks, veterinary development. CVM missionaries provide advanced training for national veterinarians, and so this too represents primarily ministering to humans (i.e., to the veterinarians themselves). And I then asked him, does CVM work with exotic

Appendix 3

animals, wildlife biology, wildlife conservation? It's the rare occasion when they do, and Kit's answer was revealing: most wildlife vets who come to them will, more often than not, have an exclusive interest in the animals and portray people as predatory. CVM is unapologetic about community transformation.ᵉ Wildlife conservation might represent a partnership niche that environmental missionaries can provide for CVM.

As for actual missionary infrastructure, CVM actively recruits potential missionaries at universities and in professional associations. There are CVM chapters at many universities such as Kansas State. CVM organizes and conducts short-term trips. But when it comes to sending career missionaries, their preferred practice is to second workers to other organizations. In other words, they help resource the veterinary medicine needs of other sending agencies. As one example, a team of SIM missionaries in Ethiopia were in need of a large animal vet component to their work among the Bunna people in the southwest. CVM happily provided the trained personnel. As a model for environmental mission agencies, the challenge will be to: (1) develop a (Christian and missional) presence in university environmental studies programs and among environmental professionals, (2) develop the network of church planting agencies for whom environmental missionaries can serve their creation care needs through secondment or other partnership relationships, and (3) nonetheless maintain an environmental missionary identity that could allow for membership (similar to "I am a CVM missionary working with SIM") and/or for the further training and resourcing that are benefits of being part of an environmental missions network.

ᵉ It strikes me that wildlife conservation is a niche that environmental missions could possibly carve into an acceptable shape that a partner like CVM would be happy to help fill. I've loved the fact that Larry Schweiger, current director of the National Wildlife Federation, is an evangelical believer. (That's right, the publisher of Ranger Rick, a Christian.) Schweiger's book is *Last Chance: Preserving Life on Earth* (Golden, CO: Fulcrum, 2009).

✣ ENVIRONMENTAL MISSIONS ✣

NOTES

1. Scott Russell Sanders, "What Is Wealth?" (speech, Prairie Festival, Land Institute, Salina, KS, September 25, 2010).
2. Greg Parsons, "Peter Harris Story," email message to author, April 9, 2011.
3. Peter Harris, *Under the Bright Wings* (Vancouver, Canada: Regent College Publishing, 1993), 20.
4. Ibid., 3.
5. Ibid., 5.
6. Ibid., 6.
7. Ibid., 9.
8. Ibid., 22.
9. Ibid., 53.
10. Thomas L. Friedman, *Hot, Flat, and Crowded* (New York: Farrar, Straus, and Giroux, 2008), 314.
11. Harris, *Wings*, 55.
12. Ibid., 57.
13. Ibid., 60.
14. John Stott, "Foreword," in Harris, *Wings,* x.
15. Harris, *Wings*, 100.
16. Ibid., 105–7.
17. Parsons, "Peter Harris Story."
18. Scott C. Sabin, *Tending to Eden* (Valley Forge, PA: Judson, 2010), 2.
19. Ibid., 10.
20. Steve Fitch, "Connectivity: Poverty and Deforestation," *Blessed Earth*, http://www.blessedearth.org/your-story/connectivity-poverty-and-deforestation (accessed July 16, 2013).
21. Sabin, *Tending*, 20.
22. Dambisa Moyo, *Dead Aid* (New York: Farrar, Straus and Giroux, 2009).
23. Sabin, *Tending*, 23.
24. Plant With Purpose, "One Year Later: Plant With Purpose Plants Over 540,000 Trees in Haiti," press release, January 12, 2011, http://www.plantwithpurpose.org/news (accessed February 28, 2012).
25. Sabin, *Tending*, 63.
26. Stephan Faris, "Heroes of the Environment 2008: Craig Sorley," *TIME Specials*, September 24, 2008.

Appendix 3

27. Craig Sorley, *Christ and Creation* (Nairobi: Care of Creation, 2009), 10.

28. Craig Sorley, *Farming that Brings Glory to God* (South Hadley, MA: Doorlight, 2011), 2.

29. Dan Fountain, ed., *Let's Restore Our Land* (Kijabe, Kenya: Today in Africa, 2007).

30. Brian Oldrieve, "The Story of Foundations for Farming," Foundations for Farming, http://www.foundationsforfarming.org/wp-content/uploads/The-Story.pdf (accessed July 16, 2013).

31. Ibid.

32. Ibid.

33. Xan Rice, "The Eco Evangelist," *The Guardian*, June 6, 2009, http://www.guardian.co.uk/environment/2009/jun/07/eco-evangelist-craig-sorley (accessed October 3, 2011).

34. Sorley, *Farming*, 28.

35. Ibid., 27.

36. Sorley, *Christ and Creation*, 115.

37. Val Shean, in *Cattle, Guns and Murder . . . or Peace?*, produced by Ron Hauenstein (Spokane, WA: acts5:20video, 2009), DVD.

38. Jean Grade Reed, "Christian Veterinary Mission: Jean Grade Reed Interview," YouTube video, uploaded by CVMUSA, May 18, 2009, http://www.youtube.com/watch?v=hjHcX46uB_g (accessed May 31, 2012; video discontinued).

39. Tom Reed, "Drs. Tom and Jean Reed, Uganda (CVM)," YouTube video, uploaded by CVMUSA, April 2, 2010, http://www.youtube.com/watch?v=dqF--lvzbl4&feature=relmfu (accessed May 31, 2012; video discontinued).

40. GoTeam, "Peace Village Update," Northwest Hills Community Church, November 11, 2010, http://www.nwhills.com/peace-village-update1 (accessed May 31, 2012).

41. Christian Veterinary Mission, "About CVM," http://www.cvmusa.org/page.aspx?pid=2694 (accessed May 31, 2012).

BIBLIOGRAPHY

"Adapt or Die." *The Economist*, September 11, 2008. http://www.economist.com/node/12208005 (accessed October 5, 2011).

Adler, Margot. "Behind the Ever-expanding American Dream House." *All Things Considered*. National Public Radio, July 4, 2006. http://www.npr.org/templates/story/story.php?storyId=5525283 (accessed October 6, 2011).

Agrimoney.com. "Chinese Hunger for Pork Could Be Corn Growers' Best Friend." March 6, 2013. http://www.agrimoney.com/feature/chinese-hunger-for-pork-could-be-corn-growers-best-friend--200.html (accessed May 21, 2013).

Andersen, Francis I. *Habakkuk: A New Translation with Introduction and Commentary*. The Anchor Yale Bible Commentaries Series, edited by John J. Collins, vol. 25. New York: Yale University Press, 2001.

Arbousset, T., and F. Daumas. *Narrative of an Exploratory Tour to the North-east of the Colony of the Cape of Good Hope*, translated by J. C. Brown. Cape Town: Saul Solomon and Co., 1846.

Astyk, Sharon, and Aaron Newton. *A Nation of Farmers: Defeating the Food Crisis on American Soil*. Gabriola, Canada: New Society, 2009.

Awehali, Brian. "Under the Eternal Sky." *Earth Island Journal* (Winter 2011): 26–30.

Barnes, Albert. *Notes on the New Testament: James, Peter, John, and Jude*. Grand Rapids: Baker, 1972.

Beisner, Calvin E. "Biblical Geography and the Dominion Mandate." *Cornwall Alliance Newsletter*, March 9, 2011.

———. *Where Garden Meets Wilderness*. Grand Rapids: Acton Institute, 1997.

Berry, Wendell. "Strachan Donnelly Lecture on Restoration and Conservation." Speech presented at Prairie Festival, Land Institute, Salina, KS, September 25, 2010.

Blackaby, Henry. *Experiencing God*. Nashville: Broadman & Holman, 1994.

Blincoe, Bob. "'Unleashing the Gospel': Perspectives Lesson #5." PowerPoint slide. http://www.perspectives.org.

Boa, Kenneth. *Conformed to His Image*. Grand Rapids: Zondervan, 2010.

Bouma-Prediger, Steven. *For the Beauty of the Earth*. Grand Rapids: Baker, 2001.

Brown, Edward R. *Our Father's World: Mobilizing the Church to Care for Creation*. Downer's Grove, IL: InterVarsity Press, 2006.

———. *When Heaven and Nature Sing*. South Hadley MA: Doorlight, 2012.

Brown, John Croumbie. *Pastoral Discourses*. Cape Town: Saul Solomon and Co., 1847.

———. "Preface." In T. Arbousset and F. Daumas. *Narrative of an Exploratory Tour to the North-east of the Colony of the Cape of Good Hope*. Translated by J. C. Brown. Cape Town: Saul Solomon and Co., 1846.

———. *Management of Crown Forests at the Cape of Good Hope Under the Old Regime and Under the New*. Edinburgh: Oliver and Boyd, 1887.

Caird, George. *The Revelation of St. John the Divine*. New York: Harper & Row, 1966.

Carey, Eustace. *Memoir of William Carey, D.D.* Hartford: Canfield & Robins, 1837.

Carey, S. Pearce. *William Carey: The Father of Modern Missions*. London: Wakeman Trust, 1923.

Bibliography

Carey, William. "Extract from a Letter of Dr. Carey, in India, to Mr. J. Cooper, of Wentworth, Yorkshire." *London Magazine*, August 15, 1823.

Carson, D. A. "Matthew." *Matthew, Mark, Luke, vol. 8. Expositor's Bible Commentary.* Grand Rapids: Zondervan, 1995.

Carter, Majora. "Discovering Where We Live: Reimagining Environmentalism." Interview by Krista Tippett. *Speaking of Faith*, January 11, 2007. http://www.onbeing.org/program/discovering-where-we-live-reimagining-environmentalism/transcript/4514.

———. *The Promised Land.* American Public Media. http://www.thepromisedland.org/wes-jackson-transcript (accessed July 15, 2013).

Cattle, Guns and Murder . . . or Peace? Produced by Ron Hauenstein. Spokane, WA: acts5:20video, 2009. DVD.

Christian Aid. *Human Tide: The Real Migration Crisis.* London: Christian Aid, 2007.

Christian Veterinary Mission. "About CVM." http://www.cvmusa.org/page.aspx?pid=2694 (accessed May 31, 2012).

Christar. "Statement of Faith." http://www.christar.org/about/statement-of-faith.html (accessed July 15, 2013).

Claiborne, Ron. "U.S. Electronic Waste Gets Sent to Africa." *ABC Good Morning America*, August 2, 2009. http://abcnews.go.com/GMA/Weekend/story?id=8215714&page=1 (accessed October 6, 2011).

Cohen, Nick. "The Curse of Black Gold." *New Statesman*, June 2, 2003. http://www.newstatesman.com/node/145564 (accessed May 23, 2012).

"Commodity Law and Legal Definition." US Legal. http://definitions.uslegal.com/c/commodity (accessed October 5, 2011).

Copeland, Luther. *World Mission, World Survival.* Nashville: Broadman, 1985.

Corbett, Steve, and Brian Fikkert. *When Helping Hurts.* Chicago: Moody Publishers, 2009.

Crossman, Eileen. *Mountain Rain.* Wheaton: Harold Shaw, 1982.

Culross, James. *William Carey.* London: Hodder & Stoughton, 1881.

Daly, Herman E., and John B. Cobb Jr. *For the Common Good: Redirecting the Economy toward Community, the Environment, and a Sustainable Future.* Boston: Beacon, 1989.

Daly, Herman E., and Joshua Farley. *Ecological Economics.* Washington, DC: Island Press, 2004.

Darr, Richard. "Protestant Missions and Earth-keeping in Southern Africa 1817–2000." PhD diss., Boston University School of Theology, 2005.

Deria, A., Z. Jezek, K. Markvart, P. Carrasco, and J. Weisfeld. "The World's Last Endemic Case of Smallpox: Surveillance and Containment Measures." *Bulletin of the World Health Organization* 85, no. 2 (1980), 279-83.

DeWitt, Calvin B., "Biogeographic and Trophic Restructuring of the Biosphere: The State of the Earth under Human Domination." *Christian Scholar's Review* 32 (2003): 347–64.

———. "Contemporary Missiology and the Biosphere." In *Antioch Agenda: Essays on the Restorative Church in Honor of Orlando E. Costas*, edited by Daniel Jeyaraj, Robert W. Pazmino, and Rodney L. Petersen, 305–28. New Delhi: ISPCK, 2007.

———. "Creation's Environmental Challenge to Evangelical Christianity." In *The Care of Creation*, edited by R. J. Berry. 60–73. Downer's Grove, IL: InterVarsity Press, 2000.

———. *Earth-wise: A Biblical Response to Environmental Issues.* Grand Rapids: CRC Publications, 1994.

———. "Seeking to Image the Order and Beauty of God's 'House.'" In *Creation-care in Ministry: Down-to-earth Christianity*, edited by W. Dayton Roberts and Paul E. Pretiz, 9–24. Wynnewood, PA: AERDO, 2000.

DeWitt, Calvin B., and Ghillean T. Prance. "ttt." In *Missionary Earth-keeping*, edited by Calvin B. DeWitt and Ghillean T. Prance, vii—x. Macon, GA: Mercer University Press, 1992.

Douglass, Justin. "The Environmental Refugee Phenomenon." *Childview* (World Vision Canada), Summer 2008, 16–21.

Bibliography

Doyle, Alister. "World Needs Refugee Re-think for Climate Victims: U.N." *Reuters*, June 6, 2011. http://www.reuters.com/article/2011/06/06/us-climate-refugees-idUSTRE7553UG20110606 (accessed October 6, 2011).

Eenigenburg, Sue, and Robynn Bliss. *Expectations and Burnout: Women Surviving the Great Commission.* Pasadena: William Carey Library, 2010.

Faris, Stephan. "Heroes of the Environment 2008: Craig Sorley." *TIME Specials*, September 24, 2008.

Fell, Nolan. "Outcasts from Eden." *New Scientist* 151 no. 2045 (August 31, 1996): 25.

Ferrarin, Alfredo. "Homo Faber, Homo Sapiens, or Homo Politicus? Protagoras and the Myth of Prometheus." *The Review of Metaphysics* 54 (2000): 289–319.

Fitch, Steve. "Connectivity: Poverty and Deforestation." *Blessed Earth.* http://www.blessedearth.org/your-story/connectivity-poverty-and-deforestation (accessed July 16, 2013).

Fountain, Dan, ed. *Let's Restore Our Land.* Kijabe, Kenya: Today in Africa, 2007.

France, R. T. *The Gospel according to Matthew: An Introduction and Commentary.* Grand Rapids: Eerdmans, 1985.

Friedman, Thomas L. *Hot, Flat, and Crowded.* New York: Farrar, Straus, and Giroux, 2008.

Geisel, Theodor Seuss. *The Lorax.* New York: Random House, 1971.

Gillis, Justin. "In Weather Chaos, a Case for Global Warming." *New York Times*, August 15, 2010, A1.

Gordon, S. D. Quiet *Talks on Prayer.* New York: Revell, 1904.

Gore, Al. *An Inconvenient Truth.* Directed by Davis Guggenheim. Hollywood: Paramount, 2006. DVD.

———. *Our Choice.* Emmaus, PA: Rodale, 2009.

GoTeam. "Peace Village Update." Northwest Hills Community Church, November 11, 2010. http://www.nwhills.com/peace-village-update1 (accessed May 31, 2012).

Goudge, Elizabeth. *My God and My All: the Life of St. Francis of Assisi*. New York: Coward-McCann, 1959.

Greenland, Paul R. and AnnaMarie L. Sheldon. *Career Opportunities in Conservation and the Environment*. New York: Checkmark Books, 2008.

Gronewold, Nathanial, and Climatewire. "Is the Flooding in Pakistan a Climate Change Disaster?" *Scientific American*, August 18, 2010. http://www.scientificamerican.com/article.cfm?id=is-the-flooding-in-pakist (accessed May 16, 2013).

Grove, Richard. "Scottish Missionaries, Evangelical Discourses and the Origins of Conservation Thinking in Southern Africa 1820–1900." *Journal of Southern African Studies* 15, no. 2 (1989): 163–87.

Hansen, Liane. "Slow but Sure Environmental Progress in Cairo." *Weekend Edition Sunday*. National Public Radio, May 4, 2008. http://www.npr.org/templates/story/story.php?storyId=90109734 (accessed October 6, 2011).

Hardin, Garret. "The Tragedy of the Commons." *Science* 162, no. 3859 (1968): 1243–48.

Harris, Peter. "Creation Care and Mission." A Rocha. http://www.arocha.org/int-en/3286-DSY.html (accessed October 5, 2011).

———. *Kingfisher's Fire*. Oxford: Monarch, 2008.

———. *Under the Bright Wings*. Vancouver, Canada: Regent College Publishing, 1993.

Hayhoe, Katherine. *A Climate for Change: Global Warming Facts for Faith-based Decisions*. New York: FaithWords, 2009.

Hays, Richard. "The Word of Reconciliation." Sermon presented at Duke Center for Reconciliation, Durham, NC, June 1, 2010. http://www.faithandleadership.com/sermons/the-word-reconciliation (accessed May 26, 2012).

Hickman, Leo. "The US Evangelicals Who Believe Environmentalism Is a 'Native Evil.'" *Environment Blog, The Guardian*, May 5, 2011. http://www.guardian.co.uk/environment/blog/2011/may/05/evangelical-christian-environmentalism-green-dragon (accessed October 6, 2011).

Bibliography

Hine, Stuart K. *Not You, but God: A Testimony to God's Faithfulness* 1st ed. n.p.: S.K. Hine, 1953.

Hobson, Wendy L., M. L. Knochel, C. L. Byington, P. C. Young, C. J. Hoff, and K. F. Buchi. "Bottled, Filtered, and Tap Water Use in Latino and Non-Latino Children." *Archives of Pediatrics and Adolescent Medicine* 161, no. 5 (May 2007), 457–61.

Houghton, John. "Sir John's Word to Pastors." Speech presented at the Center for Applied Christian Ethics, Wheaton College, January 25, 2007. http://www.wheaton.edu/CACE/CACE-Audio-and-Video (accessed October 6, 2011).

Hundert, E. J. "The Making of Homo Faber: John Locke between Ideology and History." *Journal of the History of Ideas* 33 (1972): 3–22.

"Invasive Species." Exec. Order No. 13112. February 3, 1999. http://www.invasivespeciesinfo.gov/laws/execorder.shtml (accessed October 4, 2011).

Iqbal, Anwar. "Climate Change Responsible for Floods: Experts." *Dawn*, August 23, 2010. http://archives.dawn.com/archives/41768 (accessed May 15, 2013).

Jackson, Wes. "Q&A: Wes Jackson." Interview by Jesse Finfrock. Mother Jones, October 29, 2008. http://motherjones.com/environment/2008/10/qa-wes-jackson (accessed October 6, 2011).

Jacobson, Jodi L. *Environmental Refugees: A Yardstick of Habitability.* Worldwatch Paper 86. Washington, DC: Worldwatch Institute, 1988.

Johansen, Bruce E. "Poverty and Global Warming." In *The Encyclopedia of Global Warming Science and Technology*, vol. 1, 488. Santa Barbara, CA: Greenwood, 2009.

Jones, E. Stanley. *The Christ of the Indian Road.* New York: Abingdon, 1925.

———. *Gandhi: An Interpretation.* New York: Abingdon-Cokesbury, 1948.

ENVIRONMENTAL MISSIONS

Lausanne Global Consultation on Creation Care and the Gospel. "Call to Action." St. Ann, Jamaica: Lausanne Movement, 2012. http://www.lausanne.org/en/documents/all/2012-creation-care/1881-call-to-action.html.

Lay, Robert F. *Readings in Historical Theology: Primary Sources of the Christian Faith.* Grand Rapids: Kregel, 2009.

LeBow, Victor. "Price Competition in 1955." *Journal of Retailing* 31, no. 1 (Spring 1955): 5–10, 42, 44.

Lovelock, James. *The Revenge of Gaia.* New York: Basic Books, 2006.

MacArthur, John. "The End of the Universe, Part 1." Sermon presented at Grace Community Church, Sun Valley, CA, September 7, 2008. http://www.gty.org/resources/sermons/90-360/The-End-of-the-Universe-Part-1 (accessed February 8, 2013).

Mandryk, Jason. *Operation World*, 7th ed. Colorado Springs: Biblica, 2010.

Markell, Jan. "Mixing Paganism with the Passion." *Cup of Joe* (blog), April 28, 2011. http://cupofjoe.goodfight.org/?p=1578 (accessed July 16, 2013).

McFague, Sallie. *A New Climate for Theology.* Minneapolis: Fortress, 2008.

McKibben, Bill. *Deep Economy.* New York: Holt, 2007.

———. *Eaarth: Making a Life on a Tough New Planet.* New York: Times, 2010.

Mogelonsky, Marcia. "Water off the Shelf." *American Demographics* 19, no. 4 (April 1997): 26.

Moffat, Robert. *Missionary Labours and Scenes in Southern Africa.* London: John Snow, 1842.

Moyers, Bill. *Welcome to Doomsday.* New York: New York Review of Books, 2006.

Moyo, Dambisa. *Dead Aid.* New York: Farrar, Straus and Giroux, 2009.

Myers, Norman. "Environmental Refugees: A Growing Phenomenon of the 21st Century." *Philosophical Transactions of the Royal Society of London: Biological Sciences* 356, no. 1420 (2001): 609–13.

Bibliography

National Geographic TV. "The True Cost of Gold." *Wild Chronicles.* YouTube video, 6:54. July 22, 2009. http://www.youtube.com/watch?v=lgAKeTGHx5g (accessed May 23, 2012).

Nouwen, Henri. *Life of the Beloved.* New York: Crossroad, 1992.

Ohlman, Dean. "What Is Creation Care?" *Wonder of Creation*, June 26, 2011. http://wonderofcreation.org/2011/06/26/what-is-creation-care (accessed May 18, 2013).

Oldrieve, Brian. "The Story of Foundations for Farming." *Foundations for Farming.* http://www.foundationsforfarming.org/wp-content/uploads/The-Story.pdf (accessed July 16, 2013).

Partow, Hassan. *The Mesopotamian Marshlands: Demise of an Ecosystem; Early Warning and Assessment Technical Report*, rev. 1. Nairobi: United Nations Environment Programme /DEWA/GRID, 2001.

Patel, Raj. "Mozambique's Food Riots: The True Face of Global Warming." *The Guardian*, September 4, 2010. http://www.guardian.co.uk/commentisfree/2010/sep/05/mozambique-food-riots-patel (accessed February 11, 2013).

Pearce, Fred. *With Speed and Violence: Why Scientists Fear Tipping Points in Climate Change.* Boston: Beacon, 2007.

Peck, M. Scott. *The Road Less Traveled.* New York: Touchstone, 1978.

Percy, Walker. *The Second Coming.* New York: Washington Square, 1980.

Plant With Purpose. "One Year Later: Plant With Purpose Plants Over 540,000 Trees in Haiti." Press release, January 12, 2011. http://www.plantwithpurpose.org/news (accessed February 28, 2012).

Pomerantz, Jeffrey D. "The Practice of Medicine and the First Commandment: General Considerations." *Journal of Biblical Ethics in Medicine* 1, no. 1 (2003).

Prance, Ghillean. "Faith v Science?" Interview by Nigel Bovey. *Rejesus* (blog). http://www.rejesus.co.uk/site/module/faith_v_science/P7 (accessed October 5, 2011).

Pritchard, Rusty. "Global Warming Skeptic at Religious Right Conference Apologize for Slanderous Charges." *SustainLane*, September 23, 2009. http://www.sustainlane.com/reviews/global-warming-skeptic-at-religious-right-conference-apologizes-for-slanderous-charges/MD2L-Z844ONT78J73MZZFOHI47AQI (accessed October 6, 2011; site discontinued).

Quiggle, James D. "A Brief Review of Dispensational Eschatology." First Baptist Church of Sparks, 2008. http://www.fbcsparks.org/library/Dispensational%20Eschatology.pdf (accessed May 10, 2013).

Raine, George. "Annual Ad Spending Exceeds $141 Billion / Internet Advertising Shows Largest Percentage Gain." SFGate, *San Francisco Chronicle*, March 10, 2005. http://articles.sfgate.com/2005-03-10/business/17362937_1_tns-media-intelligence-billion-spending (accessed October 6, 2011).

Reed, Jean Grade. "Christian Veterinary Mission: Jean Grade Reed Interview." YouTube video. Uploaded by CVMUSA, May 18, 2009. http://www.youtube.com/watch?v=hjHcX46uB_g (accessed May 31, 2012; video discontinued).

Reed, Tom. "Drs. Tom and Jean Reed, Uganda (CVM)." YouTube video. Uploaded by CVMUSA, April 2, 2010. http://www.youtube.com/watch?v=dqF--lvzbl4&feature=relmfu (accessed May 31, 2012; video discontinued).

Rice, Xan. "The Eco Evangelist." *The Guardian*, June 6, 2009. http://www.guardian.co.uk/environment/2009/jun/07/eco-evangelist-craig-sorley (accessed October 3, 2011).

Robert, Dana L. "Historical Trends in Missions and Earth Care." *International Bulletin of Missionary Research* 35, no. 3 (July 2011): 123–28.

———. "Historical Trends in Missions and Earth Care." Paper presented at the Overseas Ministries Study Center, December 2009.

Roberts, W. Dayton, and Paul E. Pretiz, eds. *Down-to-earth Christianity: Creation-care in Ministry*. Wynnewood, PA: EEN, 2000.

Robinson, Tri, and Jason Chatraw. *Saving God's Green Earth*. Norcross, GA: Ampelon, 2006.

Roosevelt, Theodore. "At Grand Canyon, Arizona, May 6, 1903." In *A Compilation of the Messages and Speeches of Theodore Roosevelt*, edited by Alfred Henry Lewis, 327-328. Bureau of National Literature and Art, 1906.

Rosenzweig, Michael J. *Win-Win Ecology: How the Earth's Species Can Survive in the Midst of Human Enterprise*. Oxford: Oxford University Press, 2003.

Ross, Tracy. "Hike. Pray. Protest." *Backpacker* (March 2011): 80–90.

Rowan, Chris. "Drilling for Oil Is More Risky than It Used to Be." *ScienceBlogs*, May 4, 2010. http://scienceblogs.com/highlyallochthonous/2010/05/drilling_for_oil_is_more_risky.php (accessed February 27, 2012; page discontinued).

Rubidge, Dr. "Irrigation and Tree-planting." In *The Cape and Its People*, edited by Roderick Noble, 343–56. Cape Town: J. C. Juta, 1869.

Sabin, Scott C. *Tending to Eden*. Valley Forge, PA: Judson, 2010.

Sachs, Jeffrey. *The End of Poverty: Economic Possibilities for Our Time*. New York: Penguin, 2005.

Sanders, Scott Russell. *A Conservationist Manifesto*. Bloomington: Indiana University Press, 2009.

———. "What Is Wealth?" Speech presented at Prairie Festival, Land Institute, Salina, KS, September 25, 2010.

Sarna, Nahum. *JPS Torah Commentary: Genesis*. Philadelphia: Jewish Publication Society, 1989.

Schaeffer, Francis. *Pollution and the Death of Man: The Christian View of Ecology*. Wheaton: Tyndale, 1970.

Scherer, Glenn. "Christian-right Views Are Swaying Politicians and Threatening the Environment." *Grist*, October 28, 2004. http://grist.org/politics/scherer-christian (accessed February 23, 2012).

Second Lausanne Congress on World Evangelization. "The Manila Manifesto." Lausanne Movement. http://www.lausanne.org/en/documents/manila-manifesto.html (accessed July 15, 2013).

Smith, George. *The Life of William Carey: Shoemaker and Missionary*. Middlesex, UK: Echo, 2006.

Sorley, Craig. *Christ and Creation*. Nairobi: Care of Creation, 2009.

———. *Farming that Brings Glory to God*. South Hadley, MA: Doorlight, 2011.

Spanner, Huw. "Tyrants, Stewards – or Just Kings?" In *Animals on the Agenda: Questions about Animals for Theology and Ethics*, edited by Andrew Linzey and Dorothy Yamamoto, 216–24. London: SCM, 1998.

Stevens, Michelle, and Hamid K. Ahmed. "Eco-cultural Restoration of the Mesopotamian Marshes, Southern Iraq." In *Human Dimensions of Ecological Restoration*, edited by Dave Egan, Evan E. Hjerpe, and Jesse Abrams, 289–98. Washington, DC: Island Press, 2011.

Stott, John. *The Radical Disciple*. Downer's Grove, IL: InterVarsity Press, 2010.

Third Lausanne Congress on World Evangelization. *The Cape Town Commitment*. Edited by Julia Cameron. Peabody, MA: Hendrickson, 2011.

Tobin, Noel J. "15th Sunday in OT: Hope." Catholic Diocese of Geraldton. http://www.geraldtondiocese.org.au/index.php?option=com_content&view=article&id=172:15th-sunday-in-ot-hope&catid=13:year-a&Itemid=51 (accessed May 15, 2013).

United Nations Environment Programme. *Environmental Impact of Refugees in Guinea*. March 2000. http://www.grid.unep.ch/guinea/reports/reportfinal3b.pdf (accessed October 6, 2011).

United Nations General Assembly. "Report of the World Commission on Environment and Development: Our Common Future." 1987. http://www.un-documents.net/our-common-future.pdf (accessed July 15, 2013).

Van Kooten, G. Cornelis, E. Calvin Beisner, and Pete Geddes. *A Renewed Call to Truth, Prudence, and Protection of the Poor*. Burke, VA: Cornwall Alliance, n.d.

Vu, Michelle. "Prominent Missiologist Identifies Biggest Trend in Global Mission." *Christian Post*, July 30, 2008. http://www.christianpost.com/news/prominent-missiologist-identifies-biggest-trend-in-global-mission-33570 (accessed July 16, 2013).

Bibliography

Ward, Christopher. "Yemen's Water Crisis." Lecture presented to the British-Yemeni Society, September 2000. http://www.al-bab.com/bys/articles/ward01.htm (accessed October 5, 2011).

Watt, James. "The Religious Left's Lies." *Washington Post*, May 21, 2005. http://www.washingtonpost.com/wp-dyn/content/article/2005/05/20/AR2005052001333.html (accessed July 15, 2013).

Watts, John D. W., *The Books of Joel, Obadiah, Jonah, Nahum, Habakkuk and Zephaniah.* Cambridge: Cambridge University Press, 1975.

White, Lynn Townsend, Jr. "The Historical Roots of Our Ecologic Crisis." *Science* 155, no. 3767 (March 10, 1967): 1203–7.

Wibberley, S. M. *Knowing Jesus Is Enough for Joy, Period.* Maitland, FL: Xulon, 2010.

Wilkinson, Loren. Preface to *Earthkeeping in the '90s*, edited by Loren Wilkinson, x. Grand Rapids: Eerdmans, 1991.

Willard, Dallas. *Renovation of the Heart.* Colorado Springs: New Press, 2002.

———. *The Spirit of the Disciplines.* San Francisco: HarperSanFrancisco, 1988.

Wilson, E. O. *The Creation: An Appeal to Save Life on Earth.* New York: W. W. Norton & Company, 2006.

Wilson-Hartgrove, Jonathan. *The Wisdom of Stability.* Brewster, MA: Paraclete, 2010.

Winter, Ralph D. "Twelve Frontiers of Perspective." In *Foundations of the World Christian Movement: A Larger Perspective; Course Reader,* edited by Ralph D. Winter and Beth Snodderly, 311–25. Pasadena: Institute of International Studies, 2008.

World Health Organization. "Smallpox." Media Centre, World Health Organization, 2001. http://www.who.int/mediacentre/factsheets/smallpox/en (accessed October 6, 2011; page discontinued).

Wright, Christopher J. H. The *Mission of God's People.* Grand Rapids: Zondervan, 2010.

Wright, N. T. *Simply Jesus.* San Francisco: HarperOne, 2011.

———. *Surprised by Hope.* New York: HarperCollins, 2008.

☙ ENVIRONMENTAL MISSIONS ❧

Wuthnow, Robert. *Be Very Afraid: The Cultural Response to Terrorism.* Oxford: Oxford University Press: 2010.

Zalasiewicz, Jan, M. Williams, A. Smith, T. L. Barry, A. L. Coe, P. R. Bown, P. Benchley, et al. "Are We Now Living in the Anthropocene?" *GSA Today* 18, no. 2 (2008): 4–8.

Zolli, Andrew, and Ann Marie Healy. *Resilience: Why Things Bounce Back.* New York: Free Press, 2012.

ENVIRONMENTAL MISSIONS

General Index

General Index

❧ General Index ❧

❧ General Index ❧

stewardship, 9, 24, 51, 56, 59, 64–65, 72, 92, 96, 110, 113, 122, 126, 131, 139, 143, 150–54, 163, 165, 200–02
environmental. *See* environment.
Stott, John, 53, 65–66, 89, 264, 267
Strandberg, Todd, 109
suffering, 3, 66–67, 135, 141, 164, 220, 224
Sumerian, 212, 216
Sunderban, 132
sustainability, 121, 124, 158
Sustainable South Bronx, 208
suttee, 27, 127
SWOT analysis, 8, 238

T

The End of Poverty, 207
"The Environmental Missions Prayer Digest" (EMPD), 197, 203
The Great Divorce, 70
The Journal of Retailing, 175
The Lorax, 157–61
The Radical Disciple, 65, 89
theism, 84–85
theology, 23, 52–53, 70, 97, 108, 117, 119–21, 143–45, 148
restoration, 88
Thoreau, Henry David, 5, 228
thuggi, 127, 194
Titanic, 201
tohuw, 72
Tower of Babel, 126
transcendentalism, 5–6
trash, 44, 46, 55, 117–18

Tribulation, 96–97, 100, 109, 112
seven-year, 98, 110–11
Trinitarian, 19–20, 77
tsunami, 9–10, 45, 218
Tswana, 144–46, 150

U

UAE, 124, 176
Udall, Stewart, 196
Uganda, 211, 267, 277, 282-84, 287
Ukraine, 139
UNICEF, 44–45
United Nations, 44–45, 165
Environmental Programme (UNEP), 213
Framework Convention on Climate Change (UNFCCC), 174
High Commissioner for Refugees (UNHCR), 213, 217
United States of America, 32, 106, 210
American, 5, 65, 174, 193, 195, 212, 225
Urbana conference, 218
Urdu, 7, 119, 222
Uriah, 62–63
US Center for World Mission (USCWM), 205
utilitarianism, 10–11, 30

V

Vatican City, 46
Vila Verde, 128, 266
Vishnu, 27, 179
von Humboldt, Alexander, 144–45

W

Wall-E, 130
war, 140, 213
  Gulf War, 212, 218
  World War II
    post, 229
    zone, 112
Watts, James, 140
West Africa, 216
West Antarctic. *See* Antarctic.
West Bengal, 132
  Bengali, 27, 180, 194
West Virginia, 140, 183–84, 187,
  197, 218
Western logic, 69
Wheaton College, 110
When Heaven and Nature Sing, 79
When Helping Hurts, 220–21
Where Garden Meets Wilderness, 122
Wibberly, Steve, 188–90
Wilberforce, William, 229
wilderness, 29, 61, 64–65, 71–72,
  77, 91–92, 113, 120–22, 124–
  26, 128–31, 149–50, 168
Wilderness Act, 65
Wilderness Society, 72
Willard, Dallas, 19, 117

Williamson, Mabel, 159
Wilson, E. O., 55
Wilson-Hartgrove, Jonathan, 34
Winter, Ralph, 125, 205
wisdom, 24, 34, 56, 183, 200–03
World Meteorological
  Organization, 11
World Watch List, 9, 42, 47
World Wildlife Fund, 187
worship, 10, 25, 55, 57, 71, 78, 88,
  99, 127, 139, 176, 183, 185–86,
  191–92, 194
  pir, 42–43
Wright, Chris, 59–61, 86–87, 104,
  119, 122, 135
Wright, N. T., 76, 90, 135

Y

Year of Jubilee, 168, 170
Yemen, 47, 223–24
  Yemeni, 223, 225
Young, Richard, 69

Z

Zebedee
  sons of, 178
Zinzendorf, 18, 86
Zolli, Andrew, 125–26

SCRIPTURE INDEX

❧ Scripture Index ❦

⋙ ENVIRONMENTAL MISSIONS ⋘